Mrs. J. Sadlier

The hermit of the rock

A tale of Cashel

Mrs. J. Sadlier

The hermit of the rock
A tale of Cashel

ISBN/EAN: 9783742827395

Manufactured in Europe, USA, Canada, Australia, Japa

Cover: Foto ©Andreas Hilbeck / pixelio.de

Manufactured and distributed by brebook publishing software (www.brebook.com)

Mrs. J. Sadlier

The hermit of the rock

THE
HERMIT OF THE ROCK.

A TALE OF CASHEL.

BY

MRS. J. SADLIER,

AUTHOR OF
"THE BLAKES AND FLANAGANS," "NEW LIGHTS," "BESSY CONWAY,"
"ELINOR PRESTON," "CONFEDERATE CHIEFTAINS,"
"OLD AND NEW," ETC. ETC. ETC.

DUBLIN:
M. H. GILL & SON, LTD.,
50 UPPER O'CONNELL STREET.

CONTENTS.

CHAP.		PAGE
I. HALLOW-EVE IN BRYAN'S COTTAGE,		5
II. HALLOW-EVE AT ESMOND HALL,		18
III. SHAUN THE PIPER,		31
IV. BRYAN'S STATIONS,		44
V. MARY HENNESSY HAS A VISIT, AND BRYAN ANOTHER,		57
VI. A DAY AT ESMOND HALL,		70
VII. MURDER AND MYSTERY,		83
VIII. THE EVENTS OF A NIGHT,		96
IX. UNCLE HARRY HAS AN ADVENTURE,		109
X. A MORNING ON THE ROCK,		122
XI. THE RIDE HOME,		136
XII. A WAKE AND WHAT BEFEL THEREAT,		150
XIII. A SUNDAY EVENING AT ESMOND HALL,		163
XIV. MISS MARKHAM'S STORY,		176
XV. MIDSUMMER-EVE ON THE ROCK OF CASHEL,		191
XVI. SUNSET ON THE ROCK, AND PHIL MORAN'S STORY,		204
XVII. INNER LIFE IN EFFINGHAM CASTLE,		219

CONTENTS.

CHAP.		PAGE
XVIII.	KATE COSTELLOE,	231
XIX.	AN APPARITION AT ROSE LODGE,	244
XX.	WHO KILLED MR. ERMOND,	260
XXI.	PHIL MORAN TRIES HIS LUCK,	275
XXII.	THE COUNTESS OF EFFINGHAM,	287
XXIII.	MORE VISITORS TO THE ROCK—THE CONJURER,	299
XXIV.	THE CLOSE OF THIS EVENTFUL HISTORY,	313

THE HERMIT OF THE ROCK.

CHAPTER I.

HALLOW-EVE IN BRYAN'S COTTAGE.

A RAW, cold evening was that of the last day of October, in the year 18——, a short time after the memorable "Year of Emancipation"—as the twenty-ninth year of this century is distinctively called amongst the Catholic people of Ireland. The crops were all gathered in from the rich level fields around the city of Cashel—the last potato-heap was covered out of doors, and the last load of that valuable esculent garnered in for present consumption in the farmer's household. The rich man's barns and haggards were full, and so were his byres, while even the poorest cottier had his slender stock of potatoes and turf stored away—his sole provision for the coming winter. The ancient city of Cashel, shorn of its former splendour, and dwindled down, in the vicissitudes of time, to the dimensions of a moderately-sized country town, lay dull and indistinct at the foot of the old Rock which sheltered it from the increasing violence of the wind that came sweeping from the north over the far-spreading plain. And the Rock itself loomed in solitary grandeur over the silent town, crowned with the solemn mementoes of departed glory, the ruins of many a stately edifice of other days, whose shattered walls were traced in broken and irregular lines against the grey lowering sky. The piles of masonry, so varied and distinct one from the other in the light of day, were merged in one dark solid mass as the evening mist gathered thick and heavy around them on their rocky perch. But still, like a spectral head, rose over all the weird pillar-tower, lone "chronicle of Time," keeping ward ever, through the garish day and the still night-watches, over the buried dead who sleep around and the ruins of ancient art—

The proud halls of the mighty and the calm homes of the just.

The lights in the city came out one by one, twinkling like stars through the gathering gloom. So, too, in the group of mud cabins that cower immediately beneath the great Rock, in unsightly contrast with the mouldering monuments of human grandeur towering above. Each in succession gave its faint glimmering light to the dull wintry eve, but still the Rock remained shrouded in darkness; the royal palace of Munster's kings and the lordly dwelling where princely ecclesiastics ruled of old are dark and silent now as the graves that contain the ashes of their lords; nor light nor sound comes forth from the ancient abbey that stands close by, all alike wrapped in the solemn mystery of the past, typified by the deepening gloom of the hour and the silence of death that reigns for ever in the lonely place.

The last tint of daylight was vanishing from earth and sky when the door of the smallest and poorest of the cabins at the foot of the Rock was opened with a quick, eager motion, and a woman might be seen in the aperture, her small figure dimly revealed by the light of a resin candle, which flickered through the smoky atmosphere of the miserable hut. Throwing the skirt of her blue drugget gown over her head, she made one step beyond the threshold, then stopped as if checked by a strong and sudden impulse. She cast a half-frightened, half-anxious look at the frowning walls above, and then a longer and more earnest one at the iron gate leading up the steep ascent to the ruins, muttering drearily to herself, "Isn't it a quare night for any Christian to be up *there*—of all places in the world! Sure, I know well nothing good can come of it, and many's the time I tould him so, the witless crathur!"

As she stood in an attitude of fixed attention, with eye and ear strained to the uttermost, there came from the neighbouring town certain loud noises like the banging of doors rapidly and often repeated. Shouts of laughter and merry voices came loud and distinct to the ear of the lonely watcher. A change came over her withered features as she listened, and a smile of strange meaning, half sorrow, half mockery, wreathed her thin pale lip, and shone in her dulled eyes.

"Ay, sure, it's Hol'eve night!" she muttered, "an' the fun is beginnin' already! The boys an' the girls are abroad in the streets playin' their Hol'eve thricks. They're pullin' their cabbage-stalks now in the dark, to see whether their sweethearts 'ill be crooked or straight; an' they're standin' outside the doors wid their mouths full of water listenin' for the first name that's spoken within. An' some of the girls are washin' their shifts, I'll go bail, at the south-runnin' water below; an' it's them will spread the fine supper, when the rest o' the house is all asleep, to see who'll come in to eat it, an' to turn the shift that's a-dryin' by the fireside. Vo! vo! vo! it's little they think of the throubles that may be in store for them! It's little *I* thought of them, aither, when I was like them! An' many's the thrick *I* played of a Hol'eve night,—an' didn't I see —och, didn't I—didn't I—oh, wirra! wasn't my stalk always the straightest and purtiest? It was—it was—but what came of it?—O Lord! what came of it?"

Forgetting apparently her interest in the Rock, whatever it might be at that hour, she wrung her hands, and, bursting into a passionate flood of tears, retreated into her dismal dwelling, and hastily closed the door, still repeating to herself in the same wild way, "What came of it all? what came of it all? Ah!" she suddenly added, with a startled glance around the smoky hut, "what better *could* come of it? Didn't I rake the haystack *in the Divil's* name the very last Hol'eve before— before"—— She did not finish the sentence, but, squatting down by the smouldering fire on the hearth, she clasped her hands in front of her knees, and her head sank on her chest in an attitude of helpless, hopeless, incurable woe.

The woman was first aroused from her lethargy by the raising of the door-latch, and then she started up with the energy and vivacity of youth to accost an old man, much older than herself, although she too was, or appeared to be, in close proximity to the vale of years.

"Wisha, Bryan Cullenan!" said she, "what sort of a man are you, at all, that you'd think of stayin' up there among the dead afther the stars are in the sky of a Hol'eve night? There isn't man or woman in Tipperary that 'id do it except your four bones!"

Excited as she was, she did not forget the old man's comfort, such as it was. She was down on the hearth blowing the turf fire with her apron, and, seeing it begin to emit a cheerful blaze, she drew over to the hearth a small and very rickety table, barely large enough for two cups and saucers, two plates, a third cup containing some coarse brown sugar, a diminutive milk pitcher minus the handle, and a plate containing a tempting pile of the ever-welcome potato-cake cut in triangular slices, being the four parts of a small circular cake, each piece slit in two and carefully buttered. A small white loaf, a much greater delicacy, stood also on the table. This was "the big supper" of Hallow-eve, and the old man's dim eyes brightened as he watched the preparations, for tea and white bread were luxuries seldom seen in that poor dwelling.

Slowly old Bryan took his seat on a low stool by the fire, and, leaning over it, spread forth his hands to catch the welcome heat. He seemed to have forgotten the abrupt question which had greeted his entrance, but it was not so, for when the woman began to repeat it in a sharper tone, he raised his head, and, looking at her with a somewhat sagacious smile, said, "You think I'm losin' my hearin', Cauth, aroon! but I'm not, thanks be to God! I heard what you said, mavrone, but I wonder at you to say it. Sure, you know well enough that every night is the same up there,"—pointing upwards with his thumb. "Do you think them that are abroad on Hol'eve night has power to go next or near the holy walls and the blessed graves on the Rock of Cashel? Ha! ha! ha!" he laughed or rather chuckled in a faint wheezing voice, "I'd like to see them showin' their noses where so many saints lie waitin' for the last trumpet—it wouldn't be for the good of their health if they did, and they know that well. Fairies, indeed, on the Rock of Cashel! Ha! ha! there's sperits enough there, I'm thinkin', to keep the place to themselves!"

"Christ save us!" said Cauth, setting down the little black crockery teapot on the table with a haste that came near upsetting all,—"Christ save us!" and she crossed herself with a visible shudder, "can't you let the sperits alone?"

"What harm am I doin' them, aroon?" asked Bryan innocently.

"Who says you're doin' them harm?" cried Cauth tartly. "But don't be talkin' about them! You're enough to frighten one out of their wits, so you are! Sit over now an' take your supper."

"I will, avourneen, an' God bless you! But what makes you so feard of the sperits, Cauth? Did you ever see one?"

"See one?" and Cauth shuddered again. "If I did it isn't alive I'd be now. Can't you talk of something else, you conthrary ould man you?"

"What will I talk of, then?" said Bryan, with a sort of solemn humour that contrasted oddly with the churchyard gravity of his look and manner. "What will I talk of, Cauth?"

"I was askin' a while agone what kept you so late on the Rock the night?"

Although Cauth said this, it was evidently more to change the topic than from any interest in the probable answer. Her eyes were fixed gloomily and vacantly on the blazing turf before her, and her thin lips kept moving as though she were communing with herself.

But Bryan was never the quickest of perception, so he heeded not the other's abstraction, but answered in good faith—

"I was workin' ever since I went up this mornin' at the Archbishop's tomb in the choir above. There was some bits of the beautiful carving gone off the front of it this time back, an', as luck would have it, I found some of them among the rubbish. So I was fittin' them in here an' there, an'"—

"An' you're a great fool for your pains!" broke in Cauth, starting suddenly from her reverie with the air of one who would fain get rid of her own thoughts. "Now what good does it do for you to be spendin' your time up there from mornin' till night, an' sometimes from night till mornin', in that fearsome ould rookery, where there's nothing but stones and bones and grey walls?"

"Woman!" said Bryan, with a sudden assumption of dignity and a solemnity of tone that awed Cauth into wondering silence,—"woman! what's that you say? Who are you that dares to speak so lightly of God's holy place, an' the consecrated walls, an' the bones that will come together an' rise in glory at the Day of Judgment!—why wouldn't I look after them, for if I don't who will?"

"Well you said it, Bryan Cullenan!" murmured Cauth, her head drooping on her chest, and her hands clasped convulsively as they rested on her knees,—" well you said it—who am I?— ay, who am I? There's times when I hardly know myself."

It might be that the old man was accustomed to these fits of abstraction and abrupt changes of manner in the one companion of his solitary life, for he answered soothingly, as though he spoke to a little wayward child, "Well, never mind, Cauth, never mind. I'm so much of my time all alone on the Rock above, with only shadows round about me, that I 'most forget how to speak to flesh and blood like myself. But why don't you take your supper, Cauth?"

"I'm not hungry," was the curt reply.

"But you know it's Hol'eve night, Cauth, an' you can't but eat something, if it was only for company-sake, an' in honour of the night. Why, the fairies you were talking of a while ago"—

"No, I wasn't talkin' of them—will you whisht now, Bryan! or you'll get yourself into trouble this blessed night. Fair may they come and fair may they go! sure, myself wouldn't make so free as to mention their name good or bad. But as for eatin —I couldn't do it, Bryan, I couldn't—my heart is too full thinkin' of the days that'll never come back, an'—an'"— She stopped, reached out her hand, and, taking the cup of tea that stood untasted on the table, gulped it down with feverish avidity; then, pressing her eyelids very close together, she forced back the tears that were gathering in her eyes, and started to her feet, exclaiming—

"Well! there now, haven't I the poor memory of my own? Sure, I've something better than tay for you, Bryan!"

Going to a little alcove in a corner of the hut, Cauth drew out, with an air of great importance, a black bottle, which she placed on the table with a dreary attempt at a smile, saying at the same time, "If you're done with them things, Bryan, I'll take them away."

Bryan nodded assent, with his eyes fixed inquisitively on the bottle.

"What's in it, Cauth?" he at length inquired.

"Some of the best potheen in Tipperary, Bryan, an' you're to drink the master's health in it this good Hol'eve night. Them's the orders. An' see here, Bryan?"—taking a small paper package from the cupboard,—"here's lump sugar, no less; for the young mistress said, with a sweet smile on her face, that old Bryan—meaning you, av coorse—must have his punch the night as good as the master himself. The Lord's blessin' on her every day she rises!"

"Wisha, amen, Cauth, amen, from my heart out!" said the old man, with a fervour little to be expected from him, a gleam of joy brightening his aged eyes at the thought that, poor and old and lonely as he was, there was one amongst the rich and the young and the happy that did not forget him amid all the luxurious festivity of her own stately mansion. Oh, how glad the rich can make the poor!

"Was she here the day, Cauth?" said Bryan, more cheerfully than his wont.

"No, but she sent for me this mornin', an' gave me as much tay and sugar as 'll do us every day for a month, an' this bottle for you, Bryan, on account of it's bein' the night it is, an' the lump sugar to sweeten the punch. An' see here—maybe you don't call *them* Hol'eve apples?" as she drew forth a tiny basket of the finest Russetins—or, as she called them, "rusty coats," time out of mind the favourite Hallow-eve apple in Ireland.

"Isn't God good to us, Cauth?" said the old man, drawing his stool once more to the fire, with the cup of punch in his hand (Bryan's cottage contained nor glass nor goblet), Cauth opposite with another cup containing a small quantity of the same exhilarating beverage—it was seldom either indulged, or cared to indulge, in the dangerous luxury for which mankind is indebted to John Barleycorn. "Isn't God good to us, Cauth, to send us such a friend as the young mistress? An' see what a fine load of turf we have by us—enough to put us over Christmas, anyhow. It's Dan O'Connell we may thank for that, an' a trifle I've by me ever since for a sore foot. Ah, then, did I ever tell you, Cauth, of the day I showed him over the Rock?"

Cauth answered in the negative, expressing a wish at the same time to hear all about it. Turning to a pile of turf in the corner behind her, she replenished the fire, and with a well-worn heather besom swept up the ashes from the hearth.

"You mind the day, Cauth?"—Cauth nodded assent,—"it was one of the brightest and purtiest days that came in September, and I was hard at work scrapin' the moss out of the letters on King Cormac's tomb,—you know where it is, Cauth, just in between the wall of his own chapel, God rest his soul! an' the cathedral,—well, I was workin' away as hard as I could, sayin' a trifle of prayers, too, for the good king's soul, though thinkin' to myself that it's little need he had of them, most like, when somebody says, just right behind me, 'Hillo, Bryan! you're at your old trade still, I see!' an' I started like, an' dropped the chisel out of my hand. When I turned about, who should I see but the Counsellor himself, as large as life, looking down at myself with that comical look of his that would make the dead in their graves laugh if they could only see it. He had two gentlemen with him, an' I knew in a minnit that one of them was Tom Steele, for I seen him with him once afore. So I gets out from my crib as fast as I could, an' I takes off my hat an' makes the best bow I was able, an' says I, 'You're welcome back to Cashel, Counsellor!'

"'Thank you kindly, Bryan,' says he. 'I see you haven't forgotten me.'

"'Forgotten you?' says I back again. 'Sure, that's what no one ever does that once gets an eyeful out of you.'

"With that the Counsellor laughed again, and the other gentlemen laughed too; and says Dan to me, 'Well, Bryan, for a man that's so much alone you keep the use of your tongue to admiration. But come, can you spare time to show us through the place? You know when I was here before I hadn't time to see half what was to be seen.—It was when I came down to one of those murder trials in Clonmel,' says he to the strange gentleman, 'and I was hurrying back at full speed for a general meeting of the Association that was to come off next evening'— But what's the matter with you, Cauth?" seeing that she laid down the cup and leaned back against the wall.

"There's nothing the matter with me," said Cauth testily, though her pale lips could scarce articulate the words. The next moment she sat up as before, and motioned for Bryan to go on with his narrative.

"Well, I will, Cauth, I will; but I'm afeard you're not able to sit up—you look as pale as a ghost."

"Can't you go on with your story an' never mind me? You were saying the Counsellor asked if you could spare time to take them through the ould place."

"Yis, an' of coorse I said I'd be hard run for time if I couldn't take *him* over the Rock. '*My* work,' says I, 'can stand—there's no one to hurry me, an' I've my life long to do it.'

"'Very true, Bryan,' says the Counsellor, as we turned into the ould cathedral. 'Do you know, Stacla,' says he to Tom, 'that this is our Irish Old Mortality?'—let me see, was that the word?—yis, that was it, Old Mortality,—'This,' says he, nodding his head at myself, 'this is our Irish Old Mortality.' With that the gentlemen looked at me and smiled at one another, an' though I didn't know from Adam what Old Mortality meant, I thought it couldn't be anything bad, or *he* wouldn't say it, so I took off my hat again and made a very low bow. 'Your honour,' says I, 'is very kind an' condescendin' to speak so well of a poor ould crathur like me.'

"'Not at all, Bryan, not at all,' says he. 'You're a great man, and a useful man in your own way, and, moreover, you and I are, to some extent, fellow-labourers.' Them were his very words, Cauth, as I'm a livin' man this night.

"'Why, dear bless me! how can that be?' says I, lookin' at him close to see if he was makin' fun of me or not.

"'Because,' says he, 'Bryan, you and I are both working for the future of our country—we are both clearing away the rubbish of ages—both working for the honour and glory of the Old Land!'"

"Wisha, Bryan, did the Counsellor say that?"

"As true as you're sittin' there, Cauth, he said them words! an' don't you think but it made my heart jump with joy? I declare the tears came into my eyes so that I could hardly see the way before me, an' I 'most forgot what I was about, till the Counsellor says, with that fine hearty laugh of his, 'Why, Bryan Cullanan, where are your wits gone? I think I must turn guide myself. Where's this Myler M'Grath's tomb is?' an' he walked straight to it, an' began to explain the inscription on it to the other gentleman. I had no need to speak a word there, for they all knew more about the Archbishop than I did myself. But they wanted to take a rise out of me, I could see that, an' so Tom Steele says to me in his big voice, 'Bryan,' says he, 'do you know that Myler M'Grath was the first Protestant Archbishop of Cashel?'

"'I do, your honour,' says I; 'I knew it ever since I was the height of your knee.'

"'How does it happen, then, that you take such good care of his tomb as I am told you do?'

"'For a very good reason, your honour,' says I, lookin' him straight in the face, 'because he recanted his errors before he left this world, an' had all the rites of the Church.'

"'Nonsense, man! how can you be sure of that?'

"'How can I be sure of it?" says I. 'Your honour might as well ask how can I be sure that the blessed sun will go back the night to set where he set last night, behind the mountains westward? Only I'm sure, an' double sure, that the Archbishop died a good Catholic, do you think I'd sleep many's the summer night, as I do every year of my life, right here in the choir beside his tomb?'

"'Bravo, Bryan, bravo!' cried the Counsellor and the other gentleman, clappin' their hands, and laughin' till you'd think they'd split their sides. 'What do you think of that, friend Tom? Come, come, now! look Bryan straight in the face an' tell him old Myler did right to "conform" to the religion prescribed by the Virgin Queen, or wrong to return to Catholic unity when he felt himself at the gates of death? Speak now, my man of Steel! or ever hereafter hold your tongue!'

"'Pshaw!' says Tom, turnin' on his heel an' walkin' away down the aisle, 'let the old hypocrite lie where he is——be that where it may! It matters little now to us when he was right, or when wrong!' At this the others laughed again, an' myself was afeard they'd make him angry; but they knew him better than I did, for when the Counsellor called after him to come back an' look at one of the old monuments in the wall before they'd leave the choir, he went back as cheerful as could be, an' looked just the same as if nothing at all had happened. So I took them all round an' showed them everything I could think of, an' by the time we got to the old tribute-stone near the gate, with St. Patrick risin' up from it on one side, an' the Crucifixion on the other, they were all purty well tired, I'm thinkin', and down they sat on some big stones that were lyin' a one side on the grass, just where they had a fine view of the whole, an' a beautiful sight it was, too. The sun was beginnin' to decline westward, an' the shadows of the grand ould walls were all around us, with here and there the shape of a window or a door of clear sunlight shinin' like yallow goold on the green grass. Then the Counsellor pointed out to the others all the fine elegant arches, both round and pointed, as he said, an' the pillars within an' without, an' the beautiful mullions, as he called the stone divisions where the windows used to be, an' he spoke of the carvin' over the doors, an' told the meanin' of everything, just all as one, Cauth, as if he was at the buildin' of it all; an' they talked a long while about the ould round tower, an' what it was for, an' one said one thing an' one another, but the Counsellor said it was easy to see what it was built for, an' that was to keep the rich vessels of silver an' goold belongin' to the church in the ould war-times. 'Don't you know,' says he, 'that there's an underground passage from the church to the tower—well, doesn't that prove what I'm saying to be true? Where would be the use of constructing an underground passage,'—that wasn't the word he said, Cauth, but I disremember the other—I know it began with sub—something or another—no matter, anyhow, I suppose it means the same as underground,—'where would be the use,' says he, 'of constructing an underground passage to the tower through the solid rock, if it wasn't for the purpose I have mentioned?' The others seemed to give in to that, an' after discoorsin' a while longer, they stood up to go. They turned to take another look at the ould walls, an' sure enough I never seen them lookin' so grand or so beautiful. The Counsellor's face would do you good to see it, Cauth, as he watched the sunshine dancin' and glancin' hither and thither among the broken arches, an' the pillars, an' things, an' says he then, takin' out a fine elegant white silk handkerchief out of his pocket, an' wipin' the tears from his eyes, says he, as if partly to himself, 'And such is Ireland—grand and venerable even in decay—Cashel is Ireland—Ireland is Cashel— royal still, though their greatness be of the past. But their glory shall not fade for ever. Look at the sunbeams on the old walls,' says he, turnin' to the other gentlemen,—'well, even so it is with our native land; the light of hope has never left her, and' now the sun of prosperity begins to shine again on her mountain-tops. And it will continue to shine—mark my words—when the darkness of night has settled down for ever on haughty England, her oppressor!' Them were the words he said, Cauth; for I kept sayin' them over and over to myself, by night an' by day, ever since, till I've got them by heart like a gossoon larnin' his task. There's ne'er a time I look up at the ould walls over my head, espaycially when the sun is shinin', that I don't think of Dan O'Connell, an' somehow or another his words keep singin' in my ears for all the world like one of Columbkill's prophecies. But the best of it all was what he said to myself at his off-goin'. 'Bryan,' says he,—' Bryan Cullenan! you have a great name,—your namesake, King Cormac Cullenan, was a good king and a great bishop in his day,—I'm proud to see that you take such care of these noble ruins. It is a good work, Bryan, and a pious work, too—and God will bless you for it, and the Saints of Erin will shield you from all ill. Farewell, Bryan! if we never meet again on earth, put up a prayer now and then for Dan O'Connell, while you tell your beads here among the tombs of the holy dead.' With that he slips a bright goold guinea into my hand, to buy my winter's turf, he said in a whisper. The other gentlemen gave me a half-crown apiece, so I made a good day's work of it in regard to money; but I didn't care for that half so much as I did for the honour of showin' Cashel to Counsellor O'Connell, an' hearin' all the fine beautiful words he said about the ould place that my heart is centred in. I forgot to tell you, Cauth, that he took another grand rise out of Mr. Steele as they were just leavin' the Rock. I didn't know till then that he was a Prodestan, which, indeed, is a mighty odd thing to me, an' him such a darlin' fine gentle-man, and a great friend of the people.

"'Tom,' says the Counsellor—it's the member for Clare, I hear they call him now,—'Tom,' says he, pointin' his finger down at the great new church—the Bishop's Church—in the town below,—'Tom, do you know how that came to be built?' 'No,' says Tom, 'I do not.' 'Well,' says the Counsellor, winkin' at the other gentleman,—I never can remember what name they gave him,—'it was built because the road up to the Rock here was too steep for the Protestant Archbishop Agar to drive his carriage up, and I suppose himself was too fat to walk it, though it is only a few perches, as you may perceive. So he goes to work and puts up that grand building below there, or got the Government to put it up for him. The roof was taken off this cathedral on the Rock to make lead water-pipes out of, or something of the kind, and from that day to this it has been going to ruin. See what it is to be fat, Tom!—Archbishop Agar's fat cost this noble old building its roof.' Mr. Steele got very red in the face at that, and says he, 'If I had my will of that old chap, do you know what I'd do with him? I'd put him on bread and water the rest of his days, by way of penance, then he'd soon be able to walk up here, and a little farther, too, if need were—the old Vandal!' says he, mighty angry; and at that the others laughed till the tears came into their eyes."

Here Cauth started to her feet and looked wildly around, putting back her long grey hair from off her ears to listen. "Ha! ha!" she cried, "I hear them now! That's John's voice"—

"What John? Who do you mean?" said Bryan. "I hear nothin', barrin' the wind screechin' round the ould walls on the Rock above. Sit down, Cauth, sit down,—or maybe you ought to go to bed. I'm afeard you're not well."

"Don't tell me," said Cauth, with a vehement gesture; "if that isn't the *caoine*, I never heard it. I say it's that and nothin' else—and there's men's voices in it, too! O Lord! will I hear it for ever—for ever?" She buried her face in her hands, and was silent.

Accustomed as Bryan was to the solitude of death and the grim presence of dread mortality in its relics, there was something in Cauth's voice and manner that made him shiver with an undefined sense of fear. He did not dare to rouse her from her lethargy, of whatever kind it was, but as soon as she raised her head again, he renewed his request that she would go to bed, which she did very soon after, without any allusion to what had passed.

CHAPTER II.

HALLOW-EVE AT ESMOND HALL.

WE will now take the liberty of introducing the reader to the drawing-room of Esmond Hall on that same Hallow-eve night, where the "young mistress" so gratefully and often mentioned by Bryan and Cauth was entertaining with modest though lively grace a numerous circle of visitors, all more or less connected with the family. Nothing could be more cheerful than the aspect of the spacious and lofty room, with its bright coal fire, and its crystal chandelier shedding down a flood of warm light on the gay company, the bright-hued velvet carpet, the handsome modern furniture, rosewood and marble of the latest Dublin style, the piano—one of Broadwood's grand—with its showy keyboard open to view, and near it a harp which could be set down for no other—even without hearing its silvery tones—than one of "Erard's best." A beautiful dog of the King Charles breed lay on the soft rug outside the fender, his long silken ears of glossy black reflecting the bright glow from the massive grate.

The crimson curtains were closed over the tall windows, hanging in heavy folds to the floor, and the lofty mirrors flashed back the gay scene with its richly-varied hues, its light and life and beauty. The "wind of the winter night" howling without, served but to increase the luxurious sense of comfort within, and its plaintive cadences and loud fierce swells were little heeded by the company assembled in Mrs. Esmond's drawing-room. And yet some of the guests were grave and far from young. One in particular—a stout, portly man, with short neck, square shoulders, and large globular head—would have given you the impression of a harsh, stern man as he looked at you from under his protruding brows with a glance half inquisitive, half defiant. This personage, attired in top-boots and knee-breeches of drab cassimere, with a bottle-green frock coat, black velvet vest, and scrupulously white neck-tie, occupied the seat of honour, a large Gothic arm-chair near the fireplace, with cushions of crimson velvet. He was addressed by both the lovely young hostess and her frank-looking, handsome husband as "Uncle Harry," and his presence on that occasion seemed somehow to be regarded as a very special favour. Then there was his wife, a rather favourable specimen of the Irish lady of the last generation; though somewhat stiff and formal, there was nothing forbidding in her long, thin features, and she seemed to listen with complacency, if not with any great degree of sympathy, to the joyous *badinage* of her younger relatives. This lady was "Aunt Martha."

Then there were sundry cousins, male and female, comprising a young attorney, a physician whose diploma was dated within the year, and another of some ten or twelve years' standing in the good city of Cashel. The last-named gentleman, Dr. O'Grady, had a fair-faced little wife in that goodly company, and the former, Dr. Hennessy, a sister, some years younger than himself, a gay, light-hearted brunette, whose saucy though good-natured repartees contributed largely to the general amusement. Mary Hennessy was a bright-eyed, handsome girl, with an inexhaustible fund of good humour, and her presence was everywhere greeted as heaven's sunshine——warm, genial, and enlivening. Two other young ladies were there, connections though not relatives of the Esmonds, one of whom, Bella Le Poer, was a distant relation of the elegant Lady Blessington, and the other, Harriet Markham, a pale and very interesting girl, a recent convert to Catholicity, belonging to an old but much-reduced Queen's County family. This young lady was engaged as governess in the family of a certain noble lord whose princely mansion rises but a short distance from Cashel, almost in the shade of old Killough. There was, too, a vinegar-faced old maid, the sister of Uncle Harry, familiarly called "Aunt Winn," whose natural acerbity of temper acted as a whetting-stone to the lively humour of the youngsters, and gave them no small entertainment.

Altogether it was a pleasantly-constituted party, each one marked by strong peculiarity of one kind or another, the ages and characters and professions happily assorted, and, to crown all, each known to the other in all their prominent traits of character.

Tea had been served in the drawing-room, and as the Hallow-eve sports were to come off before supper, the matter now in hand was the order to be observed. After some good-humoured discussion, the company all adjourned to the ball-room, the smooth oaken floor of which better suited that evening's entertainment than the rich carpet of the drawing-room. The youngsters were all in a state of excitement that was in itself happiness. Though all far superior to the superstitious belief of the peasantry in the fateful character of Hallow-eve, or the possibility of obtaining on that particular night a glimpse of life's untrodden path, they all, as a matter of course, assumed the greatest anxiety to "try their luck" in accordance with the spell that ruled the hour. Every face was brimful of serio-comic importance, under which each contrived to manifest a laughing incredulity, that reduced the power of fairydom to a mere myth, and the Hallow-eve observances to a pure frolic.

First came the melting of the lead in a grisset, and the pouring thereof through the wards of a key by each unmarried person in succession. This ceremony gave rise, as usual, to the most unbounded merriment, on account of the ludicrous combinations presented by the charmed lead in the various shapes it assumed falling into a shallow dish of water through the ring aforesaid. Truth to tell, the shapes were of that nondescript kind which might be construed into anything, and in that consisted the charm, for each one's lot was, therefore, predicted from the lead in the way most likely to promote the general amusement. Thus, Mary Hennessy's "cast" was interpreted by all present into a tailor's scissors, Bella Le Poer's a printing press, and Harriet Markham's a ship's rudder! It is to be remarked that the Hallow-eve lead is much more given to emblems of handicraft than any other,—it seldom meddles with the professions, though once in a while, by way of variety, perhaps a pen or a compass, perhaps a telescope, is discovered amongst the motley forms into which it resolves itself in its passage through the key. Much amusement was afforded the young people on that particular night by the result of Aunt

Winn's experiment, which was declared, after a minute and most careful investigation, to be a fiddle, indicating either a dancing master or an itinerant performer on that favourite instrument.

This announcement was received with unbounded applause, and followed by the most uproarious mirth.

"Aunt Winn is going to have a fiddler!—good gracious! good gracious!" cried Mary Hennessy; "then we shall do nothing but dance all year round!"

"Uncle Harry, do you hear that?" said Bella, in the good-natured expectation of bringing a smile to the face that even then was grave.

"I am not surprised," was the answer; "I always thought that Winn had a decided turn for music."

"Bravo! bravissimo!" cried the young men, clapping their hands, while the fair girls around made the roof ring with their light-hearted laughter. Even Aunt Martha, Uncle Harry's staid and sober helpmate, smiled condescendingly at the odd conceit; but Aunt Winn herself was highly offended, and said she deserved no better for allowing herself to be made a fool of. The very curls on either side of her high, narrow forehead—they were barrel curls of fair rotundity—seemed to swell in sympathetic indignation, and her long, thin nose assumed an alarmingly sharp point, as she rose from her seat and declared her intention of returning to the drawing-room, as "people there didn't know how to conduct themselves."

The angry spinster was, with no small difficulty, prevailed on by the host and his gentle wife not to break up the party. "For you know, Aunt Winn," said Mrs. Esmond in her sweetest tones, "we could never think of remaining here, any of us, and let you sit alone in the drawing-room,—on a night like this, too," she sportively added, "when the fairies are all on the alert to catch unwary mortals."

"Nonsense, Henrietta," said her husband gaily; "Aunt Winn wants only a little coaxing. Come, come, my fair aunt! I will take you under protection for the rest of the evening," and, drawing her arm within his, he led her back to her seat with a half smile on her face and a look of heroic determination on his, as though meaning to convey to all concerned the strength and firmness of his purpose.

A suppressed titter went round in acknowledgment of Harry's comic powers, and the lead having gone its rounds, another ordeal was instituted for the trial of each one's fate. Four plates were set on a table, one of which contained clean, another muddy water, the third some fresh clay, and the fourth a ring, drawn from the taper finger of Mrs. Esmond. The ring, in being handed to Dr. Hennessy, who arranged the plates, dropped by accident into the clay, whereat Mrs. Dr. O'Grady uttered an exclamation of horror. All eyes were immediately turned upon her, and every one asked what was the matter.

"Oh, nothing,—nothing at all," said she in a faint, languid tone, looking quite overcome at the same time; "but, dear me! Dr. Hennessy, how *could* you be so awkward? You ought to have known better! I really can't forgive you!"

"Forgive me for what, madam? I would willingly ask your pardon if I only knew the head and front of my offending. Will you have the goodness to enlighten me thereupon?"

"Some other time I will, but not now. Mrs. Harry Esmond, if I were you I would not have given the ring off my hand for any such purpose, and"— Here she stopped, and after glancing at the fair hand and then at the ring, turned up her eyes and raised her hands, with a gesture that said ever so plainly, "Well! anything to equal that!"

It was now Mrs. Esmond's turn to inquire somewhat earnestly. "What do you mean, Mrs. O'Grady?"

"Mean? Why, I mean that you did *very* wrong to give your wedding-ring for such a purpose. Any other would have done as well."

"And pray, where's the difference?" laughed Mrs. Esmond, but her voice trembled a very little. "What harm does it do the ring?"

"No harm *to the ring*, child; but—but—I wouldn't have done it, that's all!"

This trifling episode was little heeded by any of the others, and Harry, if he had noticed it, would doubtless have quizzed Mrs. O'Grady unmercifully for her old-world notions, but somehow the ill-timed remark of that sharp-sighted lady made an impression on the mind of her to whom it was addressed, which her reason strove in vain to combat. The impression was not weakened by the succeeding incidents of that evening.

The sports went on. Each of the young people was, in turn, led blindfolded to the table, and shouts of laughter greeted their groping efforts to make for the clean water and the ring. The clay, emblematic of death, and the muddy water of marriage with a widow or widower, as the case might be, were, as a matter of course, anxiously avoided.

Some did happen on the muddy water, and that was the signal for increased merriment. The attorney was one of them, whereupon the other young men clapped their hands and cried simultaneously, "The widow Gartland—the widow Gartland!" "By Jove!" added Harry Esmond, "you're a lucky dog, after all, Phil Moran."

"That's to be tried," said Dr. O'Grady, with emphasis. "Money is not always luck, and there's many a bitter curse on that same money of old Gartland's. I'd rather work my own way in life and trust to Providence than start on a fortune that was wrung from the heart's blood of the poor."

"That's because you're a fool," said Uncle Harry sententiously. "Money is money, and what is more, money is power. If I were a young fellow like Moran, with a fair chance of success, I'd go in for Gartland's houses and lands—and money too—with a heart and a half. As for the curses"—he smiled scornfully—"I'd take *them* by way of mortgage!"

Uncle Harry was a privileged person in the circle, and was tolerated, on account of his age, in a latitude of tongue accorded to no one else. The doctor contented himself, therefore, with a smile of peculiar meaning; whilst Moran laughed, and said it was time enough to balance the *pro* and *con* of that question when one had an interest in it, which, on his honour, was not his case.

"Mary! Mary! take care!" now burst from the eager circle round the table.—Mary Hennessy was trying her fortune, and her hand was hovering near the plate which contained the fateful clay. Old and young gathered round, for Mary was the favourite of all,—every eye followed the motions of her fingers as though Fate indeed hung in the balance,—again and again was the warning given, half jest, whole earnest, to take care, yet still Mary's hand, slow and wary, and moved away for a moment, *would* return to the forbidden spot. All at once, Harry Esmond extended his hand playfully, crying, "Nonsense,

Mary! that's not the plate for *you!*" but instead of drawing her hand away, as he intended, it so happened that his and hers both came down together on the damp, dark earth, and Mary's cry of terror, whether real or assumed, was echoed by Mrs. Esmond. Harry was at her side in a moment, laughing at her childish folly, and, shaking his finger at Mary Hennessy, who was herself a shade paler than usual, he declared it was all her fault, giving it, moreover, as his opinion that she had managed to see under the bandage, and, with her usual love of mischief, persisted in choosing the clay just to frighten them all.

"Upon my honour, Harry Esmond!" cried Mary, shaking back her long curls and looking at him with a saucy smile, "you are not improving in politeness since your marriage. To accuse me—Mary Hennessy—of practising deceit in a matter, positively, of life and death! Come, come, now, I think we have all had our turn at the plates."

"All but Aunt Winn," put in Moran slyly.

"Aunt Winn wants no more turns—she thanks you," was the ancient maiden's tart rejoinder, and she drew herself up to her fullest rigidity. "Every one hasn't *your* luck, Phil Moran, in regard to the muddy water—or the rusty gold the doctor was speaking of a while ago."

This speech was loudly applauded, the more so as it made the lawyer look a little sheepish; and, much mollified by the success of her well-aimed shaft, Aunt Winn smiled a vinegar smile and nodded her head several times with great self-complacency.

Perhaps gentle Mrs. Esmond was not sorry that supper was announced at that particular moment, and she took Uncle Harry's offered arm with right goodwill; while Harry, ever free and easy, followed with that gentleman's grave helpmate; and Moran went up with a dancing step to make his salaam to Mary Hennessy, with whom he joined the order of march to the tune of "The Rakes of Mallow," humming at the same time loud enough for all to hear—

"Beauing, belleing, dancing, drinking,
Lived the Rakes of Mallow."

"What a grave and reverend signor—for a lawyer!" said sprightly Mary Hennessy. "Do you ever expect to wear the ermine, or cover those locks of yours with wig judicial?"

"Undoubtedly, fair lady! thicker heads than mine have worn that venerable coiffure. Only you take the taming of me," he said, lowering his voice to a half whisper, "and you shall see me grave enough for anything."

"Oh, you incorrigible scion of the law!" said Mary, with her clear, musical laugh, "what a left-handed compliment you pay me! Let me only have the taming of you and you would be grave enough for anything! Angels and ministers of grace! heard any unfortunate damsel ever the like of that?"

"Well, but—yes or no?"

"No, decidedly; I leave you to old Gartland's gold,—the Lord forgive me," she added, with sudden seriousness, "for naming the dead so lightly!"

"Who were you naming, then?" said her brother from behind, as they entered the spacious dining-room where supper awaited them. "Will Gartland, or who?"

"What a good guess you are, Maurice!" said his sister evasively; "you should have been born in New England instead of Old Ireland."

Mary Hennessy raised her eyes as she said this, and encountered the stern gaze of Uncle Harry, who had just taken his seat near the head of the table at the right hand of the youthful lady of the mansion. She blushed consciously, without knowing why, and the man of law, seeing the blush, and mistaking the cause, interpreted the same in his own favour.

A regular Hallow-eve supper graced the well-spread board. Some of the dainties there were common to rich and poor that night, whilst others were only to be seen on the tables of the rich, though proper to a festival celebrated in every homestead from Cape Clear to Fair Head. Of the former class was the indispensable dish of "caulcannon," the plates of oaten cake, thin and white and crisp, and the tall crystal fruit stands filled with magnificent apples, the orchard's pride. To the latter class belonged the Hallow-eve goose, cooked to its highest perfection, and the rich variety of nuts, walnuts, filberts, almonds, which the poor scarce know even by name, with the delicately-flavoured hazel-nut so common in Irish woods. This is, after all, the Hallow-eve nut *par excellence*, for it alone borrows a charm from the fated night, and indicates—or is supposed to do so—the secret motions of lovers' hearts when placed in couples on the hearth within burning reach of the heat from the fire. The Hallow-eve nuts and the rosy-cheeked apples wherein the curious damsel stuck her ten new pins—throwing the tenth one away—to place it under her pillow, hoping to dream of the fated one who was to tread life's path with her!—oh, who that grew to manhood or womanhood in "dear old Ireland, gay old Ireland," land of love and of all things genial, has not watched with eagerness the capricious movements of those Hallow-eve nuts, as they sat side by side on the well-swept hearth before the clear turf fire, representing two of the company present, or, just as often, two who were absent!—what a host of bright illusions rise before the world-weary heart as memory touches on those festive hours, with the harmless mirth, the gleeful sport, that youth alone can know in perfection! What troops of loved ones, dead or distant, rise before the dreaming eye of Irish readers at thought of the Hallow-eve sports!—some—oh, many! to be seen no more on earth,—brightest and gayest and fondest, too,—others whom time and the cold, harsh world have changed almost to stone! We ask ourselves have these scenes all passed away? are we, indeed, in a *new world*, with an ever-yawning gulf between us and the past—the storied, poetical, *old-world* past?

Such thoughts as these were all unknown to the gay party round the Esmond supper-table that Hallow-eve night, for the sports and the joys of the past were still present with them—even the oldest there had not outlived the joyous celebration of "the year's stepping-stones," as some one has quaintly called the old festivals.

During supper the conversation turned again, by some singular chance, on old Will Gartland, who had, in his day, enjoyed the unenviable character of being the worst landlord in the county,—or, at least, in the barony,—for, truth to tell, few of the landlords of Tipperary County were, in that day, remarkable as good ones.

For some cause known to himself—and, it might be, to some of the others too—this disparagement of the departed spouse of the rich widow was particularly distasteful to Uncle Harry. Some contemptuous allusion having been made by Dr. Hennessy to that defunct individual, whom he styled "the oppressor of the poor," Uncle Harry filled his glass to the brim, and, standing up, said with angry vehemence, turning his scowling glance on Hennessy—

"I drink to the memory of that much-calumniated man—he was my friend and neighbour for nigh thirty years—we all knew him, all shared his hospitality—I give, then, the memory of William Gartland!"

He drained his glass to the bottom, but no one followed his example—every glass save his own either stood untasted or was turned down empty.

"So none of you will drink my toast?" said Uncle Harry, with a heightened colour on his face. "Will not you, Harry Esmond?"

"Excuse me, uncle," replied the nephew, his handsome face flushed with generous indignation ; "I had no respect for the man when living, nor have I for his memory when dead. The best thing you can do for one like him is to leave his memory where his body lies—'unwept, unhonoured'—in the earth on which his soul grovelled during life."

"Bravo, Esmond!" cried Hennessy and Moran, clapping their hands, while Dr. O'Grady, less demonstrative, slapped the table gently two or three times with his right hand by way of approval, with a quiet "Hear! hear!"

"Upon my honour, gentlemen," said Uncle Harry, with difficulty restraining his passion,—"upon my honour, I take this conduct of yours as very unkind—very disrespectful to the dead, and certainly not complimentary to the living, as far as I'm concerned." Then, as if hoping to soften the matter, he added, "Ladies, what say you?"

The ladies, as if by tacit consent, left the answer to Mary Hennessy, who was not slow in giving her opinion. "For once I entirely agree with the gentlemen. I'd as soon drink old Chadwick's[1] memory as old Gartland's—sooner, indeed, of the two, inasmuch as Gartland, being, or professing to be, a Catholic, was the more inexcusable for his cruel oppression of

[1] Mr. Chadwick, the agent of a large estate in Tipperary, was shot a few years before in broad daylight, near the ruins of Holy Cross Abbey, while superintending the erection of a police-barrack, which his own heartless tyranny, and that of others in his position, alone rendered necessary.

his Catholic tenantry. I have myself seen too many of the victims of his pound-of-flesh exactions not to hold his memory in something very like abhorrence. I tell you, sir, the whole world will one day cry out shame on the cruelty and injustice of—some Irish landlords."

"You do not include *all* in your fierce anathema," observed Uncle Harry, with forced composure.

"Certainly not, Mr. Esmond!"—she usually called him, like the others, Uncle Harry,—"God forbid I did—*under this roof!*" and she looked with moistened eyes at the young master of Esmond Hall, who was famous throughout the county as one of the best landlords in it.

Harry blushed like a young maiden at this delicate allusion to his well-known standing with the people, whilst his uncle prepared to astonish the company by an out-and-out defiance.

"Well," said he, after draining another glass, and setting it down with most convincing energy,—"well, good people, once for all, I tell you this—I despise *the people* too much to regard what they say of me, and I'd just as soon have their bad word as their good word any day in the year. I know they look on their landlords as their natural enemies, and, like cowards as they are, conspire in secret to injure them all they can, even where they don't go the length of murder. Now there's myself, for instance,—you all know that *I'm* not a bad landlord—never was—though I don't say what I *will* be, —well, you know how often my cows have been houghed, my haggard burned, and various other outrages of a similar nature perpetrated on my property. How can I speak well of my tenantry? What kindness do I owe them? I tell you I *hate* them—hate them all—man, woman, and child!"

"And maybe they don't hate *you!*" said a deep, hoarse voice not heard before at the table. It certainly came from none of the guests, and all eyes were turned on the butler, the only servant in the room, but *he* was pouring out a glass of water for Mrs. Esmond, so it could not possibly be him. Still, Uncle Harry was determined to try.

"Do you hear, you fellow?—I say, niece, what's your butler's name?—Pierce!—exactly!—I say, you Pierce! did you speak to me just now?"

"Is it me spake to your honour?" the butler replied, in such a thin, weak voice that every one laughed heartily—it was so totally unlike the voice heard but a moment before. "Do you think I'd make so free as to spoke to a gentleman unless he spoke to me? I'm a poor boy, and I don't know much, sir, but as little as I know, I know my place when the quality's to the fore. Bedad, I do, your honour!"

"Where did the voice come from, then? Would you have us believe, you rascal, that it come from the ceiling?"

"Wisha, how can I tell where it came from!" was the innocent and half-bashful answer, in a sort of whining tone that was indescribably ludicrous when compared with the stalwart proportions of the man. "Sure, nobody wonders, your honour, at anything they hear—or see, aither—on a Hol'eve night."

The rest of the company all laughed at this sally, but Uncle Harry did not laugh. He seldom did laugh, and he was nowise disposed for laughing then. He fixed his stern eyes for a moment on the butler's somewhat stolid features, and somehow, as he looked, the expression of his own face changed and his look became more earnest. At last he said through his closed teeth, "If I had my horsewhip near me, my good fellow, I'd find a back to lay it on, without going far from where I sit!"

"Uncle Harry," said the host, in accordance with a sign from his wife, "we're waiting for you to fill your glass—I've a toast to give. Are you ready? I see you are. Well, here's may we all be alive and as merry as we are now next Hallow-eve night!"

The toast was drunk with all the honours, and it seemed to restore the general good humour—even Uncle Harry so far forgot his previous irritation as to sing, at his niece's request, "One Bumper at Parting," written by Moore, to the lively air of "Moll Roe in the Morning." Nobody ever sang that song, Henrietta Esmond said, half so well as Uncle Harry; and, as if catching the inspiration of the gay, dashing music, her own sweet voice mingled with his when he came to the beautiful words—

"The sweetness that pleasure has in it
Is always so slow to come forth,
That never, alas! till the minute
It dies do we know half its worth.

> But Time, like a pitiless master,
>   Cries 'Onward!' and spurs the gay hours,
> For never does Time travel faster
>   Than when his way lies among flowers."

Then every one that could raise a note joined in the chorus, and "hearts were light, and eyes were bright," as the company left the table to finish the evening in the more refined amusements of the drawing-room. Meanwhile, the storm without increased its fury, the leafless branches of the trees swung like skeleton limbs in the fierce blast, and doors and windows creaked in dismal consonance to the wild music of the winds that came sweeping down from the stern old Rock, to rush in unimpeded fury over the broad plains of Tipperary away to the far Galtees and the distant hills of Clare. But little cared the joyous party assembled in Esmond Hall, for as none of the guests were to leave till morning light at least, what was the storm to them, or the witches and fairies who that night bestrode the blast? The louder the wind blew, the more merrily "laugh, and song, and sparkling jest went round,"— the host and hostess merriest of all the circle.

CHAPTER III.

SHAUN THE PIPER.

THE next day being All Saints' Day—Hollantide Day amongst the Irish peasantry—was, of course a holyday, of obligation. The tardy winter's morning rose clear and cold. The high wind of the previous night had dried up the clammy earth, and towards morning a sharp frost began to whiten the bare brown pastures and stubble-fields, giving the first positive indication of the near approach of winter. The red light of the dawn was just appearing over the Killough heights eastward when old Bryan Cullenan might be seen wending his homeward way from the chapel where he had just heard Mass, through one of the narrow by-streets leading off from the main street of Cashel. The old man was alone, as usual, and as he paced with slow and uncertain steps the rough pavement of the old borough, his head and shoulders bent slightly forward, and his hands crossed at the wrists in the loose sleeves of his coarse and faded brown coat,—of that make known in the rural parts of Ireland as a "big-coat"—with a large cape, namely, and a small collar turning over it,—his sharp and rather wasted features composed and thoughtful, and his gray, sunken eyes fixed on the ground as if in meditation, he looked the solitary man he was. The men and women he met all accosted him with kindness and respect, and the children as he passed smiled, and whispered to each other; "There goes Bryan, the old man of the Rock!" The urchins regarded him with a sort of feeling that was not fear, but rather something more akin to reverence. The noisiest and most mischievous of them all kept silent and demure while Bryan was in sight, and it was a notable fact that no one living remembered to have seen an ash-bag appended to the rear of Bryan Cullenan on an Ash Wednesday. That exemption, which he shared with the priests, speaks volumes for the high estimation in which the Hermit was held by the ragamuffins of Cashel town, who, like all other ragamuffins in Irish towns, take a malicious pleasure in carrying out the title of the day, by ornamenting the coat-tails and other such rear appendages of the passers-by with tiny paper bags filled with ashes. Which one of our Irish readers can boast that during their Irish life they went to chapel and got home again on an Ash Wednesday without hearing from some one passing by the sly announcement—then a startling one, too—"You have got an ash-bag on your back"?

Well, Bryan Cullenan enjoyed, as we have said, this very important immunity, with others of a similar nature, from the juvenile inhabitants of Cashel, which was the more remarkable on account of the old man's self-imposed office of expelling all such intruders from the sacred precincts of his domain on the Rock. Going home from Mass that Hollantide Day, Bryan was moving along at a pace somewhat quicker than usual, with that sliding gait peculiar to the aged, saying his prayers the while for the repose of the souls who were that morning recommended to the charitable remembrance of the congregation. Amongst them was one which would single itself out in Bryan's mind from all the others, as if demanding special attention, and though Bryan prayed fervently for all, he did, undoubtedly, offer up an extra *Pater* and *Ave* for that soul in particular. It was *Kathleen Murtha*, the mother of a poor family whom all the countryside knew to have been ejected off the lands of Harry Esmond, senior, of Rose Lodge, some two or three weeks before. The case of these Murthas made a great noise at the time, from the exceedingly trying circumstances in which they were placed. The father of the family, a thatcher by trade, had fallen off the roof of a house he had been thatching, full three months before, and had lain ever since in a helpless condition, one of his thighs having been broken, and also his collar-bone. He was a poor man, just barely supporting his family by his daily labour, and having no time to cultivate a farm, he was obliged to plant potatoes by "con-acre" in Mr. Esmond's ground, and to rent a small adjoining cottage from the same wealthy proprietor. Well, it so happened that Tim Murtha's long illness, and the want of earning consequent thereon, had completely ruined his poor family. His wife could not leave him to go out to work, even if work were to be had, and the children— three girls and one boy—were too young to be of any service; the doctor had to be paid, and that even could not have been done were it not that the neighbouring farmers made up the amount amongst themselves; the potatoes, what remained of them, were seized by Mr. Esmond's bailiffs for the "con-acre" money, and the pig that was fattening for the next fair in Cashel was sold at auction, with a goat that used to give the children milk, and a little kid, whose gambols often made them forget the hunger that was wasting away their young life. All was gone,— poverty was becoming starvation, and still, on his bed of pain, lay the so-lately strong man, his heart torn with anguish at the sight of his heart-broken wife and her thin, pale little ones cowering over the smoky embers of some brambles which the children had picked up around the fields. Not food nor drink did the cottage contain, except the can of cold water that sat on a table where the "dresser" used to be;—the "dresser" itself was gone, with the pewter plates and dishes and wooden vessels, which it had been poor Kathleen's pride to keep "like new pins." Only the shelter of the roof remained to the destitute family, and that remained not long, for on the very day that Tim Murtha crawled out of bed for the first time, Mr. Esmond's bailiffs came with certain members of "the crowbar brigade," turned Tim out on the wide world, the helpless father, the frail, drooping wife, and the wan, emaciated little children, and levelled to the ground their poor but well-loved dwelling, because "his honour didn't want such cabins so near the big house," and was glad of the opportunity to get rid of one of them.

Prayers and tears and expostulations were all in vain—Tim Murtha knew that well, so he neither wept nor prayed, but sat, with his terror-stricken family clinging around him, on a large flat stone which Kathleen's feeble arm had helped him to reach, watching with stony eyes the work of demolition that left them all houseless on a chill October day. He thought with a swelling heart of the time when his own hands built that little cottage to bring Kathleen home to—a bonny bride. He thought of the light heart that was in his breast then, and the bright hopes that danced before his eyes like fairy visions.

Scarce ten years had passed since then, and lo! the bright hopes were fled,—hunger and cold had their grasp on his heart, and, worse still, on the hearts of Kathleen and her children,—and the walls that had witnessed their humble joys, and the years of comfort his honest toil had earned, were now ruthlessly battered down before his eyes and erased from the face of the earth. What other thoughts came into the tortured mind of Tim Murtha, to the tune of the crashing walls and the falling rafters of his home, God—*and the Devil*—only know. That night the forlorn family were sheltered under the roof of a kind neighbour, himself a poor cottier too, and next day a few of "the boys" came together and threw up a shed against the side of the old Rock amongst the huts where Bryan had his home.

Not quite three weeks had passed since the Murthas were evicted from their old homestead, and now Kathleen was dead, and gone to rest. Many a visit old Bryan had paid to their dreary place of refuge during those long tedious weeks, and, truth to tell, two bright half-crowns had passed, at as many succeeding visits, from his pocket to that of Tim Murtha. That was a crown of "the Counsellor's guinea," but what of that?—"if it helped to keep the life in the poor things, it couldn't be better spent." Oh, how Bryan rejoiced then that he had divided his share with those who were more in need than himself!

But still he kept thinking of the solemn words of the priest who said Mass that morning : "*And, brethren, I recommend to your prayers, in a special manner, the soul of Kathleen Murtha.*"

"Ah!" said Bryan to himself, "there's where God's holy Church differs from the world. The poor are *her* care, and the more despised they are by the rich and the proud of this world, the dearer they are to the heart of that good Mother—if they only lived as Christians. Well, that's one comfort, anyhow!" he said, as he reached his own door, which was opened by Cauth with great alacrity; that singular specimen of womankind having been anxiously awaiting his coming.

"An' what is that?" said Cauth, as she stooped to blow up her smouldering fire; "what's the comfort now?"

"Why, just this, Cauth," said the old man, taking his seat

by the welcome fire that was now beginning to blaze up cheerily, "that the poor have one friend that never deserts them—a powerful friend, too—an' that is *Religion!* If it wasn't for Religion, an' the good, kind priest that brings her smile with him to the hovels of the poor, how could you, or I, live at all —or poor Kathleen Murtha, that's gone home now? What would become of the poor, Cauth, if it wasn't for Religion, and the hopes she keeps alive in their hearts?"

Bryan, from his solitary habits and his almost uninterrupted communion with the spirits of the dead, in the relics of their mortal bodies and the mouldering works of their hands, had acquired a certain solemnity in the expression of his thoughts which at times amounted to dignity. His speech was, moreover, thickly strewn with metaphor, and assumed now and then quite a poetical character. This was only, however, when the old man spoke in Irish, which he generally did with Cauth; but even his English was rather choice, from his frequent communication with the gentlefolks from abroad who visited the ruins on the Rock. His grave and sometimes even lofty thoughts Cauth could not, of course, understand, but his style of talking, when he did talk freely, commanded her entire admiration, and caused her to look upon the aged Hermit as something far beyond the common run of people. Be it known to the reader that Bryan and Cauth did not stand to each other in the relation of husband and wife, as might be supposed; they were strangers to each other only a year or two before, when Bryan, at the recommendation of Mrs. Esmond, and with her kind assistance, commenced housekeeping, with Cauth as *femme de charge*, for before that time poor Bryan had not a roof he could call his own, and spent most of his nights as well as his days amongst the lone mansions of the dead on his beloved Rock, coming down only to hear Mass on Sundays and holydays, and to receive from the willing hand of charity the little sustenance which he required. It was only when the inclemency of the weather drove him for shelter to the plain below that he ever asked a night's lodging. He used to say himself, when any one expressed surprise at his remaining over night on the Rock, that he had the grandest sleeping-room in all Ireland, and that was "in the king's own house." But it was not in the old palace of the Munster kings that Bryan Cullanan oftenest sought repose; he preferred the choir of the old cathedral, just by the tomb of Myler M'Grath, or the shade of the deep Saxon arch that separates the nave from the choir in Cormac's chapel.

As for Cauth, old Bryan knew no more about her than just what he saw. Who she was, or what she was, she carefully kept to herself; and Bryan, being nowise addicted to curiosity, seldom thought of what there was peculiar about her manner, unless when some wild expression, to him unaccountable, set him thinking of the probable cause of her odd ways, and the strange fits of moody thought that would come upon her at times without any apparent cause.

Her humour was somewhat caustic that Hollantide Day, and she snapped at Bryan like a cross cur when he alluded so feelingly to Kathleen Murtha's deserted state.

"She wasn't trustin' to the priest, anyhow," said she, stopping a moment with the skillet[1] in her hand, from which she was pouring out on a wooden trancher the stirabout[2] intended for Bryan's breakfast—her own share being left in the pot.

"An' sure I know that well, Cauth," said Bryan, with much feeling; "sure I know who made her bed an' kep' her clane an' comfortable ever since she came about the Rock—Oyeh! one 'most as poor as herself," he added as if to himself.

"'Deed, then, it's little I could do for her," made answer Cauth; "but there was them that could an' did give her comfort—may they never know the want of it themselves, I pray God!"

"An' who were they, Cauth?"

"That's a sayoret, Bryan," said Cauth, a little softened; "but —but—I think you might guess."

Bryan looked up from his stirabout at the shrewd, keen-looking face of Cauth, and his old eyes twinkled. "I think I do, Cauth, I think I do."

"Well, if you do, keep it to yourself, for if it came to the ears of some people—you know who I mane—it 'id make bad blood betwixt them all—so the darlin' says herself, an' she's fearful of havin' anybody's ill-will, espaycially when it's in the family."

[1] An iron pot of the smallest size is so called in Ireland.
[2] Oatmeal porridge.

"An' more's the pity, Cauth, that it *is* in the family! I declare that man's a disgrace to all belongin' to him."

"Ay, an' if it wasn't for *them* he'd a got his oats long ago!" said Cauth, with bitter emphasis.

"Whisht, whisht, Cauth! don't say that!" cried Bryan quickly, and he glanced around as if fearful that some one might possibly be within hearing.

"But I *will* say it, Bryan!" said Cauth doggedly; "an' I say, too, that there's many a one *has* got settled with before now that wasn't any better entitled to it."

Bryan dropped his spoon and looked up again; his pale, wrinkled face was flushed, and a light was shining in his aged eyes that Cauth had never seen there before.

"Woman!" said he in a grave, solemn tone, "who has made you the judge of that man's, or any other man's, evil doings? There's One above that'll judge us all."

As if a blow had stunned her, Cauth dropped heavily on the stool beside her, and buried her face in her outspread hands, murmuring in a half-audible voice, "Who am *I*? Ay, sure enough, who am I to judge any one? Oh, wirra! it's myself can tell that!"

Bryan, alarmed as he always was by Cauth's strange soliloquies, began to express his sorrow for what he had said, assuring her that he didn't mean to hurt her feelings. "But then, Cauth, I couldn't listen to the words you said and hold my peace. No, Cauth, I could not, I could not; for murder is murder, be it as it may, an' the Lord in heaven says, 'You shall do no murder.'"

At this Cauth started to her feet, and flung back the long grey hair that had fallen from under her close linen cap. "An' who has done murder, Bryan Cullenan?—who has shed blood? You needn't look at *me* with them ould fiery eyes of yours—as if there was blood on *my* hand—see there! see there!" and she stretched both her hands towards him, but suddenly drew them back and sank again on her seat, with a low, plaintive moan and a shudder.

"Christ save us!" ejaculated Bryan in an undertone; "I b'lieve it's losin' her senses the woman is! I'd best get out of her sight, I'm thinkin'."

Unnoticed by Cauth, he reached for his hat, where it hung on a peg, and, softly opening the door, left the cottage. He was taking his way, as usual, towards the Rock, and had already reached the gate leading into the hallowed enclosure, when the cheerful sound of the bagpipes struck upon his ear, and the old man paused with his hand on the latch to await the approach of the wandering minstrel, in whom he recognised an old friend. Surrounded by a troop of ragged urchins, for whose special entertainment he evidently blew his chanter at that particular moment, the piper, a little old man of threescore-five or thereabouts, moved along with the slow pace peculiar to his tribe, gladdening the hearts of his juvenile audience—and most likely his own to—with "The Reel of Tullochgorum." Ever and anon his course was impeded by the rushing and crushing of the young tatterdemalions who formed his guard of honour, each one trying to make his way nearer to the great centre of attraction; little scrupulous, moreover, as to the means employed, so that "kicks and cuffs were more plenty than ha'pence," as the piper good-humouredly observed. But still he played on, the crowd increasing by little and little as the *cortège* passed along, the merry heart of the old man growing lighter and lighter, and his music cheerier, as the acclamations of his noisy escort grew more and more uproarious. Now and then the music would suddenly cease, and the piper's voice make itself heard in tones of remonstrance rather than rebuke.

"Ah, then, childer, how can I play if you don't keep off my elbow? See that, now!—bad cess to me but you'll break my pipes, so you will! Well, now, I tell you this, if you don't keep off o' me I'll not play another tune, and that's the end of it, now!"

But it was not the end of it, as the young rogues well knew by old experience; for the piper's face belied his words, and the more he protested against playing any more, the faster and merrier went the pipes, amid the joyous shouts of the rosy urchins, who went frisking like kids to the sound of the music.

It required more than a passing glance to make a stranger sensible of the fact that the merry face of the piper wanted the light of the eyes, for the organs themselves, clear, full, and blue, gave no other indications of the visual darkness than a tremulous motion of the lids which might possibly have proceeded from some other cause. But then there was a little dog, a wiry, hard-favoured terrier, which trotted along a pace or two in advance of the piper, to whom it was evidently bound by affection still more than by the cord, one end of which encircled the neck of the animal, whilst the other was fastened to the button-hole of its master's old frieze coat by a piece of stick run through inside the garment; patiently and gently the dog moved on, suiting its pace with wonderful sagacity to that of its master, and maintaining a sort of official gravity that was proof against every trial, the effect, doubtless, of long familiarity with the noisy plaudits that usually followed the performance to which he probably considered himself a party. It was clear, then, that the piper was blind, and it was also clear that his privation sat lightly upon him, even with the weight of his sixty odd years and his houseless, homeless poverty. Shaun the piper was, indeed, one of the happiest men in all Ireland, for, like the Claddagh boatman in the ballad—

His heart was true, his wants were few,

and his pipes made him welcome wherever he went to a night's lodging and the best fare the peasant's cot or the farmer's house afforded. Even his dog—misnamed Frisk—was as welcome a visitor as himself, especially to the junior members of the humble households where he oftenest sought rest and shelter. Shaun, like most persons suffering under a like privation, had a wonderfully keen sense of hearing, and could tell people by their voices just as others do by their faces. He also knew with unerring precision every foot of ground in Tipperary, and could make his way, with Frisk alone, through many parts of Limerick, Clare, and Waterford. He had even crossed the Knockmeledown mountains, and extended his "tramp" into Cork; but somehow Frisk's sagacity failed him there, and the pipes never seemed to sound the same, and Shaun made up his mind that he and Frisk had better keep to "the old ark," so they never crossed the wild mountains again.

But we have left our friend Bryan standing too long at the gate, especially as the weather was cold and the iron latch felt like ice under his hand. A grim smile puckered his visage as he watched the triumphal approach of the minstrel, who suddenly stopped short in the middle of a bar and turned his sightless eyes towards the Rock.

"Childer," said he, "we ought to be near the gate now. I wondher is ould Bryan Callenan alive yet?"

"Oych! it's himself that is. Sure, *he'll* never die."

"Alive? Why wouldn't he? Sure, he's a ghost himself, if there's one on the Rock."

"Whisht, you sprissawn! there he is at the gate."

Here the crowd of chattering gaffers fell back right and left to make way for Bryan, who came forward with outstretched hand to greet his old acquaintance.

"You're welcome back to Cashel, Shaun!" he said in Irish. "I needn't ask how you are, for your face tells that story, and your foot is a'most as light as it was five-and-twenty years agone, when you danced the Foxhunter's Jig for the quality the night of the ould master's wedding. Frisk, my poor fellow, I'm proud to see you again!"

Frisk acknowledged the compliment by wagging his tail demurely.

"Wisha, Bryney the Rock, is this yourself?" was the piper's hearty response, as he eagerly seized and warmly shook the old man's hand. "I was just a-thinkin' to myself that if you were still above ground I'd soon hear your voice. Well, I declare I'm glad to *see* you!"

He forgot that he didn't see him, but the mischievous elves around, all eyes and ears, quickly detected the slip of the tongue.

"Oh, murdher! do you hear what he says?—he's glad to *see* him!" This was the signal for a roar of juvenile laughter, that drew a half-angry rebuke from Shaun and a whole-angry one from Bryan, both of which only tended to increase the merriment of the waggish crew.

"Put up your pipes, Shaun," said Bryan, "and come in and have some breakfast. I've a little place of my own now."

"Do you tell me so, Bryan? And where is it, agra?"

"Only a step or two back from here. Come, now! be off home with you, childer! Shaun will play no more this bout."

This unwelcome news had to be repeated by Shaun himself before it was received as true, and even then the youngsters were not got rid of till the door of Bryan's cottage hid the piper, his pipes and dog, from their eager sight.

"That was a pleasant night you were speakin' of, Bryan," said Shaun as they entered. "But I didn't know that you were there."

"'Deed an' I was, then,—wasn't the whole country there? An' full an' plenty there was for every one. A darlin' fine young gentleman the ould master was then,—the heavens be his bed this day! for it's himself was always a good friend to the poor, an' liked well to see them about him."

"Pity all the Esmonds weren't like *him!*" said the piper, with a sudden change of manner.

"His son is as good as ever he was," said Bryan, as he took the pipes and placed the piper on a stool near the fire.

"But his *brother* isn't," returned Shaun, with a degree of excitement altogether unusual. "If there's vengeance in heaven it'll come down on *him*, as sure as his name is Harry Esmond!"

"Pooh, pooh, Shaun! don't be so hard on the ould gentleman!—don't now, and God bless you! for I don't like to hear anything bad laid out for one of his name. They're a good stock, you know yourself."

"I do well, Bryan, an' that's the very raison why ould Harry shouldn't act as he does. A body doesn't wonder at the upstarts that's takin' the place of the rale quality to be hard on the ould tenants, an' trate God's poor like dogs, but I tell you, Bryan, it's against nature for an Esmond to make a brute of himself."

"A brute, Shaun!—oh vo! vo! what's comin' over you?"

"I say he *is* a brute, Bryan, take it as you will! If he wasn't, he wouldn't turn the piper from his door, and *kick tha piper's dog.*" This last came out with such strong emphasis that it was clearly the greater offence of the two.

"An' did ould Mr. Esmond do that?" questioned Bryan anxiously.

"He did Bryan, as I'm a sinner! An' if I was to die on the roadside of hunger—myself an' Frisk—I wouldn't cross his threshold again. Never fear but the grass 'll grow green enough on that same threshold, maybe afore you or I goes home yet."

"Cauth," said Bryan, for the first time addressing the old woman, who sat a silent listener in the chimney corner,—"Cauth, have you anything for Shaun to eat and drink?—the best you have isn't half good enough for him."

"Cauth?" repeated Shaun, catching at this first intimation of another being present,—"an' who is Cauth, if it's a fair question?"

Bryan would have been puzzled to answer, but Cauth relieved him of the task. "One that knows you well, Shaun, an' danced many's the time to your music years and years agone, near the foot of Slievenamon, eastward." There was an evident attempt at disguising the voice, but it could not deceive Shaun. He started, turned his head quickly towards the speaker, and said in a voice very different from his usual tone—

"Slievenamon! No, no—not there! The Lord save us all! what brings you here—all the way from"—

"Sit over an' take some breakfast," said Cauth quickly; "there's a cup of tay that'll do your ould heart good, an' some white bread from the big house. God's blessin' on the giver, an' that's young Mrs. Esmond herself! Come, Frisk, good dog! here's some could stirabout for you, an' milk too, my poor fellow."

"The milk isn't as plenty with you now, my woman, as it used to be," said Shaun in a low voice, as Bryan placed him at the little table. A change had come over the buoyant spirit that even the snows of age could not chill, and Shaun was many degrees paler than when he entered the cottage, while the happy smile had vanished from his face. Words seemed hovering on his lips which he did not care to speak, and troubled memories were evidently at work in his usually tranquil mind.

Cauth, too, appeared ill at ease, watching the piper's face with a keen, scrutinising glance, and shrinking fearfully as often as he opened his lips to speak. Bryan noticed all this, and when Shaun, having finished his scant breakfast, observed that it was time for him to be moving, the old man rose with alacrity, saying that he ought to be on the Rock long ago, there was always so much to be done there and only him to do it.

As the two old men left the cottage together, Cauth followed them to the door. "So you're goin', Shaun, without as much as sayin' 'God be with you!'"

"I declare att' so I was," said he, turning back his head. "Well, God be with you!" but he did not offer his hand.

"Will you keep my saycret?" whispered Cauth; "for God's sake do!"

"I will—God pity you!" And Shaun was gone.

CHAPTER IV

BRYAN'S STATIONS.

It was not to scrape the moss from the tombs and headstones, or to replace the precious fragments rent by time and the pitiless elements from the ancient sculptures, that Bryan Cullenan wended his way to the ruins on the Rock that cold November day. He did not forget that it was the Feast of All Saints, and therefore a holyday of obligation; but somehow he never felt perfectly at home anywhere else, and had always a misty notion that when he was not there he ought to be, and was pretty certain of being wanted. It is true the Rock had few visitors at that season, but still some there might be, and who so well as Bryan could tell them all about the old place, and the great sights that used to be seen there in the old, old times? Then, if nobody chanced to come, Bryan was never at a loss for employment, for he told his beads over and over for all sorts of pious intentions; and when he was not telling his beads, why, then his thoughts were his best companions—to borrow a phrase of his own, quoted in turn from an old story with which all of us were familiar in days of childhood. In the solitude of the ruins, which to many would have been insupportable, Bryan found his peace and happiness; on working days, working as though his subsistence depended on it, from early morning till late night, beguiling his self-imposed task the while with prayer or meditation, or mayhap the crooning of an ancient hymn, generally in the old Celtic tongue that best befitted the solemn ruins dating from Celtic ages.

The calls of nature were seldom pressing on old Bryan, whose attenuated frame required but little sustenance; and even that little he could dispense with for the better part of the twenty-four hours without much inconvenience to himself. This was partly the effect of long habit, and partly of forgetfulness, in the strange preponderance of the spiritual over the corporal in his nature during his solitary hours on the Rock. Once or twice it happened that he had been disturbed in some quaint old-world reverie by the officious kindness of Cauth coming up to summon him to his morning or noonday meal (it was only in broad daylight that Cauth would venture to set foot on the Rock), so he charged the old woman never to trouble him again on any account "in regard to the eatin' or drinkin', for when he was hungry he'd go down himself." Cauth was fain to submit, for the old man had such a way with him, as she said to herself, that nobody cared to contradict him. "It's doatin' the orathur is," was her final conclusion on that, as on many other occasions; "an' I suppose there's nothin' for it but to let him have his way." So Bryan ever after had his way as far as his solitary life on the Rock was concerned.

The hours of that holyday passed away all unnoticed by Bryan. According to his custom on such days, he made what he called his "stations," beginning at the image of St. Patrick on the great stone by the gate, and ending at the spot where the high altar of the cathedral once rose in all the grandeur of archiepiscopal pomp. Bryan had marked out for himself in the circuit of the holy places fourteen stations, corresponding with the Stations of the Cross, following, as he was fain to hope, the course by which the Sacred Host was carried in procession in the grand old times when the archbishops of Cashel were kings of Munster, and princes carried the canopy that covered the King of kings.

Long time the old man paused and prayed in the beautiful choir of Cormac's Chapel, where the altar stood of old—again at the tomb of the holy founder, close by the chapel wall—then on to the Chapel of the Apostles, roofless and bare, yet still decorated with the sculptured images of the Twelve Apostles. There, tradition says, stood, ages since, "a fair statue of a bishop," whom ancient chronicles point out as David MacKelly, Archbishop of Cashel, who died in the middle of the thirteenth century, "and was buried in the little Chapel of the Apostles." From there passed Bryan to the old abbey, whose once noble church was a goodly resting-place for the Blessed Sacrament in those grand processions of old time, when mitred abbots and cowled monks graced the choir stalls, and the stately cloisters echoed to the fall of many feet. Here was a place to pause and meditate—here where so many holy monks and sainted abbots slept the sleep of peace.

Last of all was the cathedral, with its long line of buried archbishops, many of whom are still known by name to the people and their memory fondly cherished. There was Angus, the holy prince, whose conversion from paganism by St. Patrick himself is still the theme of the winter's tale by the cottage hearth, on account of the marvellous faith of the royal convert, what time he suffered the point of Patrick's iron-shod staff to penetrate his foot without a murmur or a groan, deeming it part of the baptismal rite. There was Cormac Mac Cullenan, the holy prince-bishop, who rebuilt St. Patrick's old church and erected that chapel which still bears his name, a miracle of ancient art. There was Archbishop O'Hene, of whom chronicles tell that he was "the fountain of religion in the western parts of Europe;" and there was Archbishop O'Dunan, known to his own and after ages as "the most pious man in the Western world;" there was Archbishop Maurice, to whose learning and wisdom even the Welshman, Cambrensis, bears witness, albeit that he spoke his mind rather freely to that worthy on one memorable occasion, when, Giraldus having taunted the Irish with having no martyrs, the prelate replied: "Though our country be looked upon as barbarous, uncultivated, and cruel, yet they always have paid reverence and honour to ecclesiastics, and never could stretch out their hands against the saints of God. But now there is come a people who know how, and are accustomed to make martyrs. Henceforth Ireland, like all other countries, shall have hers." (Well you said it, Maurice of Cashel, many a martyr Ireland has had since!) There was Archbishop O'Heney, Legate-Apostolic in Ireland, and author of the *Life of St. Cuthbert of Lindisfarne*, whom he proves to have been an Irish saint;[1] there was Richard O'Hedian, one of the greatest prelates that ever swayed the crozier of Cashel, the restorer and renovator of all the buildings on the Rock, the founder of the hall for the vicars-choral; the St. Laurence O'Toole of Cashel, the prelate

[1] It is worthy of remark that Benedict XIV., in his decree regarding the offices of Irish Saints, also mentions St. Cuthbert as one of the national Saints of Ireland.

who was impeached by John Gese, the Protestant Bishop of Waterford and Lismore, in thirty articles, the principal of which were: "That he made very much of the Irish and loved none of the English;" and furthermore, "That he gave no benefice to any Englishman, and advised other bishops to the like practice." Bryan Cullenan could not have enumerated the great archbishop's claims to the admiration of posterity, but he knew him, by tradition, as one who stood up manfully for the old race; with all Munster he loved and reverenced his name, and the place of his sepulture in the old cathedral was one of the Hermit's favourite shrines. The tomb of Myler M'Grath, though from its position in the deep choir it often sheltered the old man's rest in the warm nights of summer, was yet not one of his stations; for even if the apostate prelate did recant his errors on his bed of death, he was still "Queen Bess's bishop" to all the county round, and no man or woman in Ormond wide ever breathed a blessing on his name. The stain of apostasy was not to be effaced from the memory of *an archbishop* by the private recantation of public errors persisted in for years. No, no!—prayers might be said for the repose of that late repentant soul, and many a one Bryan did say with that intention, but no prayers were offered up by him or others at the tomb where "the first Protestant Archbishop of Cashel" had mouldered into dust.

These tombs, with the old altar sites, were Bryan Cullenan's stations, but these were not all the Christian heroes whose memory gilds the ruined fanes of Cashel. Some of the greatest and holiest of the archbishops gave up their souls to God far away from the Sacred Rock, and ever as Bryan knelt before the forsaken spot where of old they ministered at the altar, he would murmur to himself, "An' sure they're not all here, the more's the pity! Isn't there Archbishop O'Hurley, the holy martyr, that suffered death and torture for the faith, that was buried in sayeret somewheres near Dublin?[1] Ay, an' many another holy bishop that died in France and Spain in the time of the troubles! Well, it's a folly to talk! England has a deal

[1] The martyrdom of Dermot O'Hurley, Archbishop of Cashel, in the reign of Elizabeth, was accompanied by circumstances of the most revolting cruelty. He was bound to a stake, his arms and legs covered over with pitch, salt, oil, and sulphur; fire was then applied so slowly that

to answer for, an' it's the black reckonin' she'll have to pay when her day of reckonin' comes!"

"But, ochone!" Bryan would sigh, as he sat himself down on the projecting base of a noble column in the aisle, after finishing his stations, and fixed his sorrowful gaze on the shattered walls of the choir, where the winter wind was making sad music as it swept in eddies through the breaches time had made,—"ochone! it's a hard thing to think that England wasn't the worst after all. Wasn't Murrogh of the Burnings worse than any Sassenach of them all? an' him of the rale ould stock, too, with Brian's own blood in his veins! Och, wirra, wirra! to think of him havin' twenty priests dragged from behind the holy althar, where they were hidin', and butchered like sheep there right in front of it—not to speak of the three thousand people he burned up in the town below! Well, well! if there's justice in heaven, Murrogh O'Brien, you have a low place in the pit of hell! Still," recollecting himself, "they say he was sorry for it all before he died—an' turned Catholic, too. Well, maybe he did,—God's grace can soften the hardest heart, we all know,—but if Murrogh of the Burnings died a good Christian, it was a meracle an' nothin' else. I declare to my heart if *he's* in heaven I'd as lieve not see him—I'd sooner have somebody else convaynient to me there—God forgive me!"

Then Bryan would endeavour to bring himself to more Christian sentiments with regard to Murrogh, but do as he would he never could school his lips or his rebellious heart to pray for his soul's repose. "If it be true that he died a Catholic," said Bryan to himself, "then he gets his share of the Church's prayers, an' can do without mine—well for him! for I'm afeard if he had no others, he wouldn't get many from me —barrin' I jist was sartin sure that he *had* no one else to pray for him. A body couldn't be *too* hard that way to any poor soul that stood in need of their prayers. Oh, musha! the Lord have mercy on all that's puttin' their punishment over them, either in the other world or this! An' sure, that reminds me, the morrow is All Souls' Day, an' I must make the stations for

the holy prelate was kept several hours in torture. He was then placed on the rack, and still persisting in his refusal to acknowledge the supremacy of Elizabeth in spiritual matters, was taken to St. Stephen's Green and there strangled.

them. I'll warrant there'll be plenty o' them about me here the night—the poor sorrowful crathurs! Please God, I must be down for first Mass in the mornin', an' to make my little offerings with the rest."

So passed the day—the evening fell, the early evening of dull November, yet Bryan was still at his dreary post, though the drizzling rain coming chill on the blast had driven him hours before to the safe shelter of Cormac's Chapel, the stone roof of which was proof alike to wind and rain. As the shadows deepened around him, where he sat under the deep arch of the portal, and the stony faces on the corbels looked grimmer and quainter through the mist, and the pillars of the blind arches within the building, but dimly seen from the entrance even in broad day, receded, as it were, from Bryan's view into the darkness that enveloped the nave and choir, the old man felt an awe creeping over him that still was not fear. It was the vigil of the dead, and with the shadows came the spirits, as Bryan firmly believed. But they were not spirits that Bryan feared—they were only "poor wandering crathurs lookin' for help," and what help Bryan could give them he cheerfully gave; in accordance with the spirit of the Church whose solemn commemoration of All Souls in the Propitiatory Sacrifice was next day to gladden the suffering spirits of the middle state—be their place of punishment where it might. To any other than Bryan Cullenan the sense of solitude and of supernatural presence would have been overwhelming, but to Bryan it was far otherwise—silence and solitude were his dream of life, and his intimate communion with the dead, and entire devotion to their memory, raised him far beyond the vulgar fear of the supernatural which superstition loves to cherish.

"Ha! ha! ha!" laughed Bryan low to himself, "to think of that foolish Cauth tellin' me not on any account to stay on the Rock this evenin' after nightfall!—as if I'd be afeard of *them* anywhere, or as if they'd do me any mischief! Aren't they about us everywhere as thick as the grass in the fields, an' still nobody sees them, the crathurs, or hears them aither,—it's little they throuble us, after all. Why, then, now what can that be? There's no livin' bein' barrin' myself that 'id be on the Rock at this hour. It must be something else."

Rising from his seat, Bryan stepped out, regardless of the rain, and strained his ear to listen. The sound was, at first, a low moaning, and Bryan whispered softly to himself, "That's some poor wanderin' sperit, anyhow. There's heavy trouble on it, I'll go bail."

All at once a soft, plaintive voice was heard singing in Irish a ditty well known in Munster, and these were the words in English—

"I could wander through the streets hand-in-hand with my true love,
I would sail the salt sea with no fortune but your love;
My nearest and my dearest I'd leave them for ever,
And you'd raise me from death if you said 'We'll ne'er sever!'"

"Well, that's a quare ghost!" said Bryan, moving a little farther in the direction of the voice. "I believe it's in the tower it is."

He moved cautiously along by the end of the great church,—the round tower standing at the angle of one arm of the transept as Cormac's Chapel nestles in the shade of the other,—but had not gone many steps when he again stood still, for the mournful caoine was rising fitfully on the breeze, and the clapping of hands was heard, and sighs and moans that seemed to come from a breaking heart.

"Christ save us!" ejaculated Bryan, and he crossed himself devoutly, "it must be the Banshee! Maybe it's a warnin' for myself; sure enough, the Banshee follows the Cullanans! Oh vo! vo! isn't that a sorrowful cry?" He was yet speaking, when the invisible singer broke again into a wild strain of music and sang, still in Irish—

"Gladly, O my blighted flower,
Sweet apple of my bosom's tree,
Would I now
Stretch me in your dark death-bower,
Beside your corpse, and lovingly
Kiss your brow.

But we'll meet ere many a day,
Nevermore to part,
For even now I feel the clay
Gath'ring round my heart."[1]

---

[1] Mangan's Translation.

"Ah!" said Bryan to himself, "I know now who it is—it's neither ghost nor Banshee, but Mad Mabel. Poor thing! poor thing! where is she, at all?"

It must be owned that Bryan's step was somewhat quicker after making this discovery than it was when he expected to see the Banshee; he speedily turned the angle of the transept wall, and there, crouching at the foot of the old pillar-tower, was a female figure, only to be distinguished from the dark objects around by the light colour of her garments. Neither the darkness nor the rain appeared to disturb the unhappy being who had chosen a place so lone and drear for her wild and mournful minstrelsy.

"Wisha, Mabel, my poor girl!" said Bryan, tenderly raising her from the wet ground, "what on earth brought you here such a night as this?"

"Husht! husht!" she replied in a cautious whisper, putting her mouth close to Bryan's ear. "They told me he was here, hidin', you know, hidin'. Isn't this Holy Cross?"

"No, no, Mabel; this is Cashel—the Rock of Cashel, you know;" and, encircling her frail form with his arm, he hurried towards the gate, anxious to get her housed with Cauth in his own cottage.

"Cashel?" she repeated in a whisper; then, as if the name awoke an echo in her darkened mind, she sang a snatch of an old song, to the air of "The Girl I Left Behind Me"—

'No more—no more in Cashel town
I'll sell my health a-raking,
Nor on days of fairs rove up and down,
Nor join the merry-making.

"Whisht! there's the Peelers—they'll hear you!—and listen hither, honest man!—if they do, they'll *hang* you—they hang everybody!"

Then all at once she broke out again with—

"The Bansha Peelers were out one night
On duty on patrolling, O!
They met a goat upon the road,
And took him to be a stroller, O!

"Good man, why don't you sing?—*he* used to sing, you know! But did you hear that he was dead?" She peered into Bryan's face through the darkness, then, pushing him away with a force that made him stagger, she cried, with a disdainful laugh—

"Get away with you, now! you're ould, an' he's young—will you not be botherin' me with your palaver? Oh, wisha! I never hear *his* voice now, at all! Where is he?—ay, that's it—he's at Holy Cross—all alone by himself, they tell me, an' that's why I want to go! An' I *must* go, too, an' be there afore the clock strikes twelve the night. Let me go now—you see I can't stay at all, at all!—

Och, among the green bushes he's waiting for me!"

Bryan had purposely kept silence, fearing lest the sound of an unfamiliar voice might frighten her so that his feeble arm could not longer hold her. But still he kept on his way, whilst the rain fell faster and heavier each passing moment. They had now reached the cottage, at the door of which stood Cauth waiting anxiously, as on the previous night, for Bryan's appearance. She was just commencing with—"Why, then, Bryan"—when the old man brushed past her with Mabel into the house.

"Wisha, Bryan! who's that you have with you?" cried Cauth, following them in; but no sooner did her eye fall on the pale face of the maniac, looking ghostly through the long damp tresses that hung over it in wild disorder, than a livid pallor overspread her own visage, and she shook like an aspen leaf. Meanwhile, Bryan had seated the miserable creature in the chimney corner, and, although the fire was blazing brightly, he threw on some additional turf, which latter act, not being agreeable to Cauth, served to arouse her from her momentary stupor.

"Now, then, what did you do that for?" she said sharply enough, considering that the turf was unquestionably Bryan's own. "Wasn't the fire good enough? One 'id think you had a turf-stack back o' the house."

"Never mind, Cauth, never mind—God is a rich provider. Come and see to poor Mabel—can't you put some clothes on her till you dry these duds she has on? She's 'most dead with the cowld an' wet, you see."

"Cowld—cowld!" muttered the girl, crouching over the

fire, and shivering all over as the kindly warmth reached her emaciated frame through the wet garments that clung around her.

"Why, then, to be sure, I'll put dry clothes on her," said Cauth, with a strange mixture of compassion and peevishness in her tone and in her face; "do you think I'm a Turk or a haythen that I wouldn't? But where did you come across her?"

"On the Rock above, an' sure it was the blessin' o' the world that I happened to be there at the time. She might have been out all night under the rain, an' maybe it's dead I'd find her in the mornin'. See how God takes care of them that can't take care of themselves! Praise an' glory to His name—He does!"

It was no so easy matter for Cauth to get the necessary change made in Mabel's apparel. She could not persuade her to leave the fire, and although Bryan went out of sight behind the jamb-wall, so as to leave the place to themselves, the difficulty still existed. The girl had taken it into her head that some sinister motive prompted the disrobement, and she resisted with all the strength that madness gives.

"If it's going to hang me you are," said she, freeing herself with a sudden jerk from the restraint of Cauth's arm, "there's no need for you to strip me, sure!——can't you hang me with my clothes on?"

Cauth tried to expostulate, but her voice failed her, and a convulsive shudder passed through her frame. The senseless prattle of the maniac was either striking some chord in her own heart, or exciting her compassion to an intolerable degree. She silently renewed her efforts, however, to take off the wet clothes, and finally succeeded, owing mainly to their tattered condition. But still, to the last, Mabel kept grumbling and protesting.

"Tut, tut! you bould jade! isn't it ashamed you ought to be to strip a dacent girl that way? Be off with you now!—not a tack more you'll get off—not a tack! Oh, murther! isn't she the robber, all out?"

When the warm, dry clothes were once on, however, Mabel's tone changed. She began to feel the comfort, and a smile overspread her wan features as, looking down at the red drugget petticoat which Cauth had put on, she said to Bryan, who had just resumed his place at the fire——

"There now, you see, I'm '*Petticoat Loose!*'[1]—I tould you so, but you wouldn't b'lieve me! Don't be afeard, ould man, I'll not hurt *you!* But don't stop me—don't, an' God bless you! for I'm on my way to Holy Cross to see *him, you know,* an' I must be back at the hill before cock-crow. There, look at *her!*" pointing with a giggling laugh at Cauth, who had dropped almost fainting on a seat,—"she's afeard of the ghost, you see!—she thinks Petticoat Loose 'll hang her—ha! ha! ha! maybe she will. She hung *me* onst—that I mayn't sin, but she did!—an' I'm walkin', walkin' ever since, an' will till the Day o' Judgment."

"The Lord save us!" muttered Cauth; "she'll be the death o' me this night, if I stay in the one house with her! Anyway, I must get the supper for them."

The supper was got accordingly—tea and oaten bread for Mabel, porridge and milk for Bryan, in which Cauth made a show of joining him, but it was plain that the appetite was wanting to her. Mabel, on the contrary, swallowed her supper greedily, and with evident relish of the tea, then a luxury little common amongst country people in any part of Ireland.

"Tay!" said Mabel very softly, looking at the liquid in her cup,—"I like tay—I get it up at the Hall." Then, as if the name had brought a thought into her mind, she turned to Bryan with quite a confidential air, "Jerry Pierce is at the Hall now—you know Jerry?—he's not hung yet—but ould Mr. Esmond says he'll hang him, an' Tim Murtha, an' everybody—an' then 'on't they hang *him?*—maybe they 'on't—no, no, hey don't hang the quality—it's *shoot* them they do!" and she lowered her voice to a hissing whisper that froze the blood in the veins of those who heard her. "You needn't look at me so, honest man! for it's truth I tell you—they do shoot the gentlemen by times"——

"Whisht, whisht, Mabel!" said Bryan in a tone of great

---

[1] A ghost, known by this appellation, was the terror of the Tipperary peasantry of that neighbourhood for years before and after the time specified—perhaps is still, for aught we know. The scene of her perambulations was a bare bleak hill, a few miles from Cashel.

alarm, knowing that walls have ears sometimes. "You said you liked tay—give her another cup, Cauth."

But Mabel would persist in the obnoxious theme, tea or no tea. "Did you ever hear of ould Chadwick—didn't they shoot him—didn't they, now? Mara said they did. An' listen hither," —pulling Bryan's head close to her,—"he said it was him—you know who I mane—there! don't say a word for your life—but there was blood spilled, now—that's God's truth—an' sich hangin' you never seen as there was after it!—ha! ha! ha! they thought to hang me too, but I hid behind King Donogh's tomb in Holy Cross Abbey abroad, an' that's how they missed of me, you see!—but they cotched him—an' they hung him, for all his purty red cheeks an' his yalla hair.

Och! what colour was your true love's hair,
And what clothes did your true love wear?
A green silk jacket, this maid replied,
And his yallow hair to his belt was tied."

A groan from Cauth here drew Bryan's attention, and a glance at her face was sufficient to show him that something unusual was the matter with her; she sat with her distended eyes fixed on vacancy, her lips and cheeks as bloodless as those of a corpse, and her hand extended as if in the act of pointing at some object.

"Blessed Mother!" cried Bryan, "what'll I do with her at all? It's dyin' she is, as sure as anything! Cauth! Cauth! what's comin' over you, woman?" and he shook her gently, but for some time received no answer.

Mabel, as if conscious that something was wrong, crept to her side, and began stroking down her hair, murmuring, "Poor thing! poor thing! did they hang somebody from you? Cry now! why don't you cry? I used to cry long ago, but I can't cry now!—I can only laugh—and sing—Och ay!—

I sing my bonny bunch of locher, O."

Cauth's features began at length to relax, and, heaving a long, deep-drawn sigh, she shuddered, looked at Mabel, and covered her face with her hands as if to shut out the sight of her.

"Bryan," said she in a choking voice, "I can't stand it any

longer! We must either get her to sleep, or I must leave the house—she'd have me as mad as herself before an hour."

"Well, I declare," said Bryan in a whisper, "I feel mighty quare myself, listenin' to her. Do, an' God bless you! try an' get her to bed—you can put her in mine, an' I'll sit up all night, for it wouldn't be safe for us both to go to sleep; she might burn the house on us, so she might, for I'm afeard it's not much she'll sleep."

With much persuasion Mabel was induced to go to bed, and, once down, she slept soundly, contrary to the expectations of her host. After a good-natured dispute about which of them should occupy the second bed, Bryan's firmness prevailed, and poor Cauth stretched her length on the straw pallet, not to sleep, but to rest her weary limbs.

CHAPTER V.

MARY HENNESSY HAS A VISIT, AND BRYAN ANOTHER.

IT was drawing towards Christmas—that is to say, about the middle of December, when four gentlemen sat together over their wine in the comfortable dining-room of an old-fashioned house in Friar Street, in the good city of Cashel. One of these was Dr. Hennessy, the host of the evening; other two, Dr. O'Grady and Attorney Moran; while the fourth was a tall grey-haired man of portly presence, whose garb, as well as his manner, indicated the priest. He was, indeed, the parish priest of Cashel, and a Dean, moreover, of the archdiocese. A grave and reverend man he was, stern enough, too, at times, but at heart the kindest of human beings, as the poor of Cashel and its vicinity knew full well. To all the oppressed of the country round Dean M'Dermot was a tower of strength, for the highest and proudest of their oppressors not seldom quailed before his scathing irony and the indomitable energy with which he defended the rights of the poor and the powerless. Far and near he was known as the protector of the widow and the orphan, the friend of the friendless, and the terror of the wicked. The fiercest faction-fight that ever raged in the streets of the old borough was suspended, at least for the time being, by the sound of the Dean's voice, or even the news of his approach. Nay, the very children in "the chapel" were so struck with awe when at the "Catechism" on Sunday afternoon he made his appearance amongst them, that their tongues were tied with fear, and the well-conned answers died away on their lips as he passed along the line abruptly questioning each in turn with characteristic abruptness, tapping his top-boots the while with the end of his riding-whip. Yet how dear he was to the hearts of his flock, young and old, the traditional respect still paid to his memory, after the lapse of many years, is the best and most convincing proof. The Dean was not much given to what are called the pleasures of the table, but he did occasionally entertain some of his principal parishioners at dinner, and could not refuse, perhaps would not if he could, accepting their hospitality in return.

Such was the venerable gentleman who occupied the head of Dr. Hennessy's table that day, a privilege everywhere accorded to him, and, indeed, to Irish parish priests generally, amongst their own parishioners of the middle class, especially where the guests are but few and all of the same circle, as was the case on that occasion. Mary Hennessy and Bella Le Poer, who had been of the party, had retired a little before, leaving the gentlemen to their politics and their wine, as Mary laughingly observed.

"Now, mind," said Mary to her brother, opening the door again for a moment,—"mind and don't stay long here, for, you know, the Esmonds and Mrs. O'Grady are coming to tea. Excuse me, Dean!" she added, with a bright smile, "I forgot, for the moment, that you were present—so in your hands I leave my request." The Dean smiled assent, and the roguish face vanished from the door, the owner of it humming "Di tanti palpiti" as she and Bella ascended the stairs arm-in-arm.

Leaving the young ladies to amuse themselves in the drawing-room pending the expected arrivals, we will return to the gentlemen in the parlour. Resuming a subject which had been previously under discussion, Dr. O'Grady said—

"It does strike me as something odd that these agrarian murders, so to speak, are of more frequent occurrence in our county than, perhaps, any other in the kingdom. Can you account for it, Dean, you that knows the country so well?"

"I account for it in this way," the Dean replied, "that perhaps there is no county in Ireland where so little *justice* has been dealt out to the people in times past, and, I am sorry to say, in times present. The natural consequence is that the oppressed have fallen, in the lapse of years, into an ugly habit of administering justice themselves—or what they consider justice—after their own wild fashion. They have long ago found out that the law is not for them, but their oppressors, therefore they fling it to the winds—excuse me, Mr. Moran!—

and take vengeance as their motto. It is much to be deplored, undoubtedly, but is not the hard-heartedness of the landlords also to be deplored, and the blind infatuation that hurries them on to their doom? All the fearful examples of swift and terrible revenge which their own eyes have seen will not induce them to treat their unhappy tenants, when in their power, with less rigorous severity."

"I believe you are right, Dean," said Dr. O'Grady. "If there weren't some such infatuation over them, surely the fate of Chadwick, shot down in broad daylight before several witnesses, would alone be a sufficient warning to them."

"For my part," said the host, "I only wonder there aren't more of the landlords shot. Upon my word and honour I do! And I think the 'Tips,' bloody and all as they are, are not half so bad as people make them out. If they were, do you think Will Gartland would have died in his bed?—or—*others* we *know* have escaped so long, with so many curses hanging over them, like the sword of Damocles, ready to fall at any moment?"

"Take care, Doctor, take care!" said the Dean, with a certain solemnity of tone that impressed the others; "such subjects are not to be treated lightly—or, indeed, at all. Murder is always heinous in the sight of God, and no circumstances can justify it. Mr. Moran, may I take the liberty of asking why you seem so unusually grave this evening? Is there anything particular coming off at the Sessions to-morrow that you are meditating a speech—come, how is it?"

"Hear! hear!" from the two doctors, and the younger pushed the decanter towards Moran, gaily saying, "Cheer up, Phil! cheer up!—all's not lost that's in danger, you know."

"Well, I don't know," said Moran significantly, "what or who you may consider in danger, Doctor, but I really do believe there's some one in danger not many miles from here. Dean, you do me more or less than justice; I could not, if I would, fix my mind on my *pros* and *cons* in any purely professional matter, where 'the feast of reason and the flow of soul' are both at my command. The fact is, I have been in low spirits all day, and cannot, for the life of me, shake off a depression that is altogether unusual with me."

"Nonsense, man!" cried the lively host; "you've been listening to Mad Mabel to-day till you've got her notions in your head. Come now, out with it; aren't we all to be hanged—hanged by the neck till we're as dead as—as Brian Boroimhe? Eh, Phil?" and he assumed a look of comical gravity that made every one smile, even the lawyer himself.

"You are an incorrigible wag, Maurice," said Moran, still in the same grave tone; "but—laugh as you may at the absurdity of the thing—I confess poor Mabel's jabbering has disturbed me more than a little this very day."

"Why, how is that, Moran?" inquired the Dean, more earnestly than might be expected.

Moran looked round before he answered, to see that no servant was in waiting, which having ascertained, he said, "I know I may speak in this company with perfect safety what I have to speak. Know then, all, that I much fear there is some mischief brewing in this neighbourhood." He paused and looked from one to the other, as if almost uncertain whether he ought to proceed.

Sundry exclamations of surprise followed, and the Dean begged to know on what grounds Moran rested his opinion.

"I am almost ashamed to tell you," said Phil, lowering his voice; "and yet I will, for I feel anxious to impart my harassing thoughts to those in whose prudence and discretion I have unbounded faith. You must know, then, sirs, that my house-keeper, Honora Quin, is a great favourite with poor Mabel who spends hours together chattering in our kitchen, and crooning her snatches of old songs. Well, to-day she came early in the forenoon, and remained most of the day with Honora. By some chance she found her way into the dining-room while I was at lunch, and do as I would, I could not get rid of her. You know how lugubrious is her usual style of talking, poor thing! and usually people do not much mind her, fortunately for themselves, but to-day she let fall words again and again which could not fail to arrest my attention."

"Ha! ha! ha!" laughed Hennessy; "well, that *is* rich!—Mad Mabel's words arrest a lawyer's attention! After that we need wonder at nothing, surely."

"You may laugh, Maurice Hennessy, but *I* cannot, I assure you."

MARY HENNESSY HAS A VISIT.

"Pray go on, Mr. Moran," said the Dean very gravely. "What were the words that excited your apprehension?"

"They were these,"—and Moran's voice again sank to a scarcely audible whisper,—"'*Odd Esmond must be shot!*'"

"Good God!" exclaimed the Dean in horror and amazement, while the blanched faces of the two doctors showed that the words had a tremendous meaning even on the lips of a maniac. "These words, you will all allow, were quite sufficient to startle any sane man having any knowledge of certain matters."

"Undoubtedly, Moran, undoubtedly; but what more did you gather from the unhappy creature's ravings?"

"Not much, my dear Dean, except that the frequent mention of Holy Cross Abbey, and twelve o'clock at night, might lead us to suppose some connection, or give some clue to the manner in which the unfortunate girl came to hear such ominous words—if hear them she did."

Here the door was suddenly thrown open, and Mary Hennessy entered, followed by Bella, both girls strangely excited, as they threw an eager, searching glance around the room.

"He is not here, then!" said Mary, pale as death. "I told you so, Bella!—I told you that was nothing earthly."

"Why, Mary, what's the matter with you?" cried her brother. Moran, almost as pale as herself, fixed his eyes on her with anxious scrutiny, but said nothing. "Who are you looking for?"

"Harry Esmond," said Bella, answering for her friend. "Has he not been here?"

"Why, of course not," cried Dr. Hennessy, with a very poor attempt at cheerfulness. "What the deuce put that in your heads, you pair of goslings?"

"Tell him, Bella—*I* can't!" said Mary, sinking heavily on a chair. "Not here," she repeated,—"not here!" her voice becoming fainter and fainter; "well, that *is* something strange!"

"My dear young ladies," said the Dean, "will you tell us what it is that has disturbed you?—you seem quite agitated."

"It would be strange if we were not," said Bella, "considering what we have seen."

"Well, well," cried Hennessy, "what *did* you see? Your own shadows on the wall, I daresay."

"No, Doctor," said Bella, with solemn earnestness, "it was not our own shadows—except aither of them could take the likeness of *Harry Esmond*."

"Harry Esmond? Nonsense!—begging your pardon, Bella."

"But how was it, Miss Le Poer?" said Dr. O'Grady. "Was it young Harry you saw, or old Harry?"

"Young Harry. We were sitting chatting by the fire in the drawing-room, I with my back towards the door, when all at once Mary called out, 'I declare there's Harry! Come, come, none of your tricks, now! You shan't frighten us *this* time. Where's Henrietta?' I turned my head, and, sure enough, there stood Harry Esmond looking in at the door, which he held half open. The light of the fire shone full on his face, and I thought I never saw him look so grave. That, however, did not surprise me, knowing what perfect command he has of his features, and supposing him bent on frightening us girls."

"Did he not speak?"

"Speak, Mr. Moran? No, *indeed*, he did not!"

Dr. Hennessy burst into a loud laugh. "Of course he did not! I know well it was a shadow you saw. One of those dim, uncertain shadows which are only seen by firelight. Ha! ha! ha! One of the poets—Cowper, I think—describes *them* most graphically," and he recited, with theatrical emphasis, those lines from "The Task":—

> "But we perhaps
> The glowing hearth may satisfy awhile
> With faint illumination, that uplifts
> The shadows to the ceiling, there by fits
> Dancing uncouthly to the quivering flame."

"I admire your smartness, Doctor," said Bella coldly; but such was not our shadow, seeing that it was *not* 'uplifted to the ceiling,' nor did it *dance*, couthly or *uncouthly*; but when Mary and I ran to the door, the figure glided away before us with a slow and noiseless step, we following all the way, till it opened the dining-room door and walked in. I had to support Mary along the hall, for she would have it that it was Harry's *fetch* we saw, whilst I maintained that it was Harry himself, playing off one of his practical jokes at our expense. But if none of you saw him come in here, whereas we both saw him enter the room, then the case is clear—it was his *fetch* we saw, believe it who may or may not."

"It is very strange," said the Dean, whilst the other gentlemen looked at each other in silence, probably connecting this singular apparition with the dark revealings of Mabel's madness. "It is certainly very strange," he repeated; "but still, young ladies, I cannot help thinking that it might be the effect of some mental hallucination. Probably you had been talking of grave subjects, if not of supernatural appearances—come now, was that the case?"

"I solemnly assure you it was not," replied the young lady; "on the contrary, Dean, we were as merry as possible, and talking of something that made us both laugh heartily. Were we not, Mary?"

"Of course we were, my dear. But there is no use saying any more about this affair. I should not like either Harry or Henrietta to hear of it—Henrietta especially, for I know it would frighten her dreadfully. The more so, on account of our seeing the *fetch* after dark, which, you know, is said to denote death to the person so seen. My God!" and she passed her hand over her brow, as one who would dispel some hideous dream.

The gentlemen were unwilling to admit, even tacitly, the supernatural character of the appearance; they would fain have laughed the girls out of their conceit, but somehow none of them felt disposed to laugh, though even that they would fain have concealed one from the other. The Dean proposed that they should adjourn to the drawing-room with the ladies, a motion which was eagerly adopted. Moran drew Mary's arm under his; and Hennessy, bowing with mock ceremony to Bella, asked with a dandified lisp if he might be allowed the unparalleled honour of escorting her upstairs.

"Just for this once," said the saucy girl, with an air of haughty condescension.

"Well, this once is all I ask—now," said the merry doctor; "but—hillo! there's music—Shaun the piper, as I live! Never came piper in better time! What say you, fair ladies! shall we not have him upstairs for the evening?"

"Of course we will, Maurice," said his sister, "after he has had some needful comfort for the inner man. How lucky it was that he came just now!"

"And how soon he let you know of his arrival?" said Moran. "The jolly old dog! what a budget of fun he is, to be sure!—and what fun he can squeeze out of those pipes of his! There's 'The Rocky Road to Dublin' for us!—won't we trip it on the light fantastic toe by and by?—that is, with the Dean's permission."

"My permission would not be wanting, Mr. Moran, were I here, but the fact is, I must be at home before your dancing will be likely to commence. I have something to do this evening that cannot be deferred."

Moran looked anxiously in his face; so did Dr. O'Grady, and a meaning glance was exchanged between the three. Nothing more was said, however, and just at that moment a loud knock at the hall door announced the arrival of the expected visitors. A moment, and the full, rich voice of Harry Esmond sounded cheerily in the hall in cordial greeting. His fine face was all in a glow after his evening ride through the frosty air, and his brown silken hair, slightly disordered, was carelessly thrown back from off one temple, leaving the outline of his head and face clearly defined. It was a fine head, not exactly indicative of the highest intelligence, but well formed withal and firmly set; whilst the face, decidedly handsome, after the Saxon rather than the Celtic type, was expressive of everything frank, manly, and generous. He was tall—that is to say, rather above the middle height, with a figure uniting strength and grace to a degree rarely seen.

"Who have you here, Maurice?" said Esmond, as he hung his coat in the hall. "I am delighted to see, or rather to hear, that you have Shaun the piper for one individual. How the fellow does bang off that merriest of tunes!" meaning "The Wind that shakes the Barley," which Shaun was then giving out in glorious style, probably hearing the gentlemen in the hall.

"That's so like you, Harry," said his friend, catching, as he always did, the gushing gaiety that came spontaneously from Esmond's heart. "You asked me a question, and rambled on to something else without waiting for an answer. We have only Moran and O'Grady, and Miss Le Poer—that is, for the evening. The Dean dined with us, but I am sorry to say he cannot remain much longer. He has some business to attend to at home. Your aunt and uncle are coming, though, and my flame, of course."

"*Your* flame? I should like to know who that is—oh, Maurice?"

"Why, Aunt Vinegar, to be sure—I beg a thousand a year— I mean Aunt Winifred."

"Well, well, mocking's catching, my fine fellow! You'll have a flame some of these days, take my word for it, cool as you are now."

"And pray how cool is that, Master Wiseacre?"

"A few degrees above zero, anyhow."

They entered the drawing-room at one door as pretty Mrs. Esmond, with Mary and Bella, entered at another. It was hard for the girls to look at Harry Esmond with anything like composure, remembering what they had seen, yet they managed to conceal their feelings tolerably well on the whole. Yet when Esmond took Mary Hennessy's hand he missed the brilliant smile that had often cheered his heart, and, starting, he looked in her face.

"Mary—Mary Hennessy—are you quite, quite well?" he asked.

"Quite, quite well," she answered, forcing a smile.

Harry shook his head, took her two hands in his, and looked at her more earnestly, then sighed and turned away, evidently not satisfied.

Before the elder Esmonds made their appearance the Dean retired, much to the regret of the company, after exchanging a few pleasant words with Shaun, who was by that time installed in the wide lobby near the drawing-room door.

"When are you coming to our house, Shaun?—you're forgetting us altogether these times."

"Wisha, long life to your reverence! it's an ill day I'd forget you, anyhow. But, to tell you the truth, your reverence, Mrs. Dwyer is mighty stingy at times, an' as cross as an ould cat, savin' your presence, sir."

"Pooh, pooh, man! never mind Mrs. Dwyer—when she's out of humour, laugh her into it; and as to the stinginess," he laughed good-naturedly, "we can easily manage that. Be sure you come, now, before you leave the neighbourhood, for I want to hear some of the old airs that no one in Tipperary can play like you."

"Glory to you, Father M'Dermot! it's myself 'ill give you the best in the pipes. I'll be over, your reverence, some day this week, God willin', an' I'll make a day of it when I do go, if it was only to spite Mrs. Dwyer." So saying, Shaun struck up "The Priest in his Boots" as the Dean descended the stairs with his host, and the other gentlemen clapped their hands, crying, "Bravo, Shaun! bravo! That was well-timed, anyhow."

When the venerable clergyman mounted his horse at the door, Dr. Hennessy, from the steps, called out, "Safe home, Dean! God be with you!" And the Dean answered, "Your wish is a good one, Doctor, and I thank you. Fare-you-well!"

It was not homeward the Dean turned his horse's head. Following Friar Street a little farther, he turned off in the direction of Rock Gate, and rode slowly along, carefully noting the cabins on either side, till at last, seeming to have found the one he wanted, he stopped at the door, and, without alighting, knocked several times with the butt end of his whip. No sound came from within, no light was seen to glimmer in the miserable hut. All was dark and silent as the grave.

"This is strange," said the Dean to himself half aloud. "Can they have left here? And yet where would they go to?"

"True for your reverence—where would they go to?" said a deep voice so close to the horse's side that the priest started. The night was pitch dark, rendering objects invisible at any distance, and a thin coat of snow lay on the ground, sufficient to deaden the sound of approaching footsteps.

"But they are gone, that is clear," said the Dean; "perhaps you can tell where to?"

"Is it me, your reverence? Oh, bad cess to the one o' me knows a thing about them! It's like they took to the road [1] at last, the crathurs!—sure, it's starvin' they wor here, for all the help they got now and then from one an' another."

"And pray who are you that seem to know so much about their affairs?"

"Oh, begorra, your reverence ought to know me well, anyhow; sure, it was yourself that christened me."

[1] To *take to the road* means, in Irish phraseology, to go out begging.

BRYAN HAS A VISIT. 67

"Yes, but that don't answer my question as to who you are."

"Does anybody hereabouts know where they're gone to? Well, your reverence, if anybody does, it's ould Bryan Cullenan—Bryney the Rock, you know—himself an' themselves were as great as pickpockets. I'll show your reverence Bryan's little place—it's only a step from here."

"If you don't tell me this instant who you are," said the Dean sternly, "I'll lay my whip over your shoulders. What's your name, I say, and where do you live? As for Bryan's cottage, I can find it out myself."

"Well, in regard to the whip, now, I'd be sorry to put your reverence to so much trouble, so I'll be biddin' you good-night, an' it's sorry I am to see you on a fool's errand!"

"What do you mean, you rascal?" said the Dean, waxing wroth, and carrying out his threat at the same time, as he thought. But his whip only fell on empty space, and a low mocking laugh sounded in his ears, as if from the rear of one of the adjacent cabins.

Muttering to himself, "What a change tyrannical oppression will make in a man or a people!" the Dean took his horse by the bridle and went straight to Bryan's cottage, which was only a few yards distant. A light was dimly visible through the solitary pane of glass that served for a window, and it so happened that, approaching the door, the Dean cast a glance on the interior. What was it that fixed his eye, and made him look long and earnestly? The only figure visible was that of Cauth, who sat sewing near the stand that held the "rosin-slut," as the peasantry call the resin candle. Bryan, if there at all, was concealed by the jamb-wall.

A thrill of some strange emotion passed through the stalwart frame of the priest as he gazed on that shrivelled hag, for such she seemed, and he said to himself, "Merciful Providence! how came she in Bryan's cottage?—and she seems quite at home. Surely the old man cannot know—he may, though, for he is a singular man in his way, and might do such a thing. Well, unless he speaks of it himself, *I* will not, that is certain! But it is very, very strange."

He knocked at the door, and Bryan himself came to open it. Great was the old man's surprise when he saw who stood without, yet he answered the Dean's "God save you, Bryan!" with a cheerful "God save you kindly, your reverence! is it you that's in it, sir?"

"And who else would it be?" said the Dean of Cashel, stepping in, whilst Bryan took hold of the bridle.

"Will I tie the baste to the door-post, your reverence?"

"No, no, Bryan—no, no; I have only a moment to stay."

"Well, but I can't leave the door open on your reverence such a night as this, an' if I shut it, maybe the baste would run away."

The Dean looked round; Canth had retreated into the furthest corner of the cabin, where the hazy light scarcely penetrated.

"I merely wished to know," said the priest, lowering his voice, "if you can tell me where the Murthas are gone."

"Gone, your reverence?" said Bryan, much amazed; "an' do you tell me they are gone?"

"Certainly; I have been knocking repeatedly at the door of the hut where they had taken shelter, and I find it is entirely deserted. Do you know anything of them?"

"Oh, the sorra thing, your reverence, the sorra thing. God help them! what's come of them, at all? Sure, it'll come down hot an' heavy on them that brought them to this!"

"Hush, Bryan, hush!" said the Dean solemnly; "those things must be left to the Great Ruler of all. It is not for you or me to judge our fellow-creatures. So you don't know anything at all about Tim, or where he's gone to?"

Before Bryan answered he looked cautiously out into the darkness, peering on every side, as if to make sure that no one was within earshot. He then moved close to the Dean, and, motioning for him to bend down his head, whispered in his ear—

"I'll tell your reverence what I wouldn't tell the face of clay barrin' yourself. Tim is not the man he used to be, at all, at all, an' I'm afeard there's something running in his mind this time back that's *not for the good of his soul!*"

He stepped back a pace, and the two exchanged a look of solemn import. "It was that very thing brought me out tonight," said the Dean in an undertone. "I have heard things that troubled me not a little, and I thought I would make an effort to prevent bloodshed."

Bryan shook his head. "I'm afeard the art o' man can't do it—but if anybody can, in coorse it's you, if you can only get speech of them."

"Which I now begin to fear will be no easy matter. Well, good-night, Bryan! We must only do our best, and leave the rest to God."

So saying, the Dean mounted his horse, and had just exchanged a last kind greeting with the old man, when a hoarse voice spoke in the hearing of both, though where it came from they could not ascertain, and it said—

"Go home, Dean M'Dermot, and let justice take its coorse— you might as well think to soften that Rock there as the hearts of them you're looking for this night."

"God bless us!" cried Bryan, "who can that be?"

"Friend," said the Dean, addressing the invisible colloquist, "it is an evil purpose that shuns the eye of God's anointed minister. Could I but speak even a few words with those persons to whom you have reference, it might be their own salvation, temporal and eternal."

A scoffing laugh was the only answer; and the Dean, seeing that nothing could then be done, reluctantly took his way homeward, leaving Bryan as ill at ease as himself, though he tried to conceal it from Cauth, who, strangely enough, made neither remark nor inquiry as to the object of the Dean's visit.

CHAPTER VI.

A DAY AT ESMOND HALL.

Two days before Christmas, the inmates of the cabins at the foot of the Rock were thrown into a state of commotion by the sight of the Esmond carriage stopping at Bryan Cullenan's door. The handsome brown livery was well known in the neighbourhood, and many heads were popped inquiringly out of doors to see what was going on. Mrs. Esmond herself was in the carriage, looking ever so pretty in her cottage-bonnet and black lace veil, with her two beautiful children, a boy of four and a girl of two years old. But, alas! there was nothing to be gathered from what took place. The footman knocked at the door; Cauth came out and dropped her curtsey; Mrs. Esmond leaned forward, smiled graciously, and said something in a low voice; whereupon Cauth curtsied again, and the carriage rolled away. This was the dumb show of the affair, and the curious neighbours dreamed of nothing more. Yet there was something more, which heard, would have set them all on the alert. "What time will you be at home, ma'am?" said Cauth to Mrs. Esmond in the very lowest whisper; "I want to speak to yourself very particular." The lady, with a look of surprise, named the hour, and Cauth made a hasty retreat into the hut, as the elegant *cortège* moved away. She never exposed herself much to the prying eyes of her neighbours, and managed her affairs so that she was seldom abroad in daylight.

Mrs. Esmond had appointed four o'clock that afternoon for Cauth's visit, and, punctual to the moment, Cauth was in waiting, not in the kitchen, which she carefully avoided, but on the gravel walk that swept up in two segments of a circle from the gates to the hall-door, around a smooth sward, in spring and summer of velvet sheen, tastefully interspersed with the choicest

A DAY AT ESMOND HALL. 71

flowering shrubs. But the turf was brown and bare that winter day, and the shrubs and plants were carefully covered to protect them from the blighting effect of the frost. The trees in the surrounding copse, too, were leafless all and bare, except where the dark green of the fir and the still darker holly stood out here and there from the sylvan desolation with the cheerless and sombre effect of light glimmering through darkness. On the gravel walk, then, Cauth took up her station, right in front of the parlour windows, which opened on a lightly-trellised verandah, as did the library on the opposite side of the hall. During the few moments that Cauth stood there, her face concealed in the hood of her cloak, she communed with her own thoughts in a way peculiar to herself.

"Isn't it a sorrowful thing, then, to see the flowers all faded and gone, and the trees bare, and the grass withered? Ay, winter's a poor time—a poor time! But there's a winter that's worse than that—*fareer gar*, there is! The spring 'ill come in a little time, and the purty flowers 'ill all pop up their heads again, and the green 'ill come back to the fields an' to the trees, and everything 'ill bloom so beautiful—even the very grass on the graves; but the green will never come back to my heart, nor the sun shine upon it aither. All withered—withered—and dead! Ochone! if a body was dead, it 'id be the less matther; but a dead heart in a livin' body—oh vo! vo! vo! how does one live, at all? By God's mercy, sure! and nothin' else, to give crathurs time to make their pace with Him. Ah! there she is, the darlin', makin' signs to me from the window. Och, wirra! why wouldn't I do it—why wouldn't I? Sure, I'd be the greatest villain on Ireland's ground if I didn't!—and I will do it if I lost my life for it." With these singular words she ascended the steps, and before she had time to ring, the door was opened by Mrs. Esmond herself, as though the lady had some vague suspicion that Cauth did not care to be seen by the servants, at least on that occasion.

"Don't you think I'm a little of a witch, Cauth?" said Mrs. Esmond, with a smile, as she pointed to one of the high-backed Gothic chairs which graced the spacious hall.

"Wisha, how is that, ma'am?"

"Why, you see I guessed that you would as soon not see any of the servants just now."

"Well, sure enough you guessed the truth, ma'am. How's the master?"

"He's very well, I thank you."

"The Lord keep him so! Och, amen! from my heart. Why, ma'am dear! sure, it isn't givin' me all this you'd be?" looking at some silver pieces which Mrs. Esmond had placed in her hand.

"Yes, yes, Cauth; that's all for you—you can provide with it what you require for Christmas. Old Dryan must not want the little comforts needful to his age—nor you either, Cauth. But hush! here comes Mr. Esmond—I hear his step on the gravel walk."

"Then listen to me, ma'am!" said Cauth, standing up, and placing her head close to that of Mrs. Esmond: "*There's them of the name that has need to keep indoors afther dark*—you know who I mane! Husht now! not a word, for God's sake! —you don't know the risk I'm runnin' in sayin' so much—not a word to any one, barrin' the master, an' let *him* give a hint *where you know* as fast as ever he can—but God love you, an' don't bring *my* name in, one way or the other!"

And, with a warning gesture to Mrs. Esmond, who seemed to have lost the power of speech, Cauth drew her hood over her face once more, and passed out with a low curtsey and a "God save your honour!" to Mr. Esmond, whom she met on the threshold.

Harry Esmond came in brimful of a steeplechase that was to come off next day a few miles from Cashel, but when he looked at his wife, wondering at her unusual silence, the ruddy hue faded from his cheek, seeing the unwonted paleness of hers and the agitation visible on every feature.

"Why, Henrietta, my love, what's the matter?" and, taking her hand tenderly, he drew her into the parlour. "Is that old woman a fortune-teller, or has she been predicting evil things for you? Sit down and tell me what means this agitation so unusual with you?"

"Harry," said his wife, as the colour came slowly back to her cheek, "that woman is no fortune-teller, but she *has* spoken words that have a strange and awful meaning."

"Indeed?" said Harry, with a somewhat incredulous air. "And what were they, pray?—or are you at liberty to repeat them?"

"I am—to you! They are these: 'There's them of the name that has need to keep indoors after dark!—you know who I mean,' the woman added, and 'let him,' meaning you, 'give a hint where you know as fast as ever he can.' Those were the words, Harry. What do you think of them?"

"I think of the whole affair this, that my dear Henrietta is more of a simpleton than I ever took her for. Who is this woman?"

"That I am not at liberty to tell you," said Mrs. Esmond, smiling at the word "simpleton," as her husband supposed she would. "But, Harry, I cannot view this matter as you do. You and I both know that the person evidently meant has enemies, and, what is worse, deserves to have them; believe me, then, this warning is not to be slighted, inasmuch as it must be kindly meant, and I must insist on your going this very day to give the hint as desired."

"Nonsense, child! how could I bring myself to convey such a message? You know the supreme contempt he has for the country-people generally, and I should only get laughed at for my pains—perhaps told to mind my own business."

"And what if you do? Consider the possible alternative!—think how you would reproach yourself if anything did happen which you, by this trifling act, might have prevented! Harry, you will not refuse me this favour?" and, taking his two hands, she looked up so beseechingly in his face that he could no longer resist.

"Well, I will go after dinner—it is now half-past four."

"Nay, you shall go now—you can dine at the Lodge—they dine at five too, you know."

"Well, I must say you are a provoking little sample of womankind," said Harry, with his habitually gay laugh; "but if it be so, why, it must, that's all;" and he rang the bell.

The tall butler appeared so very suddenly that his master said, with some surprise, "Why, Pierce, where the deuce did you come from?"

"Oh, sure, I was just on my step to the hall-door, your honour. Didn't the door-bell ring first?"

"Not that we heard. You had better go and see if any one is there."

Pierce went accordingly, opened the hall-door, and looked out, then returned with a face of artless innocence.

"Well, Pierce," said his master, laughing, "did you see any one?"

"Wisha, no, your honour!" and he rubbed his elbow after a fashion he had, and looked as foolish as might be; "still, I'd take my book oath on it that I heard the big door bell ringin' ever so loud; but, sure, it must be in my own ear it was. Ochone! maybe it's a dead-bell[1] I heard!"

Why should words like these make Mrs. Esmond start? That she could not explain even to herself, yet so it was, and by some strange association came into her mind the mysterious voice heard at the supper-table on Hallow-eve night. But none of these thoughts or fancies troubled the bright surface of Harry Esmond's soul as he said to Pierce—

"Tell Mulligan to get the roan mare saddled as fast as possible."

"The roan mare, sir? I will, your honour!—she'll be out in a jiffy." And Pierce moved away as rapidly as his natural sluggishness of motion permitted.

The roan mare, however, was not "out in a jiffy," but was, on the contrary, so long in making her appearance that Mr. Esmond, good-humoured as he was, began to lose patience, and, opening the door, went out on the steps just as Mulligan, the groom, hove in sight from the rear with the handsome roan.

"What the deuce kept you, Mulligan?" said the master, slightly annoyed; "here I have been waiting full twenty minutes."

"Twenty minutes?" cried Mulligan, a loud-spoken, red-faced man, yet fresh and honest-looking withal,—"twenty minutes, your honour? Oh, then, wait till I lay my eyes on that lazy Larry," meaning Pierce. "Why, your honour, it's not over five minutes since he came to me with the word."

"And what was he about ever since I sent him?"

"Slin-gin' about, I suppose, as usual. He said he was lookin' for me around the stables, but if he looked in the right way he needn't have looked long!"

[1] There is a very common superstition amongst the lower classes in Ireland that the sound of a bell within the ear denotes an approaching death in the family.

"Well, well, let it pass now," said Mr. Esmond; "every one is not so smart as you, Tom !—it doesn't matter so much after all. Good-bye, Henny !" and, vaulting into the saddle, he kissed his hand to his wife, who stood at the door watching him with a mixture of pride and fondness in her soft eyes.

"So you'll dine at the Lodge, Harry ?"

"Of course I must, although I shall be half an hour late— n'importe—I fly on my lady's errand dinnerless, as becomes a knight *sans peur et sans reproche*. Farewell, sweetheart !"

"Now, be home early, Harry !" called the sweet voice from the door as he rode away.

"*Nine o'clock, or never !*" was the strange answer that came clearly back on the evening breeze.

The dinner was served as usual that day at the Hall, and Pierce, in his waiting-jacket of blue striped jean, was, of course, in attendance. His mistress felt the loneliness of the table weighing upon her like a nightmare, and, anxious to be alone with her loneliness, she dismissed Pierce with the first course. But Pierce still lingered, on one pretence or another, arranging and disarranging the glasses and plate on the sideboard, placing and displacing chairs, etc., till at length Mrs. Esmond said again—

"That will do, Pierce, that will do ; you can go now."

"If it 'id be pleasin' to you, ma'am," said Pierce, "I'd make bowld to say a few words to you."

"On what subject, Pierce ?" said his mistress, looking up in surprise.

"Well, ma'am," said Pierce in his sheepish way, "it's about Tim Murtha's people—I know you wor kind and good to them when their trouble was the sorest."

"But what of them now, Pierce ?—I heard to-day that they had left the neighbourhood."

"Well, it's so said, ma'am."

"Do you know where they're gone to ?"

"Oyeh ! is it me ? Sure, it's take to the road they did, for Tim wasn't able to work or want, you see, an' they couldn't be always livin' on charity."

"Of course not, Pierce ; but it is to be hoped that poor Tim may soon be able to work again. There was no need whatever of their 'taking to the road,' as you say, and I am very sorry indeed to find that they have done so."

"God bless you, ma'am! an' it's Tim that knows your goodness well; but sure, he couldn't stay in the place at all, ma'am—he was warned off;" and Pierce's voice grew husky.

"Warned off, Pierce? What do you mean by that?" said Mrs. Esmond, much surprised.

"Why, I mane, ma'am, that Mr. Esmond of the Lodge—that's their landlord, ma'am—sent for Tim about a week ago, but Tim wasn't able to go, so he sent him word by his Scotch steward that if he didn't clear off from about Cashel altogether before the week was at an end, he'd have him put in a tight place. Poor Tim wanted to know the raison, but Sawney was mighty short, an' would only tell him that for the raison he ought to know it best himself."

"My God!" murmured Mrs. Esmond, and she raised her tearful eyes to heaven. "But surely, Pierce, Tim was not the fool to heed such a warning as that? He was not lately on Mr. Esmond's property."

"In course he wasn't, ma'am." Pierce paused a moment, then suddenly added, "Tim is a mighty paceable man, ma'am, an' he thought for quietness' sake he had better do as he was bid. He's a quiet, harmless crathur, Mrs. Esmond, that 'id do anything at all—anything at all for pace."

There was something in the tone of the man's voice as he spoke these words that drew Mrs. Esmond's eyes to his face, and she could not help noticing its singular expression. The usually stolid features were gleaming with a lurid light, a fierce intelligence, that vanished as quickly as it came even whilst the lady gazed in silent wonder. Somehow her heart sank within her, but she strove to appear calm.

"Are you any relation of Tim's?" asked Mrs. Esmond, partly to break the silence, which she felt painful.

"Is it me, ma'am? Oh, the sorra drop's blood I'm to him; that I mayn't sin if I am! but he's a fellow-crathur, you see, Mrs. Esmond; an' we were neighbour boys, too, reared at the door with one another, an' it goes hard on me to see him thrated like a dog, or worse—a dog, inagh!" he added, with a bitter laugh that sounded strangely hollow; "oh, bedad, it isn't the one way the gentlemen uses their dogs an' their tenants!"

"Pierce," said his mistress, "I am surprised to hear you

talk so. What have 'the gentlemen' ever done to you that you should speak so hard of them?"

"Not to me, ma'am! Oh no, I declare they never done me either hurt or harm, but that's bekase I fell in with the right sort. If they were all like the masther here, they might thravel the counthry night or day without any one hurtin' a hair o' their heads. It's little need there 'id be for police-barracks an' all sich things!—oh no, ma'am! *if there wasn't Chadwicks there 'id be no Graces*—or, aither, if there was law for the likes o' Tim Martha—which there isn't!—then crathurs wouldn't have to take the law in their own hands; for, Mrs. Esmond," and he drew so near her, and spoke so low, that she shrank back affrighted, —"Mrs. Esmond, ma'am, it's the last thing with one of us—I mane the poor—*when we think of sheddin' blood, or takin' away the life that we can't give back!*"

Awed by the solemnity of the man's tone and manner, Mrs. Esmond sank back almost fainting in her chair, and, covering her eyes with one hand, motioned him with the other to leave the room.

"I'm goin', ma'am," said Pierce; "but before I go, be pleased to let me say one word more. If I thought I had offended you by what I said, I'd go down on my knees to ax forgiveness, for it's you that has the good wish of the poor, an' the good word, an' the masther too, Lord's blessin' be about him!"

"Then why speak those horrid words to me?" said Mrs. Esmond faintly.

"For a raison I have, ma'am, that I can't tell you now; but don't be scared, Mrs. Esmond, don't now, an' you'll obleege me; for if all Tipperary was swimmin' in blood, *you and yours 'id walk dryshod!* I'm goin' now, ma'am, as you bid me, an' all sorts o' luck attend you till I see you again! Don't fear for Mr. Esmond—that's the masther, ma'am!"

"Fear?" cried Mrs. Esmond, starting up; "why should I fear for *him?*"

There was none to answer the question. Pierce was gone, and Mrs. Esmond felt sick at heart, oppressed with strange and gloomy forebodings. She was roused by a sad, sweet voice singing without, the sound evidently approaching the house—

"Come, all ye fair maids that do pass by,
Help me to mourn for my sailor boy!"

Mrs. Esmond went to the window, glad of anything that might change the current of her thoughts, though the words that were sung were too much in unison with them to be at all cheering.

"I shouldn't wonder if that were poor Mabel," she said to herself with tender pity. It was Mabel, now sitting on the lowermost step, singing like a lark—

"And still I'll bunch my violets,
And tie them with the locker, O!"

Oh, the exquisite music of that old air, as it gushed from the unconscious heart of the maniac; but anon it was changed for another far more sorrowful, but still more touchingly beautiful—one that is on every lip in Upper and Lower Munster—

"Shule, shule, shule agragh!
Time, alas! cannot ease my woe,
Since the lad of my heart from me did go."

"Gone! Ay, sure enough, he's gone!" muttered the forlorn wanderer, "but he said he wouldn't be long—that he'd only go down a start to Holy Cross Abbey, where some one was going to be hung!—

"Och, oft I've sat on my love's knee,
And many a fond story he told to me—
He said many things that ne'er will be—
Shule, shule, agragh!

"An' didn't he tell me about the shootin', too?—ha! ha! in coorse he did!—but *he* said it was ould Chadwick, you know, an' *they* said it was ould Esmond!"

Here Mrs. Esmond opened the door, with a face of ashy paleness.

"Who said so, Mabel? Come in, my poor girl." Mabel went accordingly. "Now, tell me who said it was 'ould Esmond'?" using her own phraseology.

"Why, the men in the abbey that dark night—don't you remember?—the dead were a-listenin' to them as well as the livin'; but *I* wasn't livin', you know," she added confidentially; "they hung *me* that time with Patrick."

"Indeed?"

"Ay, did they, an' I'm walkin', walkin' ever sence, an' will till the Day o' Judgment—och, I'm tired walkin', that's what I am!"

"You had better go to the kitchen, Mabel, and get some dinner."

"I will, ma'am;" and away she went singing—

"Ooh! I'm the girl that makes the stir
From Cork along to Skibbereen—a "——

Mrs. Esmond looked after her with a smile of ineffable pity, and then hastened to procure some warm clothing for the poor creature, saying to herself as she did so, "If she would only keep it; but, of course, she will not. I believe I have covered her half a dozen times. However, she must not go shivering from this door on a winter's day."

The servants were ordered to bring Mabel upstairs when she had had her dinner, which being done, Mrs. Esmond's own fair hands clothed her from head to foot in comfortable winter garments. Mabel appeared to watch the progress of her toilet with great complacency, and when it was done Mrs. Esmond said—

"You feel better now, Mabel, don't you?" A smile was Mabel's answer. "What do you say to me for dressing you in those nice warm clothes, Mabel?" said the lady, with a view to ascertain whether she felt or understood the change.

Mabel looked at her earnestly—very, very earnestly—as though she were trying hard to arrange her thoughts for utterance, then said slowly and distinctly—

"That no one belongin' to you may ever be hanged—or shot!" she added, as if correcting herself.

Mrs. Esmond, with a cry of horror, told the servant to take her away, and to keep her over night, if possible.

"God bless you, ma'am! you've a purty face, anyhow," said Mabel, with a low curtsey, as the girl took her arm gently to lead her away. The next moment she broke out into the wild death-song of the peasantry, clapping her hands and bending forward as if over a corpse. It was a positive relief to Mrs. Esmond's over-wrought mind when the unhappy creature was removed from her sight, but dolefully came back to the lady's ears the sad strain she sang in Irish as she paced the long and echoing hall—

"Fast-flowing tears above the grave of the rich man are shed,
But they are dried when the cold stone shuts in his narrow bed."

"May the Lord preserve him, anyhow!" sighed Mrs. Esmond, half ashamed of the fears that were gathering shape and form within her heart, at all times painfully susceptible of impressions from without. Then, as the firelight danced and flickered amongst the shadows on the wall in the darkening room, officious memory brought back the cabalistic sports of Hallow-eve—the clay and the ring—her wedding-ring—and the gloom that then, for the first time, fell on her spirits like a funeral pall. Anxious to dispel these sombre fancies, that were preying like vampires on the springs of life, and exciting her brain beyond endurance, she started up and hastened to the nursery, hoping to find in the cheerful prattle of her little ones the peace that solitude denied. She was not disappointed; for, after spending the evening with the children, and printing a farewell kiss on the rosy lips of each as they were laid for the night in their little cribs, she descended to the parlour with a lighter heart and a more hopeful spirit.

It was past eight o'clock, and she rang to order supper for half-past nine, saying to herself as she pulled the bell, "That will be time enough, for I know he dined late at Uncle Harry's."

The housemaid appeared, received the order for the cook, and also for the butler.

"I'll set the table myself, ma'am," replied the girl, "for Pierce isn't within."

"Not within? And where is he?"

"Not a know I know, ma'am, but he went out just after comin' down from you that time, an' he never came back sence. We all thought you had sent him of an arrand, maybe."

"I did not," said Mrs. Esmond, relapsing into her so-lately overcome disquietude, "and I wonder he would think of going out without so much as asking permission. Well, go down, Jane, at all events, and set the table, and tell Bessy to make haste, so that supper will be ready just to the moment."

The girl curtsied and withdrew. Mrs. Esmond took up a book and tried to read, but read she could not; listlessly she turned over the leaves of a London magazine, till she came to some fine lines of John Malcolm's on "Presentiment of Death." There she stopped and read, and read again, these stanzas in particular arresting her attention—

It comes, eclipsing pleasure's beams,
A shadow from the future cast;
'Tis secret in its source as dreams,
And traceless as the blast.

It comes, the dark, mysterious mood,—
The prophet-spirit shades the mind,
Which trembles, as autumnal wood
That "shakes without a wind!"

"The prophet-spirit?" repeated Mrs. Esmond. "I wonder if that be not the spirit that has been shaking my very soul these last weary hours!" She shuddered as she spoke, the book fell from her hand, and she sat for some moments with her languid eyes fixed on the pretty timepiece set in the belfry-tower of a miniature cathedral on the mantelshelf. The cheerful sound of the small pendulum concealed within the tower was the only sound that broke on the stillness of the too-quiet room, and its pleasant tic-tic was more than usually distinct, when, all at once, the sounds ceased, and the hands stopped precisely at the moment of half-past eight. "Well, that is strange!" muttered Mrs. Esmond. "I saw Harry wind it up this morning, and I never knew it to stop in that way before." She was so absorbed in her own feverish thoughts, however, that she forgot to set the timepiece a-going, so the pendulum stood still, with the hands pointing, like skeleton fingers, to *half-past eight!*

Time grew drearier every moment, and every moment Mrs. Esmond's anxiety increased; nine o'clock by her watch, yet still Harry came not. A moment or two after, a horse's hoofs rang on the gravel walk without—a fervent "Thank God!" escaped her pallid lips. She would have hastened to the door, but her limbs refused to carry her, and she sank again on the sofa, with her eyes fixed on the door. It opened, but instead of her husband appeared Mulligan, the groom. One glance at his face was enough. She started up, and, clasping her hands, cried, "For God's sake, Mulligan, what's the matter?"

"Oh, ma'am dear, don't be frightened,—we don't know what has happened—but—but"—

"But what?—why don't you go on? Out with it, man, whatever it is!"

"You heard that horse comin' to the door there a minute ago?

—well, ma'am, it wasn't the roan, it was one of ould Mr. Esmond's steel-greys"—

"Well, and who was the rider?"

"There was no rider, ma'am!—but och! ma'am dear, mind it wasn't our roan!"

"Nine o'clock, or never!" muttered Mrs. Esmond. Her head sank on her chest, and she would have fallen fainting to the floor had not Mulligan caught her in his arms. His cries soon brought assistance, and, leaving his mistress to the care of her terror-stricken servants, he hurried away to get the coachman and some of the neighbours to go with him along the road towards Rose Lodge to see if anything was wrong.

CHAPTER VII.

MURDER AND MYSTERY.

Mrs. Esmond was slow in recovering from that swoon, and even when consciousness did return, strength was sadly wanting. Mind and body were both prostrated, as if by some violent shock, and when her attendants proposed to her to retire to her chamber for a little while, she passively consented, whereupon two of them supported her up the stairs. They could not induce her, however, to lie down; throwing herself on her knees beside her bed, she bowed her head upon it in silent prayer, and so remained till the girls, fearing that she had fainted again, gently touched her arm. She looked up with a wintry smile on her pale features.

"Never fear, Peggy! *I'm* not dead!" The words came out, as it were, with a spasmodic effort, and a dreary emphasis on the pronoun I. "Oh, girls, let us pray — let us all pray together!"

And they did pray, the girls awed by the strange composure, the unnatural calmness of their mistress, at a moment when they could hardly restrain themselves from rushing out to join the search which they felt was going on.

Half an hour might have passed thus, when the door-bell rang. Mrs. Esmond started to her feet, gasping for breath — strove to speak, but unable to utter a word, pointed to the door. The girls understood her — one of them hurried downstairs, but did not return. Strange sounds were heard in the hall, as if of heavy feet shuffling along, and whispering voices, and stifled groans and sobs. Still Mrs. Esmond moved not, though the flitting colour on her cheek, and the fearful intensity with which her eyes rested on the door, showed the awful struggle between fear and hope that was going on within.

"Ma'am dear," said the remaining servant, "what can it be, at all? Will I go an' see?"

"Go!" The word escaped from between the firmly compressed lips, as though the speaker were scarcely conscious of its import. The girl darted off like a lapwing, and she had hardly time to descend the stairs, when a piercing scream echoed through the corridor. "Ha! that's Nora's voice! I knew it!" said Mrs. Esmond to herself,—"my God! I knew it!" and she fell senseless on the floor.

When she again opened her eyes on surrounding objects, all the women servants of the household were around her, engaged in various efforts for her recovery, one slapping the palms of her hands, another bathing her temples, whilst a third had her almost choked, holding burnt feathers under her nose. Her first look of wild inquiry was answered with a chorus of sorrowful ejaculations that confirmed her worst fears. It was but the work of a moment to spring out of bed and dash the officious attendants to one side and the other.

"Where is Harry?" cried the half-crazed wife; "where is my husband?—dead or alive, let me see him!"

No one spoke, but on the instant came from the adjoining room the most sorrowful death-cry that ever thrilled mourner's heart. Guided by the sound, Mrs. Esmond flew to the door, which was closed, but paused before she attempted to open it, her face like that of a sheeted corpse, and the cold dew oozing from her pallid brow.

"Ma'am dear, don't go in!" whispered one from behind; "for God's sake, don't!"

A scornful laugh was the answer, the door was flung open, and Mrs. Esmond stood in the presence of her husband, but not as she parted from him some hours before. Dead and cold he lay, in the clothes he had worn all day, the blood slowly trickling from a bullet wound in his temple, showing all too plainly the manner in which he had met his death. At the foot of the bed sat Mad Mabel, crooning her song of woe, and rocking her body to and fro, in dismal accordance with the wild strain she sang so piteously. Mulligan and two or three other men who were in the room draw back as the door opened; they need not have done so, for their presence was unheeded by her whose soul was that moment crushed as by an avalanche.

Mrs. Esmond stood beside the bed, looking down on the heap of clay that was her husband, but no sigh, no sound, escaped her. Every faculty of her being seemed paralysed, every limb, every feature, as it were, petrified. Her silence at such a moment was something wholly inexplicable to the simple hearts around, and the stony rigidity of her living features was more awful to their eyes even than the ghastly presence of death. People held their breath, as though fearful of disturbing a silence that yet was terrible to all. Looks of pity were exchanged, and gestures of horror, but not a word spoken. Even Mabel had ceased her wailing, and sat looking very earnestly at the motionless figure on the bed—from that her eyes wandered to the strangely-altered face of Mrs. Esmond. All at once she rose softly from her seat, glided like a spirit to her side, and, throwing her arm round her neck, began to pat her cheek with her cold hand, saying at the same time in a tone of tender pity—

"Cry now ! Why don't you cry ? Poor thing ! poor thing !"

As if Mabel's voice had broken the mighty spell that kept her senses in thrall, Mrs. Esmond started into sudden life, threw up her arms wildly, and uttered a scream so piercing, so full of anguish, that it rang in the ears of those who heard it for many a long day after. Disengaging herself from Mabel's encircling arm, she threw herself on the body of her husband and wildly called upon his name, kissing his cold lips again and again, as though hoping to restore their warmth. In vain, in vain ! Then she laid her hand on his heart, but no, no ! all was still—still as death could make it. Yet she could not, would not, believe that death *was* there. How could she realise it to herself that the stark form before her was that of her young husband, who had left her but a few short hours before in all the buoyancy of youth and health and happiness? Harry dead ! Harry Esmond dead ! No, no ! it could not be —it must be a dream, a horrible dream.

Turning for the first time, with her hand still on Esmond's heart, her eye ran round the room till it rested on the blank, terror-stricken face of Mulligan. In low, cautious tones, as if fearing to awaken the sleeper, she said, with frightful calmness—

"Mulligan, he is not dead—he *cannot* be dead ! Go directly for Dr. O'Grady and Dr. Hennessy."

"They'll be here presently, ma'am," said the poor fellow, trying hard to keep in the tears that were choking his utterance; "there's two messengers gone for them before we—we—brought the poor master home."

Again Mrs. Esmond bent down and touched the lips of her beloved and laid her trembling hand on his heart, then took up the hand that hung down over the bedside and felt for a pulse; when all this was done, the last spark of hope seemed to die out in her heart—with the stiff, cold hand pressed to her bosom, she turned again to Mulligan, and cried in a tone of heart-piercing anguish—

"Oh, Mulligan, Mulligan! who had the heart to kill *him*?"

This was the signal for a general outburst of lamentation; the grief and pity so long restrained now broke out in tears and sobs.

"Ay, you may well cry!" said Mrs. Esmond; "you have all lost a good friend! But oh, Harry, Harry! what is any one's loss to mine?" And, starting to her feet, she wrung her hands in anguish. No tear escaped her burning eyelids, and she felt as though her brain were all on fire. "Mulligan!" cried she again, with a wildness that alarmed every one,—"Mulligan! I asked you before whose work is this? Where did you find your master?"

"Och, God pity me that has to tell it!" said Mulligan. "Sure, we found him"—here a burst of tears interrupted the sad tale—"sure, we found him lying on the roadside about half way between here an' the Lodge. As for them that done the deed—well, God knows—God knows!"

"It's little matter to us," said Mrs. Esmond drearily, as she wiped away with her handkerchief the blood that disfigured poor Harry's dead face—that face late so comely and so cheering. "A time will come for all that,—now it is enough for me to know that I am a widow and my children orphans this dismal night—that I have lost the dearest and best of husbands, and my children the best of fathers! Oh, Harry, Harry! is that you that lies there so still and cold?— you that gave life and light to all around you?—oh no, no! it cannot be you!" and, raising his head on her arm, she looked with piteous earnestness on his face. "Alas! yes, it is Harry Esmond—it is *my* husband! But you cannot be dead, Harry!

oh no! you *cannot* be dead! Speak to me, Harry!—oh, in mercy speak to me—or I cannot—cannot live!"

"You must get her away—at once!" said Dr. O'Grady, who with Dr. Hennessy just then appeared at the door, both panting with excitement, and pale with horror. "Oh, Maurice, what a sight!" he whispered to his friend. "Poor, poor Harry! I fear there is little chance of our doing any good—but come, now! be a man, and brace yourself up, that we may at least do what we can."

The servants were all in motion in an instant, and the sound of the doctor's familiar voice aroused the unhappy lady. Turning round with a ghastly smile on her parted lips, she said—

"Come in—come in—you'll not disturb *him*! Oh, Dr. O'Grady, Dr. Hennessy, look what they have done to poor Harry!—he never met you without a friendly smile and a kind word; but he'll never smile again—he'll never reach the hand of welcome any more!—look here!" and, pointing to the wound on the temple, from which only an occasional drop of blood now oozed thick and dark, she fell fainting on the body of her husband.

"It is just as well," said the older practitioner. "Now take her to her own room as gently as you can, and lay her on the bed."

It was no easy task to unwind her arms from around the body, but it was at length done, and the doctors proceeded to discharge their melancholy duty, having first cleared the room of all except Mulligan.

A very few moments served to convince the doctors that Harry Esmond was, indeed, no more.

"That bullet did its work well," said Hennessy, as the two stood beside the bed looking mournfully down on the dead. "The Lord have mercy on your soul, Harry Esmond! I didn't think you had an enemy on earth! Merciful Heaven, O'Grady! who could have done such a deed?"

"Mulligan," said Dr. O'Grady, turning to that faithful servant, "they tell me you found him."

"Wisha, then, I did, sir! Ochone! ochone! I did!"

"Where! and how?"

Mulligan described the place exactly, and the position in which he found the body.

"And was there no trace of the murderer? Is there no clue to guide us—I mean the law—in bringing the wretch to justice?"

Mulligan was silent, but the next moment he said musingly, as if to himself, "How did he come to leave the roan behind, I wondher?"

"What's that you say, Mulligan?" said Hennessy quickly. "Was it not his own horse he rode?"

"Well, that's what I'm not able to tell you, sir, but I know it was one of ould Mr. Esmond's horses—the steel-grey—that galloped up to our stable this night without a rider—an' it was our own roan mare that the masther took with him."

Hennessy and O'Grady looked into each other's eyes, as if each sought to read the other's thought.

"Has Uncle Harry been sent for?" asked O'Grady.

"No, sir."

"Send Pierce off immediately, then."

"Pierce, sir?—is it Pierce?" and Mulligan began to rub his elbow.

"Yes, Pierce. You cannot go—you are wanted here, as the oldest servant of the family."

"Well, but, docthor dear, I can't send Pierce, for Pierce isn't in, or hasn't been since half-past four or five."

There was something in the tone of these words that made the gentlemen start and look fixedly at the groom. Mulligan's eyes sank consciously beneath their gaze. All at once Dr. O'Grady's hand fell heavily on his shoulder.

"Mulligan, there is something on your mind that you do not care to tell. But you need not fear to tell us, for you will have to tell all in a court of justice, and that before long. Tell me now, had this man Pierce any grudge against Mr. Esmond?"

"Not against my master, sir! O Lord, no, sir, I'll take my oath he hadn't! There was no one had any grudge against him!—vo! vo! how could they?"

"And yet they shot him!" said Hennessy, with stern emphasis; "they have killed one of the best landlords in Tipperary —one of the best friends the poor had—after that, who can ever say a word in their behalf? My poor, poor Harry! I thought you could travel the county over by night or day without any one touching a hair of your head!—and to think that others who did oppress the poor are alive and well, and you lying there dead—shot down like a dog in the flower of your youth—my noble, generous, whole-souled Harry!—you that always stood their friend when they most needed one!"

"Well, gentlemen," said Mulligan, wiping away his tears with the sleeve of his jacket, "it *does* look very bad—very, very bad at this present time—an' if any one done that deed a purpose—I mane *if they knew who was in it*—I'd disown Tipperary for ever an' a day"—

Both gentlemen turned at this and fixed their eyes on Mulligan. There was a deep meaning in his eyes, no less than in his words.

"So you think, Mulligan," said O'Grady slowly and thoughtfully, "that there might have been a mistake—a fatal mistake, if so!"

"I'll lay my life on it, sir!" said the groom, with honest warmth. "I wouldn't believe the bishop—no, nor the Pope himself, if he said it, that *my master* was shot a purpose. No, sir! it's bad enough, God knows, but it isn't as bad as that!"

"Well, well, it makes little difference, after all, how he came by his death; he is dead, God help us all this night! May the Mother of Sorrows comfort his poor wife, and protect his little orphans!" O'Grady's voice faltered as he thus spoke, and it was only after clearing his throat several times that he said to his brother doctor, "Of course, nothing can be done here till the inquest is over. We must send at once to notify the coroner;" and he raised his handkerchief to his eyes. Professionally cold and calm as O'Grady was on ordinary occasions, he was here a very child.

Mulligan was accordingly despatched with the awful intelligence to the coroner of Mr. Esmond's murder,—awful, indeed, for Dr. ——, then coroner for that district of the County Tipperary, was himself a personal friend of the deceased gentleman.

When the doctors found themselves alone together, Hennessy laid his hand on O'Grady's arm and said, "Now tell me, O'Grady, what is your opinion of all this?"

O'Grady lowered his voice to a whisper as he replied, "My opinion is that"—— He did not finish the sentence, for the door opened and Uncle Harry made his appearance. Without speaking a word, but merely nodding to the doctors, the old man approached the bed, and looked long on the lifeless form of his nephew. No outward sign gave token of what passed within, but those who watched with intense interest the bearing of that stern man under so terrible a trial, did see what they never forgot, the mighty workings of a hard, proud heart, writhing under the lash. The face was only partially seen to them, but even that partial view was not needed, for the swollen and throbbing veins on the great thick neck, and the heaving of the broad chest, sufficiently indicated the storm of passion that was raging within.

At last he turned and looked from one doctor to the other with heavy, bloodshot eyes, glaring fiercely from under his bushy brows.

"So they've killed poor Harry!" said he in a hoarse, guttural voice.

"So it appears, Mr. Esmond," sadly said O'Grady.

"Well, there's what it is to be 'a good landlord'!" There was a fierceness of sarcasm in these words that cannot be described. "If it was *I*, now, that lay there instead of Harry, people would say, I suppose, that I deserved what I got—ah! the villains! the black-hearted, cowardly villains! it's little *I* regard them!"

"Take care, Mr. Esmond, take care!" said Hennessy. "With that sight before you, how can you speak so?"

"And why not?" said Esmond fiercely.

"Because, Mr. Esmond," said Hennessy, drawing near to him, and looking him steadily in the face, "*because that bullet may have missed its mark! No man ever meant to shoot young Harry Esmond!*"

The old man started as if an adder had stung him. A ghastly paleness overspread his face, and a brighter glare flashed in his eyes. "Dr. Hennessy," he stammered out, "what do you mean?"

"I mean just what I said," replied the doctor slowly and emphatically, "that my poor friend never incurred the fearful penalty he has paid. Excuse me," said the doctor to O'Grady, "I will go and see how poor Mrs. Esmond is."

"You are impertinent, sir!—you forget yourself!" hissed the old man between his teeth.

"No, sir, I do not forget myself, or you either!" and so saying, Hennessy left the room. As he passed along the corridor to the remote apartment whither Mrs. Esmond had been conveyed, he encountered more than one group of the servants with certain women of the neighbourhood whom the news had already reached. Every soul of them was in tears, and their groans and lamentations attested the sincerity of their sorrow. Some had stories to tell of dreams they had dreamed about the poor dear master, or the mistress, God save her! or of "great trouble and confusion about the big house." And sure they knew well there was something going to happen. Others had been favoured with warnings of divers other kinds, all of which were now interpreted in the awful death of "the master" so dearly loved by all. The cook was trying hard to make herself intelligible through the sobs and tears that choked her voice, while she set forth her claims to supernatural enlightenment.

"Sure, didn't I know ever since Hal'eve night that somethin' or another was goin' to happen?"

"Wisha, how is that, Molly dear?" and all the rest dried their eyes, and held their breath to listen to one so well entitled to speak.

Molly then told, with sundry additions, the affair of the ring —the wedding-ring and the clay. When Molly had enjoyed sufficiently the simple wonder of her auditors, she proceeded to cap the climax with her own experience. "But there was something more than that," said she, "that nobody seen barrin' myself an' Nancy there."

"The Lord save us, Molly, achree! what was it?"

"Afther they wor all gone to bed that night, myself an' Nancy bein' the last in the kitchen, we thought we'd rake the ashes smooth to see if there 'id be any feet comin' or goin'. We waited to try the salt, too, so we put a thimbleful fornenst every one in the house, standin' on a plate in a cool place, an' off we went to bed."

"Well, Molly, an' what came of it?"

"As true as I'm a livin' woman this night, an' the master a dead man,—Lord receive his sowl in glory!—there was the mark of a foot in the ashes—a man's foot, too, an' for all the world about the size of his, an' it turned to'st the door."

"The Lord between us an' harm!"

"An' when we went to look at the salt, behold you, there was one thimbleful broken down, an' melted like, an' the others all standin' as straight as when we left them. Now that's as thrue as you're all standin' there, an' if you doubt my words there's Nancy Kenny can tell you the same."

Nancy groaned in corroboration, and another took up the dismal theme of the warnings. It was very remarkable, however, that in all their grief for the good master they had lost, little was said of the manner of his death, and nothing whatever of the perpetrator of the deed—whoever that might be.

When Dr. Hennessy knocked at the door of the room where Mrs. Esmond was, it was opened by Mrs. O'Grady, and he found within Mrs. Esmond, senior, and Aunt Winifred, all three having come with Uncle Harry. Mary Hennessy, it appeared, was so overcome by the dreadful shock that she was utterly unable to follow the dictates of her heart in hastening to the side of her so awfully-bereaved friend.

To the doctor's inquiry of how she found herself, Mrs. Esmond replied, in low, faint accents, "Oh, there is no fear of me—I am well enough—too well! But, Dr. Hennessy," she added, with sudden animation, raising herself from her reclining posture in a large arm-chair,—"Dr. Hennessy, do tell me, has that man Pierce yet returned?"

"I believe not. But why do you ask?—did you want him?"

"Want him?" Mrs. Esmond repeated, with a visible shudder; "oh no! no! no! The sight of him would be death—death—death!" and, moaning piteously, she fell back again in the chair.

"Why, surely, Mrs. Esmond," said the doctor, "you cannot suspect *him?*—what motive could induce *him*—or, indeed, any one else—to commit so black a crime?"

"I know not, doctor, I know not; but "—and the unhappy lady paused, gasping for breath—" but from something he said to me just before leaving the house—and after my poor—my poor Harry was gone—I fear—oh, I am almost *certain* that he sad—at least—something to do with it!" She could say no more.

The horror of this announcement blanched every cheek, and the ladies were, for once, struck dumb. It was only for a moment, however, for, long before the doctor could make up his mind as to what he should say, Aunt Winifred broke out with—

"La me! we might have known there was something bad about the fellow; don't you remember the voice we heard on Hallow-eve night?"

"Yes, and that sad affair of the ring, my dear Mrs. Esmond," subjoined Mrs. O'Grady; "you know I told you that you should not have given your wedding-ring for such a purpose! My dear, it was very thoughtless of you to do it—indeed, indeed it was! My! my! my! who could have foreseen this? —though I must say that I had a sort of presentiment that night that something very bad was going to happen. Poor dear Harry!" and, taking out her handkerchief, the sympathising friend buried her face in its snowy folds. The elder Mrs. Esmond, who sat quietly with her niece's hand clasped in hers, here made a sign to the doctor to get the others out of the room.

"My dear Mrs. Esmond," said Dr. Hennessy, anxious himself to rid her, if possible, of these Job's comforters, "had you not better lie down on the bed, and remain quiet a while? I see you are completely exhausted. Aunt Martha will stay with you, and Mrs. O'Grady and Aunt Winifred can go downstairs and attend to the household affairs. The people are already crowding in, and the house will be full of guests before morning."

The proposal was eagerly accepted by the two active ladies, who immediately retired, brimful of importance. It was hard, however, to persuade Mrs. Esmond to remain where she was.

"Oh, Dr. Hennessy!—oh, Aunt Martha!" she sobbed, "how can I stay here—and Harry so near me—*dead?*—oh no, no!—I cannot—cannot stay!" and she rose from her seat, notwithstanding the gentle efforts of Aunt Martha to prevent her. "Now, Aunt Martha, do not—do not ask to keep me!" she faltered out in tones of piteous entreaty; "he will not be long with me—let me look upon him while I can!—while I can! Oh, Aunt Martha, Aunt Martha! what will I do at all?"

A wild burst of anguish followed, and Mrs. Esmond, trembling and exhausted, was easily prevailed upon to resume her seat. It appeared to the sympathising friends who watched her so tenderly that there was in her mind, and hovering on her lips, something which she could not put in words. Aunt Martha, kind and prudent, guessed it.

"My poor Henrietta," said she, "you are thinking of—of—the laying out—but that cannot be done to-night."

"And why not?" cried Mrs. Esmond, with a start.

The old lady was silent, but the doctor spoke—

"Well, you know, my dear Mrs. Esmond," coughing slightly to gain time, "there is a certain—ah!—investigation to be made—before—before anything of that kind is done"—

"Oh, you mean the inquest?" said the widow, seized with a sudden tremor; "I had forgotten that—my God! my God!"

"What if you took her to see the children?" whispered the doctor to Aunt Martha as he turned to leave the room; "the sight of them might soften her heart and make her weep—then all were well; but I fear this horrid wildness—this dry, feverish agony."

At this juncture the door opened and Uncle Harry joined the group. The meeting between him and the heart-stricken widow of his murdered nephew was strangely silent and solemn. In silence the old man took Mrs. Esmond's hand and squeezed it very hard; in silence he seated himself by her side, drew a long, long breath that ended in a sigh, then looked through his half-closed eyes first at his wife, then at Dr. Hennessy; and last of all at his niece. As for Mrs. Esmond, she appeared but little consoled by his presence, and a darker shadow seemed to gather on her face since his entrance. She returned his greeting with her wonted gentleness, but remained silent.

"My dear niece," began Uncle Harry at length, "this is an awful visitation that has come upon us all. Who could have thought that such an end awaited our poor Harry?"

A voice here spoke from the shade of the high and richly curtained bed—"They said they'd do it—an' they did!—they said they'd hang—no, shoot ould Esmond!"

"Great God! who is that?" exclaimed Uncle Harry, while his wife turned pale as death, and Dr. Hennessy, approaching the spot whence the voice appeared to issue, led Mabel out by the hand.

"I knew it was poor Mabel," sighed the younger Mrs. Esmond.

"But how came she here?" said Uncle Harry testily.

"She must have got in when you did," observed Dr. Hennessy, "for I know she wasn't in the room before."

"Don't mind her," pleaded Mrs. Esmond, reaching out her

hand to Mabel; "she was the first to cry over—over—*him that's gone!* That's a good girl, Mabel! don't be afraid!" and she smoothed down the dark dishevelled tresses that hung over the girl's shoulders.

"I'm afraid of *him!*" said Mabel, pointing to Uncle Harry, who was regarding her with one of his keen, scowling glances. "That's ould Esmond, you know," in a half whisper to Mrs. Esmond, "and they said he was a *born devil!*"

"Hush, hush, Mabel!" whispered Mrs. Esmond eagerly.

"Let her say on," said Uncle Harry sternly. "Who said I was a born devil, Mabel?"

"Why, the men in the abbey that dark night—an' listen hither—they said they'd kill you!—ha! ha! I knew they'd do it!—it's well it wasn't hang you they did—they hang every one, you know—barrin' the gentlemen—but they shoot *them!* ha! ha! ha!—an' that's all the same—but, ochone! the purty young gentleman in the room above, what made them shoot *him?* Sure, he never done anybody any harm!—

Och, it's once I had a true love, but now I have none!"

This allusion to her husband's fate, accompanied as it was with so touching a tribute to his goodness, went straight to Mrs. Esmond's heart, and drew a torrent of tears from her eyes, to Dr. Hennessy's great relief.

"But who were *the men?*" persisted Uncle Harry, his brow darkening more and more every moment.

"Wisha, how could *I* see in the dark?" was the answer. "Ask *Jerry Pierce* up at the big house, and maybe he'll tell you! He's Kate Martha's born brother, you know! Augh! let me go now—I want to see the young master. Ochone! ochone! the black day it was when anybody made that hole in his purty white forehead!"

Dr. Hennessy flew with great alacrity to open the door for the wayward girl, and away she went along the corridor, crying and clapping her hands in all the wildness of sorrow.

"There's a terrible meaning running through her incoherent ravings," said Uncle Harry, with stern emphasis; "we must have her before the coroner in the morning. Come, doctor, let us join the gentlemen;" and, taking Hennessy's arm, they left the room together.

CHAPTER VIII.

THE EVENTS OF A NIGHT.

THE next day was Christmas Eve, and after that came Christmas Day, but the Christmas joys were clouded in many a household in and around Cashel by the awful death of the county's favourite, the gay, the generous, the all-beloved Harry Esmond. The comforts that surrounded many an otherwise cheerless hearth that Christmas-tide were the gift of him and his gentle wife, and how could the poor forget that there was sorrow at "the big house," yea, the heaviest of all sorrows! They could not forget, and they did not forget, that one of the noblest gentlemen in Tipperary lay cold and dead that day, that a blight had already fallen on the young life of their most bountiful benefactress. Few houses there were in all the countryside in which the Rosary was not said those nights for "rest to the poor young master's soul," and many a fair frolic was "nipped i' the bud" by the timely admonition of some grave senior, "Wisha, how could you think of the like an' the young master a cowld corpse the day?—och! more's the pity."

And when St. Stephen's Day came, and the "Wren-boys" perambulated the town and its vicinity bearing that diminutive specimen of the feathered tribe aloft in triumph amongst green boughs ornamented with gay streamers, the rollicking, noisy crowd hushed their obstreperous mirth whilst they passed in front of the Hall.

"Whisht, now, boys! whisht! Bad cess to you! don't you know what's in there?—Not a word, now, not a word for your lives!" —"Och! then, sure, it's the first time we ever passed *that* door without a big piece o' silver!—God rest his soul that's gone!" Such were the exclamations that stopped the bellowing mouths of the juvenile mob, but the seniors of the troop need scarcely have uttered them, for the youngest there would have neither laughed nor sung whilst passing the house of Death—that one, cast of all. A few perches past the Esmond gates, however, and the wild chorus rose higher than ever—

> "The wren, the wren, the king of all birds,
> St. Stephen's Day was caught in the furze;
> Although he is little, his family's great,
> Rise, fair lady, and give us a trate!"

This *refrain*, repeated *in recitative* with the utmost rapidity of utterance by some scores of squalling voices, was anything but musical in its character, yet heard from afar it was not without a certain wild melody, like the murmur of waves on the sandy beach. As "a lay of the olden time" the "Song of the Wren," importunate to some, was right welcome to others, bringing back long-vanished scenes, and the simple joys of other years when life was warm and young. The mourners heard it, and it made their sadness deeper yet, by contrast with the bright, untroubled past; faint and far it came to the ears of the new-made widow and Mary Hennessy, where they sat, hand locked in hand, beside the bed whereon lay the shrouded form of Harry Esmond, now decked in the mournful habiliments of the grave, awaiting its burial on the morrow; then did the two pale friends look into each other's eyes, and the weight of present woe crushed heavier on their hearts as memory brought back the merry Christmas-times that, for one of them, at least, were to come no more. The same thoughts came back with the same familiar sound to Maurice Hennessy on his daily rounds, and to Phil Noran at his desk, and he dropped the scroll over which he had been musing—it was the official report of the coroner's inquest—and a shadow fell on his thoughtful brow, and the tears welled up from his inmost heart as he murmured, "Poor, poor Harry! friend of my boyhood's years, how often have we laughed together at the merry pranks and mischievous drollery of the Wren-boys! They will miss your open hand to-day! So they ought! so they ought!" he added, starting up and pacing the room to and fro with hasty strides; "they'll all miss him, and that not to-day or to-morrow either—and that they may, from my heart out! When any one could be found amongst them hardened enough to murder young Harry Esmond, they deserve the worst that can come upon them! Such a deed is enough to draw down a curse on the whole country!"

"True for you, sir!" said his clerk, a thin-faced and rather cadaverous individual, who had the ungainly peculiarity of never looking any one straight in the face. "If it had been the old gentleman, now, a body wouldn't have cared, but his tenantry hadn't that good luck!"

"Good luck, you rascal?" said his master, turning sharp round; "how dare you say such a word in my presence?"

"Why, then, upon my credit, sir, I meant no offence," whispered the clerk; "but if it was old Esmond that got the bullet in place of Master Harry, I'm thinking, sir, there would be more dry eyes than there is the day."

"Silence, sir!" shouted Moran. "Don't let me hear any more of such talk, but go on with what you are doing."

"I will, Mr. Moran; but, to tell you the truth, sir, if it was the old fellow that was popped, I wouldn't make out the warrant so—so cheerfully."

"Cheerfully, you villain? Why, you look for all the world like a hangman!—or rather, like one whose own neck was in danger!"

"Oh, God forbid, sir, God forbid!" and the cadaverous clerk, whose name was Ned Murtha, put up his skinny hand to his neck, as if to make sure that it was *not* in danger. "But then I wish Mr. Boland had got the warrant made out at home."

"And why so, pray?"

"Well, you see, sir, it's the first warrant of the kind I ever made out, and I can't—I can't warm to the job, at all, at all! 'Deed I can't, sir!"

"Nonsense, man, nonsense! don't you think the fellow that shot Harry Esmond deserves to swing for it?"

"I know, sir, I know, but then—but then I don't care to have a hand in any one's death."

"Go on with your work, I say!—no more idle prate—there is no time to be lost."

Moran seated himself at his desk, bent again over his papers—silence reigned for a few minutes, when an exclamation from Ned made the lawyer turn quickly, just in time to see that eccentric individual throw down his pen and jump from his perch on the high office-stool.

"Confound it, Ned! what's the matter now?" cried the attorney.

"Well, it's a folly to talk, Mr. Moran," said Ned, looking every way but at him; "I can't nor I won't write them words, sir, in regard to *Jerry Pierce!*"

"You will not, eh?"

"No, sir; I wouldn't do it for all you're worth! It's against nature, so it is!"

"And why against nature?"

"Because, Mr. Moran, Jerry Pierce is a first and second cousin of my own, and—and—O Lord! if it was only the old fellow he had shot—no, no—I didn't mean that, Mr. Moran! I didn't, indeed, sir! for I won't believe he shot e'er a one, at all, till I'm full sure of it. But don't ask me, sir, if you please, to make out the warrant—Jerry and myself are too near akin, sir, for me to do it, let it be as it may. And besides, Jerry saved me a horsing[1] oust, when we were at school together, by reason of taking the fault on himself to screen me, and he as innocent as the child unborn."

Poor Ned took out a blue handkerchief spotted with white, and giving it a very determined shake before he applied it to its legitimate purpose, blubbered out, "No, Mr. Moran! I can't do *it*, sir—if I lose my place for it!"

"Well, well, Ned, you shan't lose your place for it," said Moran, coughing down his emotions—lawyer as he was, there was a large infusion of the milk of human kindness in his heart. "Go and tell Brannigan to come here—he'll make out the warrant, and you can copy that deed he was going to commence. Hurry, now, hurry!"

"I will, sir," said Ned, but he *only* said it, for his journey to the next room occupied considerably more time than the distance seemed to warrant.

"Ned Murtha," said Moran to himself, as the door closed behind him, "there's more of a heart in that ungainly body of yours than I ever gave you credit for."

[1] All our readers may not understand the nature of the service rendered on this occasion. In country schools in Ireland when a boy was convicted of any capital offence, he was hoisted on the back of another boy, and castigated to the master's "heart's content." This punishment was technically styled *horsing.*

The reader will see from this that a warrant had been issued immediately after the coroner's inquest for the arrest of "Jeremiah — commonly called Jerry — Pierce, late butler at Esmond Hall." The verdict on which this warrant was founded could nowise have been returned but for the evidence of Mrs. Esmond touching the mysterious words of Pierce, and his no less mysterious conduct on the fatal day of the murder— this, coupled with his sudden disappearance, furnished very strong presumptive evidence that, if not the principal in the atrocious crime, he was, at least, cognizant thereof, and, therefore, accessory. It was an awful suspicion, considering the relation which had existed between the supposed murderer and his victim—the unvarying kindness of the master and the apparent fidelity and gratitude of the man. In fact, no motive could be assigned for the perpetration of so foul a murder, and hence it was that the whole country cried shame on the murderer, and one general feeling of horror and of indignation pervaded the minds of all. Rich and poor were alike interested in this mysterious murder—the rich naturally inferring from it that no man's life was safe amid a population so prone to deeds of blood that not even the best of landlords was safe from their capricious malice; the poor, on the other hand, lamenting the loss of their generous friend and most bountiful benefactor, the darling of every heart, and filled with shame and confusion to think that a man could be found in Tipperary to shoot *him* in cold blood. "One of themselves, too,"—that was the worst of it. There had been murders committed even in that part of the country, where the murderers were regarded with compassion rather than abhorrence, because they had but executed the general thirst for vengeance on some hard-hearted, tyrannical landlord, the scourge of his miserable tenantry, and the avowed enemy of the people;—in this case, however, there was no sympathy for the murderer—all the popular feeling was against him; in all that eastern district of Tipperary there was not man, woman, or child who did not execrate the deed, praying with all the fervour of grateful love for the repose of Mr. Esmond's soul, and that God might comfort his desolate widow and her unconscious orphans.

Of the many humble homes to which the untimely death of young Harry Esmond brought tribulation, there was none where grief weighed so heavily as in that of Bryan Cullenan. The news had come like a thunderbolt on Cauth and Bryan, and both equally felt the crushing blow, but its effect on each was diametrically opposite. Bryan hastened at once to the Hall, "satisfied himself," as he said, "with a good cry over the poor young master," and prayed long and fervently beside his cold remains, the tears streaming from his aged eyes on the Bridgetine beads he was telling for the repose of that dear soul. During the three days and nights that the vigil of death was kept in Esmond Hall, Bryan spent the greater part of his time there, now giving out the Rosary and the Litanies amongst the country-people who thronged the kitchen and the servants' hall, now kneeling, absorbed in pious meditation, beside the state bed on which the body was laid out, that mournful privilege being tacitly conceded to the old man of the Rock.

Cauth, on the contrary, never went near the house of death. A certain gloomy wildness seemed to have taken possession of her, and she talked incoherently to herself with the strangest gesticulations. That was only when alone, however, for to Bryan she was unusually silent all those dreary days. Once, when the old man asked, was she not going up "to see the poor young master before he was laid in the cold clay, where none of them could ever see him any more," she turned on him sharply with—

"Don't be botherin' me, Bryan Cullenan! What for would I go up there?"

"Wisha, Cauth! what for does any one go up there?" said Bryan, much amazed. "Myself thought you had a great wish for the quality at the Hall!"

"Who says I haven't?" she returned still more sharply. "Go your ways, now, Bryan, an' let me alone! I hate to hear people makin' fools o' themselves, talkin' of what they know nothin' about."

Poor Bryan was fain to do her bidding, and "went his ways" to the Rock, wondering much what manner of woman Cauth might be, who, professing so much love and gratitude for "the young mistress," appeared yet so little touched by the dread sorrow that had come upon her.

"Ay, go your ways, ould man!" said Cauth, when she found herself alone; "it's little you know about them you're leavin' behind. Oh," she moaned, "if I hadn't gone next or nigh them ! if I hadn't loaded them with blessin's, maybe this heavy curse wouldn't have come down on them ! sure, I might a known how it 'id be !—why wouldn't I go an' see him, fuagh ! och, then, God help your wit, you poor foolish ould man ! isn't it on my two knees I'd walk from here to there, an' back again, if it could do *himself* or *herself* any good—but, *fareer gur!* it couldn't !—no ! no ! no ! it couldn't, an' it 'id break my heart entirely to see my poor darlin' young gentleman lyin' there kilt an' murdhered fornenst my eyes ! it would—it would ! Och ! the black villain—the black villain ! sure, the Devil himself had a hand in him, or he couldn't do the likes o' that—he couldn't spill the blood of one that never done any one any harm—one that had the blessin' of the poor, an' the good wish of high and low !"

That night when

The iron tongue of midnight had told twelve,

it so happened that Bryan Collenan found himself alone for a short space with the sheeted dead. The ladies and gentlemen were taking some refreshment in the next room, and Mrs. Esmond had been prevailed upon with much ado to lay down her weary head, even though sleep, that ever forsakes the wretched, and "flies from woe," was little to be expected for one so utterly woebegone.

All at once Bryan's solemn meditations were rudely interrupted by the sight of a tall figure standing by the bed, wrapped in a greatcoat, the cape of which was thrown over the head after the manner of a hood. Bryan's heart sank within him, and his tongue clave to his palate, so that he could not speak, even if he would. With his eyes starting from their sockets, he watched the motionless form, as it stood with head bent forward, and hands—they were large, bony hands, too—clasped tightly together, back side up, as they hung at arm's length in front. The attitude was one of mournful contemplation, but no sound was heard, not even a sigh from the unseen lips. But as Bryan gazed with his heart in his eyes, he saw some sudden emotion shake the huge frame of his mysterious fellow-watcher—one long low moan was heard, like the wail of a tortured spirit, and the figure, turning towards Bryan, raised a finger in admonition and passed slowly from the room. Oh, the horror of that moment! the icy shiver that ran from the old man's heart through every vein of his body, as, glancing up into the face which he supposed was that of a supernatural being, he recognised *the murderer—Jerry Pierce!*

Bryan used to say in after days that he often wondered how he got over the fright of that moment. He whose days, and nights too, were not seldom passed amongst the dead—he that could sleep contentedly amongst the graves on the desolate Rock of Cashel, no whit alarmed by the possibility of some of their occupants

Revisiting the glimpses of the moon,—

he was paralysed with terror by the sight of that mortal man. His first impulse was to cry out and give the alarm now that he found his tongue unloosed from the spell of that dread presence; but Bryan was a cautious man, an exceeding cautious man, and he made it a rule in every emergency to "think twice and speak once," so he thought twice then, and concluded—just as "the quality" came in again from the other room—firstly, that there was no great chance of catching Pierce by that time, and secondly, that it might be the death of the young mistress if she came to hear that the murderer of her husband had been there in the silent midnight to look upon the lifeless remains of his victim. So Bryan crept from the room unnoticed by any one, and was making his way to the kitchen, when in the hall he found a crowd assembled round one of the maid-servants, who seemed obstinately bent on fainting away directly, from which overt act divers of her fellow-servants, aided by a number of the wakepeople from below, were violently endeavouring to dissuade her.

"Och! let me alone!" hysterically cried, or rather sobbed, the entirely overcome damsel, as she wriggled and twisted in the arms of the sympathising assistants; "sure, I'll never be the better of it—never—never!—och! I'll faint—I'll faint!"

"Wisha, don't now! don't, achree!—you'll be over it soon, please God!—it's only a wakeness."

"What did you see, *a colleen?*"

"Och! och! what did I see!—why, I seen—I seen—*Jerry Pierce!!*—Och! I'm goin'—I'm goin'!"

Exclamations of horror were heard on every side. "Jerry Pierce!! the Lord in heaven save us!—ah, then, where did you see him, *acushla?*"

"I met him—on the stairs abroad—comin' down—an' the cape of his big coat up over his head—oh! oh!—an' his eyes lookin' at me like—like live coals!"

"Oyeh! it's his fetch she seen!"—ran round the circle in a loud whisper,—"it's well if she *does* get over it, the crathur!"

"There, there! she's goin'!"

"If she is, she can use her feet well—and her tongue too," said Bryan to himself as he passed on towards the kitchen, cruelly indifferent to the precarious condition of the fainting fair one, but much occupied with the thoughts of the apparition which had frightened himself no less than her. Notwithstanding Bryan's silence, the news soon spread all over the house, and every soul in it, with the single exception of its widowed mistress and Uncle Harry—of whom all stood in too much awe to tell him anything—had heard the awful tale of Jerry Pierce's fetch being seen walking about the house. Then did Mary Hennessy and Bella Le Poer remind each other of the shadowy form *they* had seen only ten or twelve days before, and, coupling that with this, they shudderingly concluded—as did most of those at the wake—that this appearance was possibly in advance of the wretched man's impending doom.

There was another that saw Jerry Pierce that night—a comely, dark-haired damsel, by name Celia Mulquin, who kept house for her uncle, a road contractor, named Larry Dwyer, within a stone's throw of the Esmond gate. The uncle and his two strapping sons were long since abed and sleeping soundly, as evinced by the somewhat unmusical chorus executed *in trio* by that number of nasal organs on the loft which covered "the room,"—another over the kitchen being Celia's sleeping apartment, both reached by a ladder; the middle space, or that end of the kitchen where was the fireplace, shaded from the door by the jamb-wall, had no covering over it but the thatch and wattles of the roof.

Celia was sitting in a very desponding attitude before the yet unraked fire, looking with fixed, unconscious eyes down into the red *greshaugh*, the ashes of the burned sods which had all day long made "the back" for the light "slane turf" that formed the fire. It was hard to say what Celia was thinking of just then, but it must have been something very painful to her heart, judging by the paleness of her round fair cheek and the sad expression of her soft blue eyes. By and by the vacant look vanished, and a world of sorrow was suddenly in motion all over the girl's smooth features. Tears began at length to moisten her eyelids, and, raising the two corners of her checked apron, she held them to her eyes, her chest heaving violently under the coloured kerchief so modestly folded over it. Suddenly she started, turned her head in the attitude of listening, then stood up and crossed herself, her eyes fixed with a frightened look on the little window that pierced the front wall of the house a few feet from the ground.

"Christ save us!" muttered the girl; "who can it be at this dead hour o' the night!——why, sure——sure it can't be *him* !"

The pallor deepened on her face, but she stepped on tiptoe to the window; nothing was there to be seen but the pitchy darkness of the night. A tap was now heard at the door, and thither went Celia with the same stealthy pace. Putting her ear close to the door, she listened for a repetition of the sound —it came not again in the same form, but a voice spoke through the keyhole—

"Celia darlin', won't you let me in? If you're by yourself, do, for God's sake! I want to speak to you."

Celia knew the voice, and it brought the rich colour back to her cheek, though the flush passed away as quickly as it came. For a moment she stood irresolute, but her soft woman's heart prevailed, and she opened the door with as little noise as possible. Jerry Pierce stood without, but the next moment he stood within, close by the jamb-wall. The girl retreated as far as the front wall would let her, but that was only a few feet.

"Celia," said the man in a thick, hoarse whisper, "are you afeard of me too?"

"I'm not *afeard* of you," she answered in the same low tone; "I know you'll not harm *me;* but——but——oh, what——what brings you here, you poor misfortunate man?"

"Bekase I'm hunted like a wild baste already, an' they'll be apt to hunt me down soon, an' then I could never say to you what I *must* say, dead or alive. Are they all gone to bed?"

" Hours an' hours ago—don't you hear them snorin'?"

" May I sit down, then, for a little start by the fire?" whispered the deep voice; " I'm shiverin' with the cowld, Celia, an' it'll be long, long before I see your face again—maybe never!" The girl could not resist this sorrowful appeal, so, placing the light in a position which threw the broad fireplace and the greater part of the kitchen in shade, she proceeded to hang a thick cloth before the window, so that none could look in from without, and then placed a low seat for Jerry in the corner just by the jamb. Taking her own station on the opposite side of the fire, she sat with her eyes cast down, her cheek and lip pale as ashes, and her clasped hands resting on her knees. For a few moments both were silent, Pierce cowering over the fire, while his large limbs trembled, partly with cold, partly with misery and desolation.

" Maybe you're hungry?" questioned the girl in a choking voice, without raising her eyes, and without naming his name.

A sort of low, convulsive laugh gurgled in the man's throat as, starting at her voice, he replied, " No, I didn't come here to ask charity; I had my supper—thanks to them that gave it to me."

" Well, what—what—did you want with me?" still without looking up.

" Want with *you*?" repeated the man in a half-angry tone, but the next moment he added somewhat more mildly, " Oyeh, Celia! it's althered times with us when you'd ax me such a question. But och! och! sure, the faut isn't yours, mavrone mavrone, it is *not!*"

" I ask you again, what did you come here for?"

" I'll tell you that—do you believe me guilty of what's laid to my charge?"

" How can I *dis*believe it?" asked Celia sadly. " An' och! och! but it's the hard thing to think that—that "——

" That what?"

" That you'd be guilty of the likes of that."

" But you think I am?"

" Wisha, God help me! what can I think?" And the tears began to fall unheeded from Celia's eyes.

In a moment Pierce was beside her, and would have taken her hand, but that she stoutly resisted, drawing her seat away from him with a look that was partly fear, partly anger.

"Don't—don't—lay a hand on me, unless you want to kill me too!"

She was sorry for the word almost before it had passed her lips, but she made no effort to recall it. Its effect on Pierce was like that of a stunning blow; he was struck dumb, and for a moment could only look at the terrified girl with eyes of blank bewilderment. At last he sighed, and that sigh passed shivering through his whole body, his blue lips parted, and he said, clasping his hands together, and letting his head fall heavily on his chest, "Then I am—I am—a murderer!"

When he raised his head again, there was a ghastly smile on his face, and he looked more like a corpse than a living being; his hands were clasped tight across his breast, as though to restrain its wild throbbings; it was some moments before he could speak, gasping for breath the while, Celia watching him with eyes distended by horror and amazement. At last he spoke in a hissing whisper that made the blood curdle in her veins—

"Well, now, *that's* what brought me here the night!"

"What?"

"Why, you know the promise of marriage that's betwixt us —well, I came to give mine back—it'll soon be all over with me, an' I don't want to have you afeard of me comin' back on account o' the promise—when—when—I'm gone!"[1]

Celia Mulquin leaned forward and looked into his eyes with a wild, searching gaze,—as she looked, her features gradually relaxed, her lips parted with something like a smile, if a smile could come at such a moment. Slowly, very slowly, she spoke— "I'll not give you back your promise, then; for, livin' or dead, Jerry Pierce, if I don't marry *you*, I'll marry no one else. If that's what you came for, you have your answer!"

Jerry Pierce sprang to his feet with an energy that frightened poor Celia. A gleam of wild, passionate joy flashed across his features like red lightning over the black thunder-cloud.

"I *have* my answer," he said in the subdued tones that

[1] This superstition is common in all parts of Ireland. If one of two betrothed lovers die, it is considered as certain as anything, not of faith, can be, that he or she will haunt the living party to the promise until it be cancelled between them.

caution required,—" I have my answer, an' I'll go! Now I can face death, an' shame, an' all that's before me; for I know there's one true heart that—that loves me still, black and odious as I am! God be with you, achorra macree!"

"Whisht, whisht!" said the girl earnestly; "how dare you name that *Holy Name?*"

"I can dare more than that," was the answer. He stooped towards her, and, before she could prevent him, kissed her pale lips once, twice, thrice. "Don't be angry, Celia, that's the first kiss, and maybe the last, but *it isn't the kiss of a murderer!*— you'll think of them words, darlin', an' they'll comfort your poor heart when I'm maybe swingin' on the gibbet!"

He was gone before Celia could make herself conscious of what he had said.

CHAPTER IX.

UNCLE HARRY HAS AN ADVENTURE.

At the chapel door in Cashel on the following Sunday there was a crowd gathered, after last Mass, discussing, of course, the murder of young Mr. Esmond. There generally is a crowd after Mass, I am forced to confess, at every church and chapel door, discussing all manner of topics; but on the day in question the crowd was even greater than usual, and there was no diversity in the subjects under discussion—all were chattering away for dear life on the one engrossing theme of the murder, all the more engrossing for being horrible, and, moreover, mysterious. Many were the wild and strange rumours already afloat in relation to the murder and its probable causes, for people will have causes for everything, and where there are none on hand, they will make them to order. Some would have it that Pierce had an old spite against Master Harry since one day long ago he was out following the hunt as a game-boy, and the young master said or did something to him that was rankling in his mind ever since, till he got the chance of being revenged. Others always knew, they said, that there was something very bad in that Jerry Pierce; whilst others went further still, and said, with a sagacious wink or a shake of the head, that there was "a bad drop in them Pierces altogether." This capped the climax, the more so as it was something entirely new, for the Pierces, though poor cottiers from father to son, had always been in good repute with their neighbours, and this was the first actual blemish on their fair name. But there are always people ready, on such occasions, "to help the lame dog over the stile," as they say in Ireland, which means, in plain English, to speed an ill story on its way. "When a man's down, down with him," is the common order of things, and that in more countries than our dear Celtic Ireland. There are *lame dogs* in every country, and charitable people in abundance to "help them over the stile." But to our story.

The Dean himself had spoken for a full hour after Mass on the awful crime just committed in their midst, the disgrace of which fell, he said, on the whole community, until such time, at least, as the murderer was brought to justice. He had warned the people against aiding or assisting in concealing him from the officers of the law, saying that his crime was of the most revolting character, without one extenuating circumstance to lessen its enormity in the sight of God or man. He had paid an affectionate tribute to the virtues of the deceased gentleman, and spoke even with tears of the loss he was to the whole country both as a landlord and a magistrate. "When young Harry Esmond," said he, "was on the bench, the poor man always knew he had a friend that would see justice done him; and as a landlord," said he, "where will you find his equal?—which of you, his tenants, ever went from his office-door with anything but a blessing on your lips? Well, he is gone; this upright magistrate—this kind, easy landlord—this honourable, noble-hearted gentleman is gone from amongst us— cut down in the pride of his manhood, in the bloom of his youth, like a young tree lightning-blasted. And, alas! alas! that I should have to say it!—cut down by the hand of violence—the red hand of *murder!*—oh, horrible, most horrible it is to think of, for if people slay their friends and benefactors, what can be said in their favour? Nothing, nothing; they close the lips of their friends, and make their name odious to those who know them not. Murder is always abominable in the sight of God, and on no account justifiable. There are times, however, when people will pretend to make excuses, and soften down the horror of the crime by alleged provocation of one kind or another; but here, as you all know, there is, or can be, no palliation of a deed which stands out in the calendar of crime as a black and brutal murder. As for the perpetrator of the deed, may God convert him, and bring him to a sense of his wickedness before justice overtakes him, as it surely will, even in this world, if there be a just God in heaven! And mark well my words—the man or woman that has act or part in concealing that unhappy man from the officers of justice will be accountable for it before God and the laws of his country!"

This discourse, as may well be supposed, had made a deep impression on the minds of all, and, in fact, closed every heart against the murderer.

And so, as I said before, every tongue was loud in condemnation of the crime, whilst showing cause for its commission. All at once, a little old woman in a red cloak, with the hood drawn over her face, stumped out from the midst of the crowd, and stood on the open green with both hands resting on her stick, regarding the different speakers with a strange expression of scorn on the only part of her face that was visible beneath the hood. After listening a few moments longer, she broke out into a shrill, derisive laugh that immediately drew all eyes to her strange figure and stranger attitude, and it so happened that the clatter of voices ceased at once, and a hush fell on the so-lately noisy crowd.

"Ha! ha! ha!" laughed the hag again, "much you all know about it!—jist as much as the crows that are makin' game of you up yondher in the trees!—Ugh! ugh! ugh! go home about your business, I'd advise you, an' let the poor boy alone that never done you any harm!—Ugh! ugh! ugh! isn't it funny to hear people talkin' of what they know nothing about? But I tell you again"——and she raised her stick and pointed it at the crowd——"let *Jerry Pierce* alone, or ye'll not be thankful to yourselves!"

Away she hobbled, leaving her hearers bewildered and confused, for a whisper had run through the crowd while she spoke—"It's the fairy-woman of the hill! Christ between us an' harm!"

A heavy shower of rain could not have dispersed the crowd more quickly than the sound of that woman's voice; but as they scattered in all directions through the town and the adjoining country, groups might be seen here and there with their heads together, and in low, cautious tones might also be heard as the parting salutation—"So it's best take care, anyhow, an' not anger *her*."

In the course of that Sunday afternoon, Mr. and Mrs. Esmond of Rose Lodge paid a visit to their widowed niece, with whom Aunt Winifred had been staying ever since the fatal night that had quenched in blood the light of Esmond Hall. Mary Hennessy and Bella Le Poer were also there, to Mrs. Esmond's greater consolation, for their tender and judicious kindness was balm to her bruised and broken heart. No visitors were as yet admitted, save only the nearest relatives, and the house, late so full of life and animation, was gloomy as a funeral vault. The very servants, as they glided around in their deep mourning costume, were grave and sad as mutes at a funeral, and the merry voices of the children were hushed and silent. As for the fair mistress of the mansion, no smile had yet crossed her visage, and but few words escaped her bloodless lips, as she lay from day to day in her high-backed chair, a pale drooping flower, fading slowly away in the sight of the two devoted friends who watched her with more than sister's love. As on that first dreary night, the presence of Uncle Harry seemed somehow to discompose her, though she evidently strove to hide her disquiet, fearing, doubtless, to give him pain. But her tell-tale features refused to keep the secret, and the old man's keen eye speedily detected the emotion she vainly sought to repress. Declining Mrs. Esmond's faint invitation to remain for dinner, he rose abruptly, saying to his wife—

"Come, Martha, it will be night before we get home." He glanced at the timepiece over the mantel. "Why, how is that, Henrietta?—your clock is not going."

"No," said Mrs. Esmond, with more energy than she had of late manifested; "it stopped, I suppose, when Harry's heart did, and *it shall never go again*—at least, while I am its owner."

"What! do you mean to say it stopped at *that hour*, on that night?" and he pointed to the hands.

"My eyes saw it."

"Great God! it was about *the very moment!*" and the old man leaned on the back of a chair for support, his eyes still fixed on the timepiece.

"You think so, uncle?"

"There is no doubt of it," said Aunt Martha, her face pale as ashes. "It was about eight o'clock when he left our door, and half an hour would likely have brought him to—to—the fatal spot."

"True!—most true!" murmured Uncle Harry, as if to himself.

"But tell me, uncle," said Mrs. Esmond, with a spasmodic effort, "how it happened that it was your horse my poor fellow rode at the time, instead of the roan mare he took from here?"

"Oh, that, my dear, is easily explained," Uncle Harry carelessly replied. "The roan got lame with him on the way, and when my groom came to examine how it was, he found that a nail in one of the fore-shoes had pierced the hoof, and the animal was in downright pain, so we had to send directly for the blacksmith to take off the shoe, and a hard job it was to get it off. Of course Harry had nothing for it but to leave her behind, and take one of my horses."

"Dear me!" groaned Aunt Winifred, "it was most unfortunate."

"What was?" said her brother snappishly.

"Why, the change of horses, brother! You know there is such a thing as luck, after all, and I do think that grey of ours was unlucky to poor Harry!—I shall never go out with her again—never—never! But, mercy on us! you needn't look so cross; one would think you meant to bite my nose off!"

"No danger of that, Winny," said her brother maliciously; "my chance of getting you off my hands is small enough now without taking so unnatural a means of spoiling your *beauty!* Good-bye, Henny, my poor child; try and keep up your heart as well as you can."

"I will, sir," was the dreamy, listless answer, as the mourner received and returned Aunt Martha's kind farewell greeting. As for Miss Esmond, she stiffened herself to the rigidity of a colossal poker, and, not deigning to notice her brother's parting nod, extended the long fingers of her right hand to her sister-in-law, saying as she did so—

"Well, Martha, my dear, though he's *my* brother, I must say that you have got the greatest bear of a husband in all Tipperary. You have indeed!"

At another time this little manifestation of temper on the part of Aunt Winifred would have given much amusement, but there was none to notice it then, and in grave silence the party separated.

8

The early night was already close at hand when Mr. Esmond stepped into the gig where his wife was already seated. As he took the reins from Mulligan, he placed a half-crown in his hand, which Mulligan acknowledged by a very low bow and a "Long life to your honour, an' safe home, sir!" Then, lowering his voice, he added, "I'd make the bay step out, your honour, if I was you—there do be ghosts an' things abroad afther dusk, an' you've a lonesome bit of a road before you. Safe home, sir!" he said aloud, and, making a sign to Mr. Esmond to say nothing, he hurried off to open the gates, then bowed again as the gig rolled out on the high road, and distinctly uttered the words, "Take care!"

"What did Mulligan say, my dear?" asked Mrs. Esmond when they were fairly started.

"He said to-morrow would be a fine day," replied her husband with characteristic gruffness, as he leaned forward to apply the whip to the shining flanks of his horse, though the animal needed no such hint to make haste home.

Mrs. Esmond made no further attempt at conversation, and the ill-matched pair were whirled along for a mile and better through the chilly air of the winter evening without again exchanging words. Both were wrapt apparently in their own thoughts, and gloomy thoughts they were, too, for neither could forget that about the same hour less than a week ago, one near and dear to them left his home in happy unconsciousness that he was to see it nevermore.

As the evening shades fell colder and darker on the wintry landscape, the sense of loneliness began to press on the stout heart of Mr. Esmond, and he was glad to break the silence that he now felt oppressive. He addressed some trifling observation to his wife, but had not yet received an answer when the horse, shying at some object on the roadside, pricked up his ears, tossed his head, and began to prance in a backward direction that was anything but safe, seeing that a gravel-pit full of yellow muddy water bounded the road at that particular spot.

Mrs. Esmond's scream of terror frightened the animal still more; back—back he went, notwithstanding the desperate efforts made by the strong arm that was urging him forward; back—back he reared, till the wheels of the gig were within a foot of the water edge. Mrs. Esmond, crying, "Holy Mary!

Mother of God! pray for us!" was about to throw herself out of the gig at all hazards, when a tall man appeared at the horse's head, laid hold of the bridle, and with one jerk, and a soothing "Wo! wo!" drew the frightened animal out on the road, the gig lumbering heavily at his heels.

The fervent thanksgiving that escaped from Mrs. Esmond's ashy lips was for once echoed by her husband, with a hearty acknowledgment of the timely assistance that had saved them both from an awful death.

"You have saved our lives this night," said he.

"Undher God, sir—undher God," put in the tall man, stooping to pick up a bag he had thrown from his shoulder.

"Oh, of course—of course!—that's understood. But who and what are you? tell me that before you go, for if I live I'll reward you well."

"I'm not goin' yit," was the answer; "I'll walk a little ways further with you, for fear the baste might shy again, or something."

"But who are you? what is your name?"

"Well, my name isn't worth your honour's knowin', but I'm the poor man that asked charity from you there back o' the hill, an' didn't get it."

"My God!" murmured Mrs. Esmond in an audible whisper, and she pressed close to her husband as the tall beggarman appeared at her side of the vehicle.

"Don't be afeard, ma'am!" said he in a voice that sounded as if it came from a barrel; "any company's better than none sometimes—especially on a lonesome road of a dark night."

Mrs. Esmond said no more, and the sturdy beggarman trudged along, staff in hand, by her side, keeping pace with the horse even at a brisk trot. The few belated stragglers who passed along one way or the other, exchanging a brief salutation with the self-appointed guide, passed cheerily on, most of them whistling some lively air, as if to counteract the sombre influence of the hour.

On and on went the gig, and on went the tall beggarman beside it, bag on back and staff in hand. The one half of Mr. Esmond's homeward road was already passed, when the horse pricked up his ears again, glanced fearfully at one side of the road where stood an old limekiln, its rude masonry partly concealed by the overhanging branches of a huge alderbush. In an instant the beggarman had hold of the bridle, and his strong arm speedily brought the scared animal to subjection. A slight noise was heard as it were in the kiln—a dark form was visible for a moment, one word issued from the throat of the man at the horse's head—the word was "REMEMBER!"—in the twinkling of an eye the figure vanished, and the horse sped lightly on his way. Mrs. Esmond breathed more freely, she knew not why.

A little farther on, the beggarman stopped, and laid his hand on the rein. "You'll soon be at home now, Mr. Esmond," said he in his deep, guttural tones; "the baste won't shy any more, I'm thinkin', so I'll be biddin' you good-night; an' it's one advice I'll give you, never refuse a poor man or a poor woman a charity when they ask it for God's sake,—an' listen to what I'm goin' to say, your honour,"—he leaned over the wheel and spoke in a whisper,—"you're the last man in Tipperary that ought to be out afther nightfall. Now go your ways!"

"But, my very worthy fellow," said Mr. Esmond, "will you not tell me to whom I am so deeply indebted this night?"

"Maybe you wouldn't thank me if I did," said the man gruffly; "ask me no questions and I'll tell you no lies. Go on now, as fast as you can, or maybe there's worse than a quarry before you; an' mind what I tell you—be merciful to the poor, or their curse 'ill fall on you where I can't save you!"

Bounding like an antelope over the ditch, he disappeared, and it is hardly necessary to say that Mr. Esmond's bay flew home at a gallop.

The first act of Mr. Esmond after reaching home was to send post-haste for the Dean and Attorney Moran. Pending their arrival dinner was served, but seldom was meal less honoured at the well-appointed table of Rose Lodge. The old gentleman was far too much excited to think of eating; with his bushy brows knit together, and his sharp grey eyes fixed in moody thought, he sat leaning back in his chair, scarcely deigning to answer the repeated entreaties of his wife to eat something.

At last, seeing that the lady had finished her very slight repast, he said, pushing back his chair with characteristic *brusquerie,* "If you're done now, Martha, I wish you would have those things removed. I wonder how people can eat under such circumstances."

Mrs. Esmond made no reply—she was, indeed, a most submissive wife at all times; the dishes were removed, and fruit and wine placed on the table. The old gentleman drank off a glass of Madeira, then looked at his wife and said—

"That was a confoundedly queer chap, that beggarman!— didn't you think so, Martha?"

"I really can't say, my dear, what I thought of him, or of anything else at the time, I was so frightened."

"What!" said the husband ironically; "at the prospect of a cold bath? Well, I own it wasn't over inviting such a night as this. But you know that chilling prospective was only for a moment."

"Was there no other danger but that of the quarry?" said Mrs. Esmond pointedly.

"Oh, true, there was the limekiln,—but that needn't have shocked your weak nerves, seeing that there was no fire in it. They couldn't roast you, you know, without fire!—ha! ha! ha!"

A second and a third glass of the sparkling Madeira had somewhat exhilarated the old man's spirits, though his humour was still bitter.

"I am sorry, my dear," said Mrs. Esmond quietly, "that I can't compliment you on your wit. Now, I think *I* wasn't the only one whose *nerves*, weak or strong, were shocked on this occasion."

"Of course not, my dear; there was the horse"—

"Well, what was it that frightened the horse first and last?"

"I'm sure I can't tell—except it was a ghost; horses, you know, can see a spirit where human optics are at fault."

The cool sarcasm of Mr. Esmond's tone and manner did undoubtedly ruffle his wife's temper not a little. That amiable gentleman took sufficient pains on all occasions to show his unbounded contempt for female understanding generally, which he was wont to epigrammise by grammatical comparison as weak —weaker—weakest. But, for reasons sufficiently clear to herself, Mrs. Esmond was more than usually susceptible to his pointless sarcasm.

"Harry," said she, with much earnestness of look and tone, "if I were alone, I, for one, would not have been afraid of either the living or the dead."

"Zounds, madam! what do you mean by that!" cried her husband fiercely.

"No blustering, Harry—no blustering !" said his wife calmly but firmly. "What I mean to say is this, that my fears were for you,"—drawing back and pointing at him with her finger,— "*not for myself.* I feared that *the blow might fall this time where it was meant to fall before !* You understand—I see you do; I will therefore leave you to your own thoughts, which may, in your case, be the best companions, commending to your farther attention the old adage, 'It is ill playing with edged tools.'"

Before Mr. Esmond had recovered the effect of this stunning blow, the door-bell gave intimation that one or both of the anxiously-expected visitors had arrived, and Mrs. Esmond vanished by one door as the Dean and the man of law entered by another.

Mr. Esmond, recovering by a violent effort from the stunning effect of his wife's home-thrust, advanced with outstretched hand to greet his guests.

"Well, Mr. Esmond," said the Dean, when, having warmed his hands over the fire, he turned and faced his host, " you see we have promptly obeyed your summons, though, as regards myself, I would rather have waited a little, seeing that I had but just returned from a sick call, some three miles away."

"I'm very sorry indeed," said Mr. Esmond, "but my business is very urgent, and would not by any means wait."

"Well, what is your business?" and the Dean exchanged a significant glance with Moran, who had coolly taken his place at the table for the refreshment of his inner man,—" what is your business, sir ? It must be of grave importance when you send in all haste for the priest and the lawyer."

"It is of grave importance—the very gravest importance, Dean M'Dermot !" emphatically said Mr. Esmond, as he threw himself back in his chair opposite the Dean, and looked first in his face, then in Moran's, to see how they took this startling announcement. "Do you know that I have discovered the existence of a conspiracy ?"

"A conspiracy, Mr. Esmond?" cried his hearers simultaneously.

"Yes, a conspiracy!—a conspiracy against me—Harry Esmond, of Rose Lodge?—a conspiracy to take away my life—to murder me!!"

"Bless me, Mr. Esmond, you astonish me!" said the Dean. What Moran would have said we know not, for it so happened that he was seized just then with a troublesome fit of coughing that made him very red in the face, and obliged him to apply his handkerchief to his eyes very suspiciously often.

"*I thought* I should astonish you," went on Mr. Esmond, wholly absorbed in his own ideas. "But you will be more astonished when I tell you that I have a strong suspicion, almost amounting to certainty, that my poor nephew fell a victim to this same diabolical agency."

"Ah, indeed? and what reason have you to think so?" The half-credulous look vanished from the Dean's massive features, and Moran's cough suddenly ceased to trouble him.

"Sit down, Dean, and I'll tell you all about it, then let you and Moran judge for yourselves."

The details of the evening's adventures were listened to with much interest by the two gentlemen, a glance of surprise being exchanged between them at certain points of the narrative.

"Now what do you think of that?" said Mr. Esmond in conclusion. "Am I, or am I not, justified in thinking that there is a conspiracy on foot to murder me, as my nephew has been murdered, in cold blood—in fact, to exterminate the Esmonds? What say you, Dean? what say you, Moran?"

The priest shook his head and replied that he did not see how that followed from the premises.

"You would have much trouble to make out your case, my dear sir, in a court of law," said Moran. "For my part, I see no proof whatever of a conspiracy in what you have been telling us."

"Indeed! Well, I must say your faculties are more obtuse than I ever supposed they were. And you, Dean! I am astonished that *you* do not see further into this affair! Now, what is your opinion of that beggarman?"

"Why, upon my word, Mr. Esmond," the Dean replied in the

caustic tone he could well employ at times,—" upon my word,
I think him a very fine fellow, and that on your own showing.
You don't mean to find fault with him, do you, for saving your
life ?"

"Saving my life, indeed ? I tell you that was all a sham!"

"Then your horse must have been in the fault."

"Pshaw! the horse?—who frightened the horse? Tell me
that, now!"

"Why, perhaps the beggarman—or his bag!"

"Yes, that may do for the quarry, but then there must have
been another individual, with or without a bag, in waiting at
the limekiln!"

"Very true, Mr. Esmond—very true;" and the Dean began
poking the fire with a meditative air, while Moran took out his
note-book and wrote, more, apparently, to satisfy the self-
opinionated old man than from any necessity there was to
commit the affair to paper.

"Humph! humph!" soliloquised Moran as his pen flew over
the paper with professional rapidity; "let us see now how the
case stands. Mr. Esmond deposes that being on his way from
Esmond Hall to Rose Lodge, his horse took fright, and by a
retrograde movement towards a stone quarry in the vicinity
would have precipitated deponent and his wife thereinto, had
not a beggarman, *minus* bag, caught hold of the bridle, and persuaded the obstinate animal to resume his onward course. Is
not that right, Mr. Esmond?"

"Perfectly correct, sir—perfectly correct."

"Whereabout said beggarman, *plus* bag, walked by the side
of the gig till a certain limekiln was reached, where and when
deponent's horse took fright again, when said beggarman, with
felonious intent, as deponent sayeth, did again take forcible
possession of the reins, and enunciating the remarkable word
'Remember,' whether addressed to the horse or some unknown
individual deponent sayeth not—not having the fear of God
before his eyes, did feloniously lead the animal some distance
on his way, then and there feloniously betaking himself to parts
unknown—all which facts do clearly indicate in the mind of
this deponent a dangerous conspiracy against his life. Am I
still correct, Mr. Esmond?"

"Yes—on the whole; but—ahem!" pulling up his collar,

and establishing his head therein with a vehement jerk, "pray, Mr. Moran, what is your own opinion of the matter?"

"My opinion," said Moran gravely, "is, that you owe your *life twice* to that same beggarman during that short journey!"

"And yours, Dean?"

"Precisely the same as Mr. Moran's. No reasonable doubt can be entertained that your life *was* in danger from some concealed enemy, and that you owe your safety, and perhaps that of your wife, to the protecting presence of that mendicant"—

"Oh, hang the mendicant!" angrily broke in Esmond. "If I don't clear the country of these sturdy bang-beggars before I'm many weeks older, never call me an efficient magistrate—that's all!"

"Well, Moran, after that we may go, I think," said the Dean, rising, as did Moran, both looking the indignation they felt. "We have learned two useful lessons to-night, one of which is never to save any one's life without permission asked and received; the other is, never to obey a summons from Rose Lodge without a written certificate of actual necessity. A good evening, Mr. Esmond!"

And, declining all entreaties to remain longer, the gentlemen mounted their horses and bade adieu to Rose Lodge.

CHAPTER X.

A MORNING ON THE ROCK.

JANUARY passed away with its cold, clear days, and February duly fulfilled its allotted task of *filling the dyke;* snow had fallen in unusual quantities, making the farmer's heart glad with the prospect of rich fields and abundant crops. The first days of the month were so mild and fair that the country-people were no little alarmed, because of an old saying amongst them that *all the months in the year curse a fair February.* St. Bridget's Day, the first of the month, was a dry, sunny day, only just cold enough to make outdoor exercise agreeable, and as soon as old Bryan could get "a mouthful to eat" after Mass, he went up to the Rock to make his "stations," which having done, he went about his work of restoration, talking to himself as usual. He had no lack of employment that day, for a storm which had raged with great violence for full twenty-four hours in the last week of January had covered the surface of the sacred enclosure with fragments from the ruins. Notwithstanding that Bryan had been labouring for some days to repair what he could of the damage, many stones lay scattered around, some whole, some broken in their fall, while amongst them were seen not a few fragments from the rare old sculptures on the walls and arches; here a leaf from a tall Corinthian column, there the round cheek of a stone cherub from one of the corbels of the arches; again, the corner of some mural tablet, or a piece from a monumental slab which, split for long, had at length yielded to the might of the storm, and, wrenched from its home of ages, was hurled from on high to swell the heap of rubbish on the floor of nave or chancel, aisle or transept, as the case might be. Everywhere these wrecks of the recent storm met Bryan's eye, not so numerous, it is true, as they had been, but still enough to make the old man's heart ache, the more so as many of the fragments were far beyond his power to restore, on account of the height from which they had fallen, and their hopelessly shattered condition.

"Well, well," said Bryan, "patience is a virtue, an' if I can't replace them all, sure I will a good many of them. So in honour of the blessed and holy St. Bridget, I'll begin my work this day."

With all the ardour and energy of "sweet five-and-twenty," Bryan addressed himself to that labour of love, which to any other but a man of primitive faith and primitive simplicity would have appeared insufferably tedious, but to him who had grown grey in the loving service of the Saints of Cashel, preserving their monumental remains as far as one poor solitary mortal could from the devastation of wind and rain—to him it was happiness purer than the coarse, carnal-minded worldling ever knows to set about repairing the effects of every passing storm that shook the sacred walls of Cashel.

After working a while in silence, Bryan began, as he often did, to croon an ancient ditty, on this occasion an old Carmelite hymn, known and sung in every rural district of Ireland to the old, old air which Moore has wedded to the sweetly tender song, "Come rest in this Bosom"—

> "Och, when the loud trumpet sounds over the deep,
> And wakens each nation out of their long sleep—
> Och, it's then you'll see thousands come crowding along
> To the valley of Josaphat, it's there we'll all throng."

Mavrone! what a sight that'll be!—an' maybe Cashel won't turn out the grand company entirely! If they'll only let poor Bryan Cullenan jist walk behind them, a long ways off, when they're on their march to the valley—well, sure, it's great presumption for me to think o' the like, but somehow I think they'll all have a *grugh* for poor Bryan, that used to keep the weeds an' the long grass from chokin' up their tombs, and take care of the fine ould walls they built to the glory of God in the ancient days of Erin—

> Och, there you'll see Carmelites in glorious array,
> And we will be with them if we work our way.

Well, that's a fine promise, anyhow! God grant us grace to
'work our way'!"

Another while of assiduous work and silent meditation, and
then Bryan commenced again, to another old-world air both sad
and dreary—

> "Down by Killarney's banks I strayed,
>   Down by a floating wave,
> A holy hermit I espied,
>   Lying prostrate in his cave.

"Well, now, that must be a fine place for a hermit!" soliloquised Bryan; "I declare but it must. They say that Kil-
larney is a wondherful place, with wood and water to no end,
an' mountains, an' rocks, an' all sich things—an' fairies that
hates the world out for the antic tricks they play, an' the
sweet music they make in the bright moonlight nights when
the ladies an' gentlemen do go out a-boatin' on the lakes. I often
heard the quality that comes here on their tower talkin' about
it, till my ould heart would be jumpin' out o' my mouth; and
then I'd begin to think of the ould hermit—what a fine time
he had of it there, an' what a fine place it must be to make
one's soul in!—

> His eyes ofttimes to heaven he raised,
>   And thus exclaimed he,
> 'Adieu, adieu, thou faithless world,
>   Thou ne'er wast made for me!'"

"Poor man! poor man! that must have been when he was dyin',
I suppose. Och! an' sure it is 'a faithless world'!" and Bryan
sighed dolorously; "jist go no farther than the poor young
master—to think of *him* bein' shot like a dog, an' by them that
was on his own flure, an' eatin' an' drinkin' of his share for
months and months! Well, sure enough it was a horrid murder," he went on, though in an undertone; "in all my born
days I never heard the likes of it. Och! my poor young
gentleman! but it was the hard, hard thing for any one to take
your life, an' you so young, so handsome, an' so good—so good!
The Lord receive you in glory this day, I pray, through the in-
tercession of the blessed an' holy St. Bridget. As for him that
cut your days short—well, well, I'll leave *him* to God—he's bad
enough as he is, an' I'll only pray that the good an' merciful God

may bring him to repentance! It's mighty strange that he can't be taken, an' the people all agin him as they are!—

> To Thee, dear Lord, we recommend
> Our brethren late departed;
> Grant that their souls may ever be
> Amongst the saints and martyrs!
> O Virgin Mother, intercede!
> Protect them by your banner,
> And help them at the judgment-seat.
> O Lord, have mercy on them![1]

Amen, amen, sweet Jesus! espaycially *him* that was taken so sudden!—och! och! an' more was the pity!" he muttered low to himself.

The heavy sigh, or groan, that accompanied the words was heard, though not the words themselves, by two young ladies who had just reached the spot, all unnoticed by Bryan.

"Bryan," said one of them, the taller of the two, "I would wager a trifle that I know what you are thinking of."

The old man started as though a cannon were discharged close to his ear. Turning hastily, he looked at one and the other of his visitors, then smiled and took off his hat, and bowed very low.

"Well, I declare, Miss Mary, but you took a start out of me—you an' Miss Power! But long life to you both! sure, it's always proud I am to see you, espaycially up here on the Rock where I'm in a manner at home. But in regard to your knowin' what I was thinkin' of, bedad, if you do, you bate the women of Mungret all to nothing!"

"The women of Mungret?" repeated Mary Hennessy, for she it was, as may be supposed, whom Bryan addressed as "Miss

---

[1] The air of this old hymn of the people is exceedingly solemn and beautiful. There is some reason to think, however, that neither it nor the hymn is extensively known in Ireland. The author heard it once, many, many years ago, in her early days, under circumstances that fixed its wild, sweet melody in her fancy for ever after. Passing with some friends the "chapel" of her native place—which stood in a solitary and beautiful spot on the outskirts of the populous town—one fine summer's evening when day was fading into night, she was surprised to hear the sound of music from within, a thing by no means usual on week-days. Entering, she found a few pious persons singing this old hymn for the dead, and as the solemn chorus echoed through the deserted chapel in the silence of the shadowy twilight, the effect was indescribably fine.

Mary." "Well, I have often heard of the *women of Mungret*, but I really never thought of asking what manner of women they were whose wisdom has come down to us in the form of a proverb. Can *you* enlighten us on that point, Bryan? I know you are a sort of walking repository of ancient lore."

"Well, it's a folly to talk, Miss Mary, a body does see an' hear a sight o' things in threescore-and-ten years, but the most of what I know of 'ancient lore,' as you call it, I larned here among the ould walls, from hearin' the quality talkin' of all such things when I do be showin' them round the Rock."

"Well, I suppose you can tell us all about the women of Mungret and their *wisdom*, can you not?"

"In coorse I can. But I'm ashamed to see you an' Miss Power[1] standin' so long on your feet; if it was summer-time, now, you'd be at no loss for a sate," and he glanced mournfully around on the fragments of plinth and capital that strewed the nave of the cathedral.

"Oh, never mind us," said the young ladies in a breath; "we'd as soon stand as sit. But pray go on with your story."

"Well, Miss Mary, I'll tell you the story as I heard Father Heenan of Killenaule tellin' it to two English gentlemen one day here on the Rock. A long time ago, when there was a great college here at Cashel, an' another at Mungret, in the County Limerick, westwards, there was a power of fine larned men in both places, but Mungret got the applause all over Ireland, an' even beyond sea everywhere, for the wonderful great skill they had in all sorts of larnin', espaycially what Father Heenan called the *dead* languages. Myself doesn't know what in the world sort of languages *them* can be—barrin' they'd be what the priests spake to the evil sperits when they're layin' them in the Red Say, or anywhere. Anyhow, that's what Father Heenan said, I'm sartin sure of that. Well, Mungret bein' famous for the dead languages, an' the fame of that house bein' noised abroad, as I told you before, the hands of our college here—that's Cashel—took a notion that they'd send some of their best men to Mungret below, to try the skill of the people there, or whether it was true what every one said about them

---

[1] So the country-people always called the Le Poers, and that, I believe, was the origin of the name *Power*, now so common in the south of Ireland.

in regard to the dead languages. So when the head men of Mungret got word of what was goin' on, they were a little daunted, you may be sure, for fear their students wouldn't be able to answer all the questions that 'id be put to them, an' that they'd be ruined entirely, an' disgraced for aver, in regard to *the dead languages*, so well becomes them, doesn't they dress up some of the best of the students in women's clothes, an' some of the monks, that were great larned men entirely, like plain countrymen goin' to their work, an' they sends them all off to scatter hither an' thither along the road that the Cashel men were to thravel on their way there. Well, what would ye have of it, but when the fine venerable ould gentlemen from Cashel got within three or four miles or so of Mungret, an' began to ask how far they had to go, or maybe which was the way, when they'd come to a cross-ronds or the like, they were always answered in *the dead languages*"—

"Oh, nonsense, Bryan!" cried Miss Hennessy a little impatiently; "the dead languages are Greek and Latin, and some others not spoken now."

"Well, well, miss, I suppose you know best," said Bryan submissively; "anyhow, there wasn't a man or woman they spoke to but answered them in"—

"Greek or Latin."

"In Greek or Latin, then, if that's what the dead languages manes,—so the gentlemen from Cashel here began to look at one another, an' shake their heads, an' at long last they put their heads together, an' says they, 'Where's the use in *our* goin' to Mungret, when all the country-people around the abbey— even the very women—speak the dead—ahem!—Greek an' Latin —as well as we do ourselves? What chance would we have with the monks and the students? Maybe it's worsted we'd be ourselves instead of puzzling them.' So with that they turns on their heel an' comes straight back to Cashel without ever goin' next or near Mungret"—

"And so"—

"An' so, ever since then, Miss Mary, it's a byword in the place, *You're as wise as the women of Mungret*, more by token they weren't women at all, but fine well-spoken young students that were great hands entirely at *the dead languages*, an' I suppose the *livin'* too—if there be such things."

At this the young ladies laughed, assuring Bryan that there were such things as living languages—"And what is more, Bryan," added Bella, "you are speaking a living language yourself."

"Is it me spakin' a livin' language?" and the old man turned on the fair friends a look of simple wonder that much amused them, accustomed as they were to his guileless ways. "Oh, now I see it's makin' game of me ye are—as, in coorse, you have every right to do—me spakin' a livin' language!—well, now, if that doesn't flog all! As if *I* could spake any language, either livin' or dead."

The lesson which our Hermit might have received in the interesting science of philology was prevented for that time, at least, by the arrival of another party, whose advent appeared to throw the young ladies into a pretty little state of excitement, a nervous tremor, as it were, that would have puzzled any observant spectator. The party consisted of a pale, lady-like young person, very plainly attired, two pretty little damsels of some ten and twelve respectively, a comely gentleman with a fine Pickwickian cast of countenance, a very white cravat, in the folds of which his soft fleshy chin, or rather chins, lay snugly imbedded, and an exceedingly smooth suit of black, the nether garments of that demi-length vulgarly called knee-breeches, with, to all these attributes of respectability super-added, a goodly rotundity of that central region of the human *corpus* which in Shakespeare's "justice" was said to be "with good capon lined"—whatever the *lining* might have been in the case before us, the exterior was undoubtedly both "fair and round;" lastly, there was a tall, dignified personage of some thirty-eight or forty years, not remarkably handsome, yet strikingly noble in appearance, and with just that set of features which ordinarily express both superiority of intellect and that consciousness of the same which in some faces might be set down as approaching to superciliousness; this, however, was by no means the case in the very marked face of the gentleman in question, whose manners withal were singularly unpretending, though marked by a certain degree of reserve, and a coolness that might or might not be constitutional. This personage was no other than the Earl of Effingham, the fat gentleman, Rev. Mr. Goodchild, his chaplain, the two little girls, his daughters,

Lady Ann and Lady Emma Cartwright, and the young lady, their governess, Miss Markham, whom our readers will remember as forming one of the pleasant party assembled on Hallow-eve night under the hospitable roof of Esmond Hall.

"Bryan," said Miss Markham, after she had shaken hands with the other young ladies, "these gentlemen are desirous of seeing the ruins. Will it be convenient for you to show them now?" And she smiled in her pensive way, well knowing that Bryan lived for nothing else but to take care of the ruins and to "show" them.

"Wisha, then, it is convaynient, Miss Markham, ah' why wouldn't it? What am I here for only to show the place to the ladies and gentlemen when they come on their tower?"

"My very worthy old man," said the rosy chaplain, whose enunciation of syllables and final letters was remarkably full and distinct,—"my very worthy old man, I am told you are something of an antiquarian."

"An anti-what, your honour?"

"An anti-quarian," repeated the chaplain slowly and with great complacency. "I presume you know what that is?"

"Well, no," said Bryan, with a gentle shake of his old head, "I can't say I do. Maybe it's anti-trinitar-ian you mane, sir?" he slowly added, as his thoughts reverted to the hedge-school of his childish days, and the word that looked so awfully grand and terrifically long at the head of the much-dreaded words of seven syllables somewhere near the end of his "Universal."[1]

The ladies all smiled, and even the grave dignity of Lord Effingham was put to the test; but the good parson would have there and then undertaken to enlighten Bryan on the difference between "antiquarian" and "antitrinitarian" had not the peer interposed.

"We have heard," said he, "that there is no one now living who knows so much about these magnificent ruins as you do— that is, if you are the Hermit of the Rock."

"Well, your honour," said Bryan bashfully, "I b'lieve there's

[1] The *Universal Spelling-Book* of the last generation—in Ireland, at least—still traditionally remembered in connection with "The Town in Danger of a Siege," the edifying history of "Tommy and Harry," and that graceless "Boy in the Apple-tree" who would not yield to moral suasion.

some that calls me so, but it's only a nickname, sir, that the quality gave me, for I'm no hermit, at all, you see, or anything in the wide world but a poor ould man that takes care of the ruins here, an' shows the ladies an' gentlemen through the place when they come from furrin parts or anywhere to have a sight of it."

The two little girls had been eyeing the Hermit with much curiosity, and the elder of the two suddenly exclaimed, loud enough to be heard by all present—

"La, Miss Markham! what a very funny-looking old man he is! and don't he speak queer?" How much further the young lady would have committed her party there is no saying, for Miss Markham, with a crimson cheek, drew her to her side, with a whispered "Fie, Lady Ann! fie, fie!" that effectually silenced the young chatterbox for that time at least.

"Miss Markham," said the Earl, with a grave smile, "you forgot to introduce your young friends."

"Excuse me, my lord, for I am sometimes forgetful,"—she did not say what was really the case, that she could not well have taken the liberty of introducing friends of hers to him,—"permit me now to repair my unaccountable oversight."

The peer bowed with lofty grace to Miss Hennessy, more condescendingly to Miss Le Poer, whose name arrested his attention.

"Le Poer!" he repeated, as his eagle eye scanned her girlish features; "what! any relation to the ever-charming Countess of Blessington?"

"Not much of a relation, my lord," said Bella, blushing to find herself for the first time in her short life in actual *parlance* with a peer of the realm; "there is a relationship, I know, but of what degree I do *not* know."

"Be it as it may, I am pleased to make your acquaintance, Miss Le Poer," was the courteous reply, as the party prepared to follow Bryan, the chaplain, note-book in hand, close at the old man's side.

"Now we shall have some fun," whispered Harriet Markham to her young friends; "the chaplain, bless his heart! is somewhat of a character in his way, and cherishes, moreover, a supreme contempt for all things popish. It is, I believe, a grievous thorn in the good man's side that the primary education of the Ladies Cartwright is entrusted to one who has lapsed from Anglicanism and turned her back on the Thirty-nine Articles! Do but listen to him and Bryan!"

"Friend *cicerone*," began the law-church chaplain, "I presume you have many distinguished visitors here from time to time?"

"Well, we do, then, have some very grand people now an' then," rejoined the Hermit; "but my name isn't Chris-roomey, or Chitch-rony, or whatsoever that was you said,—it's Cullenan, your honour—*Bryan Cullenan!*" with strong emphasis on the name.

"But, my good friend, you mistake me," said the reverend gentleman apologetically; "I did not mean to address you by name just then; I merely said *cicerone*, which means *a guide*."

This explanation appeared to satisfy Bryan, who was now putting on his official dignity.

"Who was the greatest personage you ever had here? You have had the Primate, I suppose?—I mean the Protestant Primate, of course."

"Is it him? is it ould Beresford? Oh, then, much about him, an far less!" cried Bryan indignantly; "it's betwixt two minds myself was when the ould rap was here, whether I'd show him the place or not, an' I put a penance on myself for doin' it!—Primate, inagh! it's the hopeful Primate *he* is!"[1]

A low titter was heard in the rear, speedily suppressed, however, on the part of the young ladies by a side-view of the Earl's face, graver and darker even than its wont. Lord Effingham was a staunch supporter of "the Establishment."

"My good Mr. Cullenan," said the chaplain, his nose swelled with anger, yet his voice over-exceedingly calm,—"my good Mr. Cullenan—my very respectable old anchoret?—

"I told you before," said Bryan, with a testiness foreign to his nature, "that my name was *Bryan Cullenan*—now I tell it

---

[1] Most of our readers are well acquainted with the obnoxious character of the Beresfords and the hatred with which they are regarded by the peasantry, not only of Munster, where they are chiefly located, but of all parts of Ireland. Indeed, their possessions were scattered all over the country, and their character was everywhere the same. The late Marquis of Waterford was, with all his wildness, the best Beresford amongst them, and with all his faults he was rather a favourite with the people. To his credit be it said, he was far from being a bad landlord.

to you onst for all!—for a big man you have a mighty short memory! Now, to save you the throuble of askin' any more questions about the grand people that was here in *my time*, I'll jist tell you who was the greatest man I ever showed over the Rock—an' that was *Dan O'Connell!*"

"Dan O'Connell?" cried Mr. Goodchild, recoiling from Bryan as if he had suddenly put forth the horns of Beelzebub. "You must be losing your senses, old man!"

"'Deed, then, I'm not, your honour! Sure, the world knows that the Counsellor is the greatest man in all Ireland, barrin' the bishops an' archbishops—that's our own, I mane, an' it isn't much time *they* have to be travellin' about, seein' sights—they have something else to mind, God help them! Another great man we had here one day was Father Tom Maguire—in coorse your honour has heard of him—him that had the great discussion with Pope—Pope and Maguire, you know?"

"I know nothing about the man," fibbed Mr. Goodchild, with the petulance of a very froward *child.*

"Oh, naughty Mr. Goodchild!" whispered Harriet to Mary; "only hear what he says!—he knows nothing about *Father Tom Maguire!*"

The chaplain had evidently got enough of Bryan's company so he turned away to examine, as he said, the architectural features of the building.

"Mind your steps, then," quoth Bryan, "for if you don't you'll be apt to get a toss over some o' these stones that the storm brought down the other night." Then, stopping for a moment to look after the parson, he said, as if to himself, "Well, now, where in the world did *he* come from? Sure, I thought every one knew Father Tom Maguire! He's a mighty quare ould gentleman, anyhow, whosomever he is!"

They were now in the chapel, and Bryan pointed out to the Earl—the ladies were all familiar with the scene—the place where the high altar stood of old, and near by, the tomb of Myler M'Grath.

"Was he not Archbishop of Cashel?" said the Earl.

"Well, he was, an' he was not," replied the Hermit.

"How is that, friend?"

"Why, your honour, he was only Queen Elizabeth's arch bishop, an' in coorse Queen Elizabeth had no more power than you or I to make a bishop, let alone an archbishop—so we never give him anything but 'Myler M'Grath,' an' that same is too good for him, for he was a disgrace to his name, on account of sellin' his faith for a good livin'. Still, there's some people says that he *came back* afore his death, so we pray for his poor soul, hopin' that God may forgive him his sins, an' espaycially the shame an' the sorrow he brought to all good Christians! The Lord forgive him, an' I forgive him, poor unfortunate man! But isn't that a fine elegant tomb they put over him?"

"Very fine indeed, for the time at which it was erected."

"There's none of our own bishops here that has so fine a one, an' more's the pity," said Bryan mournfully; "but no matter for that, *they* don't need anything like that to keep them in the people's minds. They'll never be forgotten, anyhow! Husht, now!" and he lowered his voice to a whisper, and made a sign to the children to be silent; "this is the place, your honour, where the Holy Sacrifice used to be offered up, so I never allow any noise to be here." When they left the chancel he said aloud, "Where the *Verbum caro factum* used to be said for hundreds an' hundreds of years"—the old man bent his knee at the awful words, as did the three young ladies—"there ought to be silence for ever—an' there will, too, while God spares me life. A time will come when the altars will rise again on the Rock of Cashel, an' the unbloody Sacrifice of the New Law will be offered here again, an' psalms will be sung, an' organs play, an' the people that will see that day will rejoice, for Ireland will then be a nation again, and Cashel may be 'Cashel of the Bishops,' though it'll never be 'Cashel of the Kings' any more!"

As the old man thus spoke, his aged eyes flashed with a strange and fitful light that gradually illumined his whole features, a flush suffused his hollow cheek, and a smile, as it were, of exultation wreathed his pale lips. His look was fixed as if on some point far off in the future, and the whole character of the face was so transformed, as it were, by the proud vision passing before the eye of the spirit, that it was hard to recognise the meek, subdued, and somewhat emaciated face of old Bryan. The ladies glanced instinctively at the Earl; he was regarding the old man with a look of surprise mingled with curiosity, whilst even the children pulled Miss Markham's sleeve on either side and pointed in silence to the strange old man, the like of whom they had never seen. The rapt expression, however, was visible but for a moment—gradually the light faded away, and the smile vanished, and Bryan said in his usual tone, as if to himself—

"My old bones will be white and bare by that time; an' my soul with God, I humbly trust—well, no matter, though I'll not be here on earth to see it, I'll see it from above, an' that'll be better, for there I'll have the holy saints of Cashel all before me in their heavenly glory! There'll be no Murroghs there!" he added, addressing his listeners in the same calm, soliloquising tone,—"no, nor any Harrys, or Elizabeths, or Oliver Cromwells! That's one great comfort, anyhow!—we'll have heaven to ourselves!"

"Who do you mean by *we*, Bryan?" said the Earl.

The old man looked up in the cold, dark face of the speaker and scanned it for a moment, then glanced significantly at the young ladies, whom he knew to be Catholics, shook his head, and replied evasively—

"Why, then, *all good Christians*, please your honour!"

The Earl smiled,—his smile was very pleasing as it shone for a moment on the dark, well-formed features,—but he made no further remark. The chaplain now rejoined the party, taking care, however, to keep at a safe distance from Bryan, and they made the circuit of the sacred enclosure, examining everything worth seeing, and listening with marked surprise—on the part, at least, of the Earl and his chaplain—to the explanations of old Bryan, so beautiful in their simplicity, yet so learned in their admirable reconciliation of all the splendid monuments with the purposes of Catholic worship in the grand old ages of the past, with which the old man seemed as familiar as though he had in the body witnessed their glories. Even the ultra-Protestant Goodchild heard with amazement the simple eloquence which faith and fervour, more powerful than rhetoric, gave to the tongue of the old *cicerone*.

"I am told," said the Earl, as the party emerged from the last of the buildings, and stood on the verge of the Rock, looking out over the magnificent plain,—"I am told, Bryan, that you spend whole days here working amongst these ruins, endeavouring to preserve them from the ravages of time, without any hope of remuneration."

"An' what better work could I be at?" said Bryan sharply. "As for payment, what payment could I get *here* that I'd care anything about?—I'll be paid in heaven, please the Lord!" And, reverently baring his aged head, the old man raised his eyes upwards with an expression that faith and hope could alone impart to the face of man.

"You sleep here at night, too, sometimes?"

"It's the place I like best to sleep in."

"And you are not afraid?"

"Afraid?" repeated Bryan, with a look bordering on contempt. "Well, now, that's a good joke, anyhow!—afraid on the Rock of Cashel!—athen, where would a body be safe if it wasn't here on St. Patrick's Rock, with these consecrated walls about one, an' the holy dead below, an' the voices of saints singing hymns an' psalms all about one in the darkness of the night—how could I be afraid on the Rock of Cashel by day or by night?" With these words ringing in their ears, the party bade adieu to the strange old man, with a gratuity from the Earl that astonished his simple heart.

CHAPTER XI.

THE RIDE HOME.

As our party stood for a moment enjoying the fair prospect ere they descended from the Rock, old Bryan, having carefully hidden away his golden treasure from the eye of day, called after the young ladies, with all of whom he was familiar from their frequent visits to the ruins—

"Take care, ladies, that none of ye'd be tempted, standin there, to take the leap that Queen Gormlaith did once upon a time!"

"Why, what leap did she take, Bryan?"

"Well, I can't tell you that, Miss Mary, bekase why, I never heard it myself, but she took a great leap here at Cashel —maybe from the side o' the Rock, for all as I know; she must ha' been a great leaper that same Queen Gormlaith, for the ould chronicles tell that

> Gormlaith took three leaps,
> Which a woman shall never take (again),
> A leap at Ath-cliath (Dublin), a leap at Teamhair (Tara),
> A leap at Caiseal of the goblets over all."[1]

At this the ladies laughed and the gentlemen smiled.

"And pray, Bryan, who was this Queen Gormley?" asked Mary Hennessy.

"Wisha, then, Miss Mary!—unless she's far belied, it doesn't matter much who she was, for by all accounts she was no great

---

[1] "Annals of the Four Masters." According to these famous annalists, this Gormlaith (pronounced Gormley) was daughter of a chief of Offaly, who died A.D. 928, and wife of a Danish king of Dublin, Aulaf or Auliffe by name. O'Donoghoe, in his *Memoirs of the O'Briens*, says that she had the great monarch Brian Boroimhe for a second husband, and was repudiated by that good prince for her shameless immorality.

things. They say she was Brian Boromhe's second or third wife, an' that he had to put her away clane and cliver on account of the bad life she led. Sure, it's easy known she wasn't a dacent woman, or it isn't leapin' she'd be, the tory! like a lump of a gossoon, or a wild goat!"

"I see you are no admirer of female gymnastics, Bryan," said Lord Effingham, with a smile, as the young ladies walked on in silence, not caring to notice Bryan's concluding remark.

"I'm no admirer," quoth Bryan, "of anything faymale barrin' what's dacent an' proper."

It is hard to say what meaning the old man attached to the word *gymnastics*. Perhaps he understood it in the same sense as Biddy Moriarty, the Pill Lane fishwoman, did O'Connell's *hypothenuse* or *parallelogram* in his memorable mathematical scolding match with that renowned vendor of "Dublin Bay herrings" and other piscal edibles.

"Your honour, sir," said Bryan, after coughing in vain once or twice to arrest attention, "maybe you'd be good enough to let me know who you are, for I'm sure it's none o' the common sort you are, anyhow."

And he stood with his hat in his hand, sharp and cold as the day was.

"Why, Bryan," said Miss Markham, "I thought you knew all the quality for miles around. This gentleman is the Earl of Effingham."

"The Earl of Effingham!" cried Bryan, in a state of ludicrous amazement,—"the great English lord from the Castle below!—an' me talkin' to him just all as one as if he was only a bit of a buddagh!"

"Never mind, Bryan—never mind," said the Earl, with kind condescension; "you said nothing but what was very polite."

"Barrin' to the ould gentleman here;" and Bryan nodded over his shoulder towards the chaplain, who was loitering a pace or two behind, examining the ancient tribute-stone, with the rude sculptures thereupon. "Now, might a body make free to ask who is *he*?"

On being told, Bryan nodded sagaciously, and smiled to himself.

"Ay, ay! I might ha' known he was some kind of a preacher — he looks for all the world as if he was fed on

Lady Farnham's fat bacon! Well, God be with your honour's lordship, anyhow! Sure, I often heard people say that you were a rale gentleman every inch of you, only mighty grand, as in coorse you ought to be! Isn't it a beautiful fine country around here, my lord? I'm sure you never seen the beat of it in England beyant."

"Well, I cannot say I did, Bryan, though we have some 'beautiful fine countries' in England too;" and the Earl smiled.

"You have? Well, see that, now! But I was goin' to tell your honour's lordship that for all so rich a country as you have before you now, an' all the fine cattle an' sheep that's grazin' in it, there was a time, they say, when it was all as one as a desert."

"Oh, you mean, probably, the very early times before the country was settled?"

"No, my lord, I do not; I mane the days of Queen Elizabeth, or, as we always call her, Queen Bess—that's ould Harry's daughter, your lordship knows—the *Vargin Queen*—ahem! as Cobbett calls her—did you ever read Cobbett's *Reformation*, my lord?"

"I believe not."

"Oh, well, now, see here, that's the greatest book that ever was prented—it 'id be worth your lordship's while to read it, an' then you'd know all about Queen Bess an' her ould baste of a father, Harry the Eighth."

"I shall certainly pay my respects to Mr. Cobbett at the first opportunity," said the Earl, with imperturbable gravity.

"Queen Elizabeth was a great benefactor to Ireland," said the chaplain, his short nose curling upwards in evangelical anger; "she did more to pacify this country than any sovereign that ever reigned in England."

"Well, I declare, now," said Bryan, eyeing him with a half-comical look,—"I declare, now, if your reverence—ahem! was tellin' lies all your life, you're tellin' God's truth now—Queen Bess was the greatest hand at pacifyin' Ireland that ever tried a hand at it—barrin' Oliver Cromwell! Sure, didn't Bess pacify the country abroad fornenst us there to that degree that they say there was scarce the lowin' of a cow or the voice of a ploughman to be heard from the far end of Kerry to the gates of Cashel. Now, that's what I call pacifyin', your reverence, bekase, you see, where the people's all dead there's sure to be pace an' quietness—an' for that very raison the Rock of Cashel is the quietest place in all Munster! Oh, bedad, yis, they might all throw their caps at the Vargin Queen for pacifyin'—herself an' Noll, the Divil's butcher!"

"Oh! oh! oh!" said Mr. Goodchild, holding up his hands in pious horror; "of a surety the poison of the adder is on this man's lip, and the sting of the wasp under his tongue. Hear how he blasphemes the holy ones of God!"

"I deny it, sir," said Bryan, with sharp emphasis; "I deny that Queen Bess an' Oliver Cromwell were the holy ones of God—it's you that's blasphemin' to say the like!"

"Oh, Popery! Popery!" groaned the chaplain, as the Earl took him by the arm and hurried him down the steep descent; "oh, Popery! what a foul-mouthed beast thou art—yea, verily, the beast of beasts!—My good young lady," to Miss Markham, "I am extremely sorry for having been induced to visit this popish place, the *locum tenens* whereof is a most violent and rabid Papist."

"Now, pray, Mr. Goodchild, do not blame *me*," said Harriet, with meek gravity, throwing at the same time a sly look at her friends; "you know that so far from 'inducing' you to visit the Rock, which is, I admit, a very exceedingly popish place, I warned you over and over that old Bryan would most probably try your patience. Did I not, my lord?" and she turned with downcast eyes to the Earl.

"You certainly did, Miss Markham," his lordship gravely replied; "I can bear witness that you gave Mr. Goodchild fair warning of what he had to expect from the Hermit of the Rock. You know, my dear sir, old Bryan is somewhat of a character"——

"Excuse me, my lord, but his name were better *Briar* than *Bryan!*—old Briar!—ha! ha! ha!" The really good-natured chaplain laughed till his fat sides shook at what he considered his excellent pun, and the smile that appeared for a moment on every face he complacently accepted as the tribute of general admiration. All at once came back his usual placidity. "You seem thoughtful, Miss Markham," said he, the large expansion of his heart taking in at the moment all mankind, even a votary of Rome,—"thinking, doubtless, of the woeful doom that hath fallen on yonder stronghold of superstition?"

"Not exactly," said Harriet, with much coolness; "I was thinking, rather, of that celebrated juvenile 'little Johnny Horner' on the memorable occasion when he

——— sat in the corner,
Eating his Christmas pie.

You cannot but remember, my dear sir, the highly poetical lines that follow—

He put in his thumb
And took out a plum,
And said, 'What a good boy am I!'

How ineffably gracious the face of Johnny Horner must have looked then!—just like yours, my dear Mr. Goodchild, under the happy consciousness of Christian perfection."

The compliment was not so graciously received as it ought to have been, and the young ladies remarked with suppressed glee that the chaplain moved away soon after from Miss Markham's vicinity, devoting his attention to the children, who, in all the buoyant freshness of life's early spring, were gambolling in advance of the party, commenting in their own way on the new and strange objects that came under their eyes.

At the foot of the hill the carriage was found in waiting and, declining with thanks the Earl's polite offer of "setting them down," Mary and Bella turned off in the direction of Gallows Hill.

"What! going to visit the fairy-woman?" said Harriet, with a meaning smile, as she glanced towards the clay mansion of that potent charmer, partially visible from where they stood, its low thatched roof dotted here and there with the green of the darnel and the chickenweed, while a tufted sallow projecting over the one gable which protruded into view from behind a shoulder of the hill, gave it a picturesque and shady look.

"Fie, fie, Harriet!" was the half-serious, half-playful answer of Mary; while Bella only shook her little clenched fist at the speaker, tossed back her saucy curls, and with a smiling bow to the party in general, tripped after her friend.

"What charming young ladies your friends are, Miss Markham!" said the chaplain, anxious, no doubt, to exhibit his good taste.

"They are well enough—for Romanists," was the arch reply.

"What a superb group of ruins!" said Lord Effingham, glancing over the bold outlines of the towering walls, so stately even in decay. "After all, the past greatness of Ireland cannot be treated as a myth whilst such monuments as these remain to attest it."

"Pooh, pooh, my lord! what are those ruins compared with the Acropolis or the Colosseum"—

"Or the Pyramids?" suggested the Earl, by way of capping the climax, and he smiled at the eagerness with which the good man hastened to throw Cashel in the shade.

"Or the Pyramids — precisely, my lord! or any other of the great relics of the past. But then, how could it be expected that an insignificant little island like this should produce anything very great?"

"Well, I must say," replied the Earl, with caustic humour, "that to be 'an insignificant island,' Ireland has done wonders in the way of producing things great. Now, I am decidedly of opinion, my dear sir, that those buildings on the Rock of Cashel, so varied in their character, so massive in their construction, so romantic in their situation, so impressive in their solitary grandeur, and so mournful in their utter ruin and desolation, are no whit inferior in interest even to the Acropolis itself—or, indeed, to any ruin or ruins with which I am acquainted."

Harriet Markham raised her eyes to Lord Effingham's face for one moment, and a smile of wonderful sweetness brightened her pale, spiritual features; her lips parted as though she were about to speak, but, blushing, as it were, at her own boldness, she resisted the impulse, and turned her eyes again on the weird old walls now draped in the gorgeous noontide rays of the clear, cold February day.

"I am bound to submit to your lordship's judgment," said the obsequious chaplain, "but I confess I was not prepared to hear such—such"—

"Such classico-heretical opinions?—say on, and fear not! Well, my very dear and reverend friend, even at the risk of being set down as a heretic against the received principles of taste, I am free to admit that Christian ruins are at all times more interesting to me than those which date from pagan times and were associated with pagan worship."

"Pardon me, my lord!" said the chaplain, his rosy face waxing crimson red; "I should like to know what other than pagan worship was practised there?" pointing backwards to the Rock.

"Nay, Mr. Goodchild," said the Earl very gravely, "with all the corruptions attributed to the Roman Church—mind, I say *attributed*, Miss Markham—I believe it cannot be denied that she is a *Christian* Church."

"*A* Christian Church?" said Harriet, her eyes flashing with the fire of a spirit that would no longer be restrained, "say rather, my lord, *the* Christian Church! The Church that has risen like the sun over the ruins of paganism—the Church that unites all the ages and all the nations in one eternal act of homage to the Almighty Ruler of the world. Look there, my lord!" and she cast a glance of withering scorn on the crest-fallen pillar of the law-church; "you admire those ruins as noble monuments of ancient art, attesting the former greatness of a now impoverished people—but think, my lord, of the ages that look down from those shattered walls, from the height of yon pillar-tower, and the glories that gild them with everlasting fame. And the memories of Cashel are *Christian* memories, Mr. Goodchild—at least, what history and tradition have both preserved. That mystic tower may, indeed, date from pagan times, and probably does, but all the other buildings are of purely Christian origin, save and except the royal palace of the Munster kings. And, indeed, for ages long the very princes who ruled in Cashel were consecrated bishops."

A contemptuous "Humph!" from the chaplain and a cold "Indeed!" from the Earl would have discouraged a less ardent spirit than that of Harriet Markham; but the effect was directly opposite on hers, for the bright intelligence that burned within her was lit at the lamp of faith, and where the honour of religion was concerned she was all life and warmth. Here her country and her faith were both in question, and she could not sit by a passive listener. Yet she spoke with a modesty and a womanly grace that at once disarmed angry criticism.

"If your lordship has no objection," said she, looking timidly at the stately peer, "I will bring from the treasure-chamber of the past, for Mr. Goodchild's edification, a very few of the Christian memories connected with yonder ruined shrines."

The Earl bowed assent. The chaplain groaned in spirit, but, seeing there was no alternative short of actual rudeness, he prepared himself to listen, fortifying his mental position with a pinch of Lundy Foot's best.

Their little ladyships, delighted at the prospect of a story, bestowed sundry caresses on their "dear, sweet, darling Miss Markham," who, smiling on her pupils, entered at once on her task.

What Harriet told is known, we hope, to most of our readers, so we shall not follow her in her rapid and picturesque description of the historic glories of Cashel. She told of St. Patrick, how he founded the first Christian church on the Rock, which was royal even then, and in the shade of the old pillar-tower, which had in still earlier ages "reared the sacred flame," rose the cross-crowned roof of the Christian temple. Of Angus she told, the royal convert of Patrick, with his childlike simplicity of faith and most excellent humility; of Cormac the king-bishop, of whom the ancient annals say that "his loss was mournful, for he was a king, a bishop, an anchorite, a scribe, and profoundly learned in the Scotic (i.e. Irish) tongue,"— Cormac the historian, the elegant scholar—but, alas! the too-gentle and too-yielding prince, persuaded by ambitious courtiers to enter upon the dangerous trade of war in defence of his dominions, in which bloody contest he lost his life, and Ireland, in him, one of her greatest sons. And of Flaherty, his successor, Harriet told, who, having been one of the ill advisers of the late king, was so stricken with sorrow and remorse, seeing the evil which his counsels had mainly brought upon the land and the people, that he speedily laid aside his episcopal office and his royal state, flung from him the mitre and the crown, and, retiring to an abbey which he founded in a wild and lonely spot on a small island in a lake (now a bog),[1] he there ended

[1] The Abbey of Monahinch, even the ruins of which have now almost disappeared, was still in tolerably good preservation when Dr. Ledwich wrote, some sixty or seventy years since. According to that and other antiquaries, the abbey must have been both grand and beautiful, presenting many features of extraordinary interest. It was situate on the confines of Queen's County and Tipperary, but chiefly in the latter county.

his life in the austerity of penance common in those days of faith and fervour. "If your lordship will take the trouble," said Harriet, "to look into Ledwich's *Antiquities of Ireland*, at 'Monahincha,' you will be repaid, I assure you, by the very interesting account he gives of the enormous labour and industry evinced by the monks in conveying the materials for their magnificent structures not only from the opposite side of the lake, but from a considerable distance inland, the island being then only accessible in canoes, hollowed, he says, out of excavated trees. You will then, I think, admit that the monks of those mediæval times could not have been so *lazy* as people would have us believe."

Blushing at her own earnestness, Harriet stopped short, and glanced furtively at her auditors. There was a smile on Mr. Goodchild's face, a smile half benevolent, half incredulous, and he was tapping his snuff-box with prodigious energy and determination, as though the king-abbot of Monahinch were bodily encased therein, and the punishment of his folly had devolved on the worthy chaplain. Lord Effingham's haughty lip was curled with something very like a sneer as he coldly replied—

"I should not have thought you were so much of an antiquarian, Miss Markham. Your reference to Ledwich is quite superfluous after your own *learned* description. Why, you can really draw 'sermons from stones,' if not 'books from running brooks.'"

There were two islands in the lake, now a bog, and on each was situated some of the monastic buildings. One was called the Men's Island, and contained an abbey and oratory; the Women's Island contained a small chapel; and a locality on the firm land, exterior to the bog, contained a second abbey. "Sculpture," says Ledwich, "seems here to have exhausted her treasures. A nebule moulding adorns the outward semicircle of the portal, a double nebule with beads the second, a chevron the third, interspersed with the triangular frette, roses, and other ornaments. It is also decorated with chalices artfully made at every section of the stone so as to conceal the joint. . . . By some accident ashen keys have been dropped on the walls of this building; in a number of years they have become large trees. Their roots have insinuated into every crevice, burst the walls everywhere, and threaten the whole with ruin." Hence the almost total disappearance of these interesting structures. Ledwich further says, "Adjoining the abbey, on the north side, was the prior's chamber, which communicated with the church by a door with a Gothic arch."

"My lord," said Harriet, reddening to the very temples, "I know it is not now the fashion for ladies to devote attention to such matters, much less to speak of them, but my father was a votary of the past, and whether it be for good or ill to me, his only daughter, I was early imbued with his passionate love for ancient lore and the glories that perish not with time. An antiquarian I am not, my lord, in the sense in which you apply the word, but simply a lover of the storied past, especially of this my native land. You, an Englishman, can scarcely understand the love that we Irish cherish for 'our own loved land of sorrow,' the fond pride with which we turn over to the departed glories of the fair land, and dream

> Of chieftains, now forgot, who beamed
> The foremost then in fame;
> Of bards who, once immortal deemed,
> Now sleep without a name."

"Englishmen, like other men," the Earl replied, "can understand many things for which they do not get credit. But pray, Miss Markham, is your Cashel chronicle at an end?"

"I see our journey is, at all events," rejoined the lady, with a smile of doubtful meaning. "I regret to deprive Mr. Goodchild of the martyrology of Cashel—and Cashel has literally a *martyrology.* I am bound to crave your lordship's pardon too,"—her look was very arch just then,—"for I know you would have been much entertained by the account of the various tortures and punishments, pains and penalties, inflicted on divers of the archbishops of Cashel by *Act of Parliament.*"

"Some other time," said his lordship, with an ironical bow.

"Ah! at our next visit to Cashel, perhaps," blandly suggested Goodchild, rubbing his fat hands in a small ecstasy at what he considered a capital hit. He, of course, interpreted Lord Effingham's coldness according to his own wishes, and measured his impressions of Cashel by his own. Perhaps he was right, perhaps wrong.

The carriage had just turned into the long and shady avenue leading to the Castle—shady even then, if not with the fresh foliage of the sycamore, the beech, and the poplar, at least with the shadow of the dark-hued "evergreen pine," the laurel, and the dapper spruce, planted at intervals along the double row of tall shade-trees that bordered the noble avenue. All at once the little girls broke out into divers exclamations of wonder.

"Oh, do look, papa!—Miss Markham, see! see!—oh dear! what strange people!"

Following the direction of their eyes, Harriet saw moving along on the sward that fringed the carriage-way on either side two figures, in whom she at once recognised Mad Mabel and Shaun the piper.

"And, dear! dear! what an ugly little dog!" cried the little Lady Ann, meaning poor Frisk, who was trotting in advance as usual.

"If your lordship has no objection," said Harriet, "the young ladies may now have a specimen of rustic minstrelsy. There is the famous Shaun the piper, and if you will only have the goodness to tell William to drive slower, I know he will 'give us a tune,' as he says himself."

The check-string was pulled accordingly, and the carriage rolled slowly along the level avenue till it came within a few yards of Shaun, when he all at once struck up "The Wind that shakes the Barley" with a vigour and spirit that made the horses prick up their ears and champ their bits as though they felt very much inclined to try what they could do at a reel.

"What barbarous music!" said Goodchild; "it is only fit for savages!"

"It is good enough, surely, for 'wild Irishry'!" said Harriet with a smile; then, leaning her head out of the window, she accosted the piper—"Many thanks, friend, for your music. Where may you be going now?"

"Wisha, then, I was goin' to try my luck at the Castle. I never was up there, at all, at all, an' they say there's a fine darlin' lady in it a-tachin' of the lord's daughters, that's a great friend entirely to the likes of us, an' mighty fond of the ould music."

"Well, that is true enough, Shaun, but the lady of whom you speak may not be at liberty to draw 'the likes of you,' as you say, about the house, seeing that she is only employed there."

"Oh, Miss Markham, do have him come!—oh, pray do!" cried the two little girls in a breath. "Papa, mayn't he come? We shall be so delighted!"

"Be delighted, then!" said the Earl, smiling down in the eager little faces upturned to his. "Give him a general invitation," he said, addressing Miss Markham.

"Lord Effingham says you will be welcome at the Castle whenever you choose to come," said Harriet to the piper.

"And is the lord here himself? An' maybe you're the beautiful young lady that loves the ould ancient music?"

"*The lord is here*," laughed Miss Markham, "and I am the lady that loves the old music—but as for the *beautiful* lady, I am sorry to say we have no lady of that description in Effingham Castle."

"Now, don't say that, miss! don't say that," cried Shaun, with much quickness. "Sure, I know by your voice you're as fair an' as sweet as the flowers in May. Long life and success to your ladyship!"

"You see, my lord," said Harriet, "our Irish piper has the peerage at his finger ends! But what have you to say to Lord Effingham, Shaun?"

"'Deed, then, I've nothing to say to him but what's good, an' very good. Sure, only he's the right sort of a gentleman he wouldn't have the good wish of the people as he has, an' them not knowing much about him, at all, at all!"

"There, my lord, there's a specimen of Irish heart-logic for you," said Harriet archly.

"I accept the compliment," said the Earl, "and I thank you, friend, for your good opinion. The gates of Effingham Castle shall be always open to you and that four-footed friend of yours."

"I humbly thank your lordship," said Shaun, with his lowest bow, and the blood coursed merrily through his old veins, and the lightness of long-vanished youth was in his step for the moment as he moved on playing "Planxty Drury."

"But who is the girl?" said Lord Effingham, struck with Mabel's sad and singular appearance.

Harriet sighed as she turned her eyes on the poor witless creature, who had been watching the inmates of the carriage with the closest attention and in very unusual silence. "Ah! that, my lord, is a poor wreck of humanity—the people call her Mad Mabel. She is a minstrel too, in her way. Why so silent, Mabel? Have you no news for me?"

"Oh, wisha, news?—what news 'id I have? But they're goin' to hang Jerry Pierce—did you hear that?"

"Is it possible, Mabel?"

"It's truth I tell you,—an' listen hither," coming ever close to the carriage, "Celia Mulquin an' me is goin' away together to the well o' the world's end—you know where that is? Och, no! that isn't it," she added in a desponding tone; "sure, it's down at Holy Cross Patrick is, an' I dunna where they'll put Jerry Pierce when they hang *him*—maybe in that dark van't where they put young Mr. Esmond."

The carriage stopped, as if the coachman wanted to let those within have the full benefit of Mabel's wild prattle. All at once Shaun changed the gay fantastic measure of his "Planxty" for the love-sweet "Shule aroon," and Mabel, catching up the strain, sang in her dreamy, unconscious way—

> "Och! if I was on yonder hill,
> It's there I'd sit and cry my fill,
> Till every tear would turn a mill,
> As' go dhi me vourneen shaun.[1]

Oych! it's little I cry now! I used to cry a long time ago before they took *him* away from me, but the tears are all gone —all gone. Come now, Shaun! let us be off," and she seized the piper by the arm; "the fun 'ill be all over before we get to Holy Cross, an' I want you an' me to dance a jig on King Dough's tomb the night—no, behind it, where I hid from the men that killed ould Esmond!—ha! ha! they wanted to kill *me* that time, but I was too many for them!—so now, Shaun, put the best foot foremost,—step out, man!—augh! maybe it's goin' to hang that purty lady in the coach they are—or shoot her, or somethin', an' then she'll be walkin', walkin' ever, like me an' Celia Mulquin. Ochone! but I'm tired, tired—an' my heart is sore!"

There was a mournful pathos in the tone and the words that drew tears to Harriet's eyes.

"A strange being, that," said the Earl carelessly, as the carriage rolled away.

"An Irish *Blanche*, my lord,—her story much the same, only sadder still."

[1] And may my love come safe.

"By her madness hangs a tale, of course?"

"A tale?—ay, a tale of horror, of blood, and of"——

"Of love stronger than death!" subjoined Lord Effingham, with a chilling smile that was more than half a sneer.

"Yes, even of that, my lord," said Harriet promptly.

"It were worth the hearing, if so," said the peer in the same ironical tone. "I see the children are dying, as you ladies say, to hear the story. Could you not gratify their curiosity some of these first evenings—when Mr. Goodchild and I are within hearing—and Mrs. Pakenham—if in humour to listen?"

"Most willingly, my lord, if Mr. Goodchild will promise to keep awake to hear me?"

"My dear Miss Markham!"—began the chaplain, by way of entering a protest against the implied charge.

"My dear Mr. Goodchild, I freely forgive you for steeping your senses in sweet forgetfulness during my late prosy narrative," said Harriet, with a smile,—"on condition, however, that you lend me your ears, as Marc Antony says in the play, when I come to unfold the sad tale, not exactly of poor Mabel's wrongs, but of her sorrows."

The chaplain, ashamed of being so literally "caught napping," the more so as he detected an incipient smile on his patron's face, was but too well pleased to get rid of the subject with an unconditional promise. The carriage stopping just then, Mrs. Pakenham's portly figure was soon visible in the vestibule of Effingham Castle, and poor Mabel was, for the time, forgotten in the important business of "lunching," for which the drive through the frosty air and the long visit to the Rock had duly disposed the party.

CHAPTER XII.

A WAKE AND WHAT BEFEL THEREAT.

THE weeks and months rolled by, the snows of February and the winds of March and the soft dewy showers of April had all passed away, and still Jerry Pierce was a wanderer on the earth, with the brand of Cain on his brow, eluding the vigilance of the police, in what way no one could tell, notwithstanding that a tempting reward had been offered for his apprehension, and to all appearance the popular feeling was as strong against him as it ever had been. It was the last day of April, the charmed May-eve, and the little boys and girls were abroad in the dewy meadows gathering the golden May-flowers to strew before the house-doors for the welcoming of the summer.[1]

In the grey light of the closing evening sat Cauth by the door, with her stocking on her arm, listening to the pleasant sounds from the fields and meadows, and ever as she plied her needles muttering drearily to herself, as was her custom when alone.

"Wisha, but it's merry ye all are now," she said half aloud "as merry as crickets!—that's right! go on with your gallivantin', make the best of it while ye can!—I'll go bail ye'll not be so merry this night twel'month—some o' ye, anyhow! Ah, the poor foolish crathurs! isn't it badly off they are to know what's before them?—most o' them 'ill know it time enough!"

"That's the truest word you ever spoke," said a man who just then stood on the threshold before her; "it's little pleasure

---

[1] In Ireland the summer commences with the merry month of May—the spring with February and Candlemas Day, as the Feast of the Purification is there called, from the blessed candles then distributed amongst the people.

they'd expect in this world if they knew it as well as you and me, Cauth."

"Well, I declare you have the odds o' me, honest man!" said Cauth, startled a little by his sudden appearance.

"That may be," said the man gruffly, "but it's askin' your help I am, for God's sake, an' it matters little whether you know me or not. I know *you*, at any rate."

"Wisha, God help your wit, poor man!" said Cauth in a softened tone, "it's little I have to give any one. It's a sign you *don't* know me, though you say you do, when you ask me for charity."

"Much or little, you can give something, an' you must, too, for I have a sick child at home—*at home*," he repeated, with something like a chuckling laugh,—"a motherless child, too, without a bite or a sup to give her, an' she cryin' for somethin' to ate. They tell me," he added, with hysterical wildness,—"they tell me it's the hunger o' death that's on the darlin'! Woman! woman! give me somethin' for her, if it's only a mouthful!"

"Oh vo! vo!" said Cauth, rising quickly; "sure, I'd keep it out o' my own mouth an' give it, if that's the way it is with you!" And, going to the little alcove, she took out a piece of oaten cake, then poured some buttermilk into a porringer (*i.e.* tin cup), and gave it to the man, who had stepped inside the door, and stood shivering in his tattered garments waiting to receive the precious aliments, miserable though they were.

"There's the best I have for you," continued Cauth, as the man put the bread in the wallet that hung empty over his shoulder; "if it was a little while agone, I could give you somethin' better, but, ochone! since the black sorrow came on the poor mistress at the Hall above, there's many a thing we miss that we used to have. It's the good lady she was, all out, till that curse-o'-God villain murdhered the darlin' young master, but sure, sure, we couldn't have the face to go next or nigh her now! Go your ways, honest man; an' as I gave you that charity in the honour o' God, I lay it on you to say a Pather an' Ave for Mr. Esmond's sowl."

"Don't be layin' anythin' on *me*!" said the man fiercely. "I'll say no Pather an' Aves for the bit that's to save my child's life. That's the laste I may have !" And he was rushing out of the hut when Cauth caught him by the arm.

"You're a bad man," said she, "or you wouldn't say the likes o' that !"

"Wisha, thank you kindly," said the man in a tone of bitter mockery, "an' sure it's a *good woman* yourself is, ———," he named a name in a low, guttural whisper, and then darted off, leaving Cauth like one spellbound. Long she stood looking vacantly down on the floor, her features fixed and rigid, and her long skinny arms hanging, as it were, powerless by either side. At last she staggered to her seat near the door, and, heaving a deep-drawn sigh, leaned her head against the wall.

"Och, then," she murmured sadly, "them that 'id tell me of a May-eve long ago that it 'id ever come to this with me! Sure, nobody knows what's before them. But I thought—I thought I could hide myself here, an' I see I can't! I believe there's no rest for me aboveground!"

She was roused from her dreamy cogitations by the sound of Mabel's wild, sweet voice singing outside—

"Och! beware of meeting Rinardine
All on the mountain high!

Wisha! what's come of all the snails? an' the ne'er a bit o yarra can I find, at all, an' they tell me it's May-eve, an' what'll I do for the yarra?"[1]

"Lord save us!" muttered Cauth; "there's that poor cracked Mabel! I hope it isn't in here she'd be comin'! The lonesome crathur! it's lookin' for the yarra she is, an' the snail! Oyeh! oyeh! see how she gropes along on the ground—she's for all the world like a ghost!—an' worse than a ghost she is to us!" And she shuddered as she watched the spectral-looking figure gliding in a stooping posture through the deepening shades in her search for the charmed plant.

[1] The pulling of the yarrow after nightfall is one of the principal "charms" proper to May-eve amongst the peasant girls of Ireland. Another is placing a snail (also captured after the stars are in the sky) between two plates, in hopes that during the night it would trace in snail-hand the initial letters of the *fated name* on one or other of the plates. All these May-eve "tricks," like those of Hallow-eve, are of purely pagan origin, the first of November and the first of May being the two great festivals of the year amongst the pagan Irish.

"The sight of her makes me shiver all over," said Cauth, "an' when she gets a-talkin' about things, it makes me 'most as mad as herself to hear her! She'll not get in here the night, that's for sartin! An' it's a hard thing, too, to shut her out bekase she's afflicted! But sure, I can't help it—I wouldn't do it if I could!"

And so saying, she softly closed the door, whilst Mabel went on with her fruitless search, singing the while—

"He says, my purty fair maid, I like your offer well,
But I'm engaged already, the truth to you to tell,
Unto another damsel who is to be my bride,
A wealthy grazier's daughter down by the Shannon side."

The next moment, as usual with her, the strain was changed to that most doleful ditty—

"Och! it's on the banks o' Cla-dy I'm told he does remain!"—

perhaps more in accordance with her own wild and gloomy fancies.

Later in the evening, when the full moon was shining down in silvery splendour on the old Rock and the ivied ruins and the richly-varied plain stretching far and away beneath, Mad Mabel stole with a creeping pace to the door of Larry Mulquin's cottage, and, raising the latch, glided in. Celia was alone, spinning by the fire, her father and brothers being gone respectively "on their cail-lie."[1] There was a troubled look on Celia's face, and the rich bloom had faded from her cheek; ever as her foot turned the wheel, and the delicate flaxen thread passed lightly through her fingers, a deeper shade fell on her shrunken features, and the tremulous motion of her lips denoted the workings of the heart within. So wrapt was she in her own sad thoughts that she heeded not the raising of the latch, and the first intimation she had of Mabel's presence was her squatting on the floor beside her, looking silently up in her face through the dishevelled tresses of her long hair. A low scream escaped Celia at the sudden appearance of the ghostly face and figure, but, instantly recognising Mabel, she drew a long breath, and forced a smile that was ghastly on her face as sunlight on a new-made grave.

[1] i.e. to a neighbour's house to spend the evening.

"Wisha, Mabel! is it you that's in it?—the ne'er a bit but you took a start out o' me!"

"Husht!" whispered Mabel, raising her finger, "don't say a word for your life—the pealers are out, you know, this purty moonlight night, looking for Jerry Pierce an' every one;" then, forgetting her own injunction, she began singing—

> "Ooh! it's my delight of a shining night
> In the season of the year."

Celia shook like an aspen leaf at the mention of Pierce's name, and she cast a shrinking look around.

"Take care now, Mabel, what you say!" she whispered, but remembering how useless it was to warn the poor creature of anything, she adopted the wiser course of turning her attention from the dangerous subject.

"What did you come here for, Mabel?" said she very gently. "Did you want to speak to me?"

"Look here," said Mabel, "see what I brought you."

And opening a dock-leaf she held in her hand, she showed its contents to Celia, looking eagerly up in her face the while, as if to note her satisfaction.

"It's May-eve, you know."

"Ah, poor Mabel!" sighed Celia, and she sadly shook her head; "I want no snails now, nor yarra neither. No, nor the May-dew.[1] All that's past an' gone!"

"But don't you want to see Jerry's name on the plate jist for onst before they hang him?"

Celia, with a groan and a shudder, covered her face with her hands, murmuring, "Mabel! Mabel! for God's sake hold your tongue!"

"I will, avourneen, I will," said Mabel, rising. "So you'll not take the yarra, afther me goin' out a-purpose to pull it for you?"

"Yis, yis, I'll take it," cried Celia, snatching it from her, in hopes of getting rid of her the sooner.

"An' you'll put it under your head, achree? an' you'll see

---

[1] Another beautiful and highly poetical custom of the Irish peasant girls is that of gathering the first May-dew to bathe their faces. For that purpose they go out before sunrise on "May-morning" (as the first morning of the fair month is distinctively styled) and gather the dew from the leaves and flowers.

the beautiful fine drame you'll have about the hangin'. They wouldn't let me see Patrick hangin', you know," she added confidentially, "but maybe they'd let you go and see Jerry when it comes *his* turn. If they do, be sure an' bring me with you, for I think it's the greatest thing in the whole world to see any one a-hangin'. Och! och!" she added, with a piteous moan, "I wish they'd hang *me* at onst, an' be done with it, for I'm tired walkin', walkin' ever, and never gettin' to my journey's end."

"Where are you going now, Mabel?" Celia asked, moving with her towards the door.

"I'm goin' to the graveyard, to see if Jerry be there, an' if he is, I'll tell him you want him."

"To the graveyard, Mabel!—Lord save us! what 'id bring him there?" Celia asked, affrighted, without waiting to think of the folly of heeding Mabel's wild ravings.

"Well, I wasn't spakin' to him that night I seen him at the vau't lookin' at the letters on the front of it. You mind that night, Celia? it was a purty bright night, for all the world sich another as this. The sperits were all out that night in the purty moonlight, an' Patrick an' myself walked round an' round the ould walls an' the graves on the Rock above, an' then we went down to Hore Abbey, an' we sat discoorsin' there a while about one thing an' another, an' watchin' the fairies divartin' themselves, an' chasin' one another in an' out through the ould windows an' arches an' things, an' then, mavrone! off we went to Holy Cross, but jist as we got there the cock crew, an' poor Patrick had to go,—but listen hither, Celia! he said Jerry Pierce was goin' to be hung some o' these days, an' then you an' me, an' Jerry an' him, an' all the rest o' the sperits, 'id have the finest times you ever seen! Och, well! I must be goin'——it's tired I am——tired, tired——an' the heart athin me is as heavy as lead——it's a load to carry, so it is! I wish Jerry Pierce hadn't shot the purty young gentleman, an' made that ugly hole in his white forehead——och! what made him do it, at all?"

So saying, poor Mabel glided away noiselessly as she came, leaving Celia well pleased to get rid of her (to her) torturing prattle, which had somehow renewed all her troubles in her mind, and left her a prey to the most excruciating misery,

Still the silent moon shone down on the slumbering earth as calmly as though no stormy passion, no gnawing grief, was at work amongst the children of men. But the world never sleeps, and the peaceful sheen of the cold pale moonbeams as they rested on the earth and on the dwellings of men, was but a mockery after all. Beneath the glittering guise which nature wore that night the tide of human life was rushing on, and hearts were throbbing in the wildness of grief, and burning with the fever of mighty passion.

Leaving the old borough behind, with all its quaint and picturesque irregularity of outline, and its striking contrasts, and the shadows lurking amongst its silent avenues, we will take our way up the side of Gallows Hill to the mud cabin beneath the alderbush, where the fairy-woman dwelt in charmed solitude, her lonely hut fenced round, as it were, by popular superstition. On ordinary occasions neither bolt nor bar secured the door, a latch with a string being more than sufficient for the exclusion of all without and the protection of all within. Indeed, there was little in the place to tempt cupidity. The hut was divided midway by a partition of wattles covered with clay, which partition being only the height of the side wall, left all the space to the roof open, and gave access to the little room beyond simply by cutting itself some three feet short, leaving the breadth of a doorway at one end. The outer apartment was the kitchen, if kitchen it could be called. It had neither jamb-wall nor hob; the only provision for making fire being a few large flat stones loosely laid on the clay floor, an opening in the roof above giving egress to the smoke, or at least as much of it as chanced to take an upward direction. A small pile of dry brambles lay in one corner, but the fire on the hearth at this time was composed of a species of fuel probably only known amongst the peasantry of Ireland. A quantity of "seeds," that is to say, the outer husks of the oats, was heaped on the stones against the blackened wall; the front of the heap was burning, emitting a much more cheerful blaze than might be supposed from the nature of the fuel, and close by sat the hag who owned the cabin, stirring in the fresh "seeds" from time to time with a primitive sort of tongs formed of a piece of iron hoop bent in two and brought almost close together at the ends. Beyond her, next the wall, were two little children, a boy and a girl, cowering over the poor substitute for a fire, their half-covered bodies and their pinched faces conveying a picture of the dreariest and most abject destitution. A ghastly light was thrown on the group from the inner chamber, where a still more pitiable sight was visible through the doorless aperture in the partition. On a straw pallet, which usually served for the fairy-woman's couch, lay the dead form of a young child, the face only visible over the wretched covering of the poor bed. And a face of touching beauty it was, in its sweet repose, though sadly pinched, and stamped with that premature oldness so often seen in the children of the very poor. But the pale golden hair that shaded the small fair forehead and the delicate outlines of the marble-like features made a picture fair though sad to look upon. Death had there nothing repulsive, nothing stern; it was the image of rest, tranquil, happy rest, no more.

Not such was the face of the solitary watcher by that bed of death—a man of spare proportions, haggard features, wild and restless eyes, and shaggy brows knitted into an ominous frown. The garments of the man had been patched in many places, but other rents here and there showed either the want of a friendly hand to mend the tattered garment, perhaps the increasing neglect that follows and accompanies increasing misery, perhaps both. The man was the same who had asked and received charity from Cauth, but the charity had come too late. His child was dead when he returned all panting and eager with his poor prize. One heavy groan was all that escaped him when his eye fell on the dead face; but, handing the bread and milk to his remaining little girl to divide between herself and her brother, who was still younger, he drew a stool to the bedside, and muttering, "Thank God she's gone at last!" he had never stirred from the same posture all the long hours that had come and gone since then. A resin dip was burning beside the bed in one of those stands improvised for the purpose, rising some three feet from a wooden block that rested on the floor. Bare and unsightly were the clay walls of the little room, unrelieved by even one article of furniture, save and except the straw pallet and the round three-legged stool on which sat the desolate father. All was poverty, sheer, unmitigated poverty, in its most cheerless aspect; yet there was one redeeming quality in the squalid misery of the place, and that was its remarkable cleanliness, truly remarkable under the circumstances.

All at once the door opened, and another man made his appearance, stooped as if beneath the weight of years, yet of stout proportions withal, judging from the faint light in the cabin. The stoop soon vanished when once the door was closed, and the children uttered an exclamation of pleasure that drew a sharp rebuke from the ancient crone. She turned her head, however, and nodded to the new-comer with a curt salutation in Irish.

"Is Tim within?"

"Athen, why wouldn't he?—Nelly's dead."

"Dead?" cried the man, with a sudden start,—"little Nelly dead? You're not in earnest, vanithee!"

"Maybe I'm not—go in there an' see!" pointing to the inner room.

The children began to cry, but were speedily silenced by a threatening gesture from the hag. The man passed on into the room.

"I'll slip out now, childer," whispered the old woman to her young companions; "I didn't care to go and leave him by himself with the corpse, but I'll go now an' I'll see if I can't get somethin' to lay her out in. Mind you don't let the fire out till I come back;" and, wrapping her old red cloak about her, she left the cottage.

A tall and sinewy form was that of the man who now stood beside the wretched pallet, looking down on the little wax-like image so ineffably calm and serene. The father had only noticed his entrance by a listless nod, and then sank again into his gloomy reverie.

"Poor Nelly!" said the tall man, as he wiped away the fast-falling tears with the sleeve of his old frieze coat,—"poor girleen! is that the way with you?" After a moment's silence he spoke again. "Well, Tim, maybe it's best as it is. God is good to us, afther all!"

"Good to us?" cried the other fiercely. "Where's the goodness, I'd wish to know? It's aisy for you to talk, that doesn't know what a father's heart is!"

"Maybe I do as well as you? If I hadn't a father's heart

myself for these poor childer, I wouldn't be the man I am the night, an' I think you ought to know that."

The other started to his feet, his face, late so pale, flushed crimson red. "There it is again, now!" he said in thick, guttural tones; "will you never be done talkin' that way?"

"I wouldn't talk that way, Tim, only you take it out o' me. You're a mighty quare man, now, that's what you are. But there's no use talkin' an' wranglin'. When did Nelly die?"

"There a little while after dusk, when I was down about the town tryin' to get a mouthful for her to ate. She died of hunger at last!" His look grew darker and fiercer. "That's another nail in *his* coffin! There's Nora yit, an' Patsey, I'll go bail they'll both go like their mother an' Nelly—an' when they do *we'll clinch all the nails*—ho! ho! ho!" and the man laughed with horrible glee.

"Tim! Tim!" said the other, "what's comin' over you, at all?"

"Oh, the sorra thing's comin' over me—I'm in my parfit senses, an' sure you can't say I'm talkin' rashly when I tell you I'll wait till the childer's all dead wid hunger an' want before I settle with them that killed mother an' childer both. Sure, if I waited till I'd be dead myself, there 'id be nobody then to do the business."

"Tim Murtha!" said his companion, fixing his eyes on him with a wild and troubled look,—"Tim Murtha! the hand of God is heavy on us! Blood is blood, an' the stain of it can never be washed away, an' the voice of it cries from the ground for vengeance on the murderer!"

A change came over the haggard face of Tim Murtha. Slowly he turned on the speaker, and the two stood looking into each other's eyes with a strange and ghostly meaning. At last Tim Murtha spoke, and his voice was strangely hollow.

"Blood is blood, I know, but revenge is sweet!"

"God forgive you, Tim! you have a heart as hard as a stone! Now, I'd give all the money I ever seen, an' twice as much more, if that deed wasn't done yit, an' *you're* only thinkin' of"—

"Nobody doubts you," said Tim, with scornful emphasis; "it's your own neck that's throublin' you, an' not *the deed!* Why don't you get out of the way altogether, like a man, an' not be hangin' about here like a moth round a candle, till they catch you at last, an' then your life isn't worth a pin ? But I know what you're up to !"

"You do ?"

"I do—as well as if I was standin' within you."

"Out with it, then !"

"No, I won't; but mind, I tell you, Jerry Pierce. I'll be even with you if you think to play any of your tricks on me !"

It was Jerry Pierce himself who stood there listening, with a thunder-cloud on his brow and a lurid lightning in his eye. A storm of passion was raging in his heart, and his very brain throbbed and burned like molten lead; his huge frame shook like an aspen leaf; he darted one fiery look at Tim, and the man shrank back affrighted. His momentary terror brought Pierce back to recollection, and he smiled a grim and bitter smile.

"No wonder you'd be afeard," said he, "*of Jerry Pierce the murderer.* But don't fear," he added in a softer tone, "I wouldn't touch a hair of your head for all the goold in the Queen's mint—an' all on the 'count of the weenie crathurs that she left behind her. Poor Nelly !" and, stooping down, he kissed the little dead face, while his tears fell over it like rain, —" poor little darlin' ! you that I loved best among them is gone now, but I wouldn't hurt *your father*, Nelly, or the man that owned your poor mother !"

"Give us the hand, Jerry !" said Tim in a choking voice. "I know the thruth's in you, afther all; but why, why don't you get out o' the way ? Sure, you can't expect to escape for ever, an' you keepin' under their very nose."

"Never you mind that," Pierce replied. "I'll live till my time comes, in spite of them all. But why isn't the poor darlin' laid out ?"

"For the best o' raisons," said Tim, with his ghastly smile, "because there was nothin' to lay her out *in.*"

"It's not so *now,*" made answer the vanithee from behind; she had entered unperceived by either of the men. "Get out of the way, now, till I do what's fit to be done."

"What are you goin' to do ?"

"What's that to you, Tim Murtha ? Do what I bid you, an' that's all !"

Just as the men went into the kitchen, a low tap was heard at the door, and Tim Murtha, much excited, would have pushed Jerry back into the room, but the old woman told him shortly to "let him be." "Do you think any one is comin' here afther him?" she added, with the proud consciousness of power. "Go an' open the door—it's Ned Murtha that's in it."

Sure enough it was Ned Murtha, and Tim and Jerry exchanged looks at what they supposed the supernatural knowledge of the vanithee. It never occurred to either that she had herself apprised him of what had happened and therefore expected him to come. As Ned turned after closing the door, his eyes fell on Jerry Pierce, and the colour instantly forsook his face.

"The Lord in heaven save us, Jerry!" he said in a low, cautious whisper; "is it here I have you? Why, it's out o' your mind you are to be goin' about this way!"

"Never mind, Ned—never mind," said Pierce, with bitter emphasis; "they can but hang me, afther all, an' they can't do that, aither, till my time has come! But what brought you here? Did you hear of poor Nelly's death?"

Before Ned could answer, the vanithee came out and told them all to go in and see the corpse. At the same time she threw some brambles on the fire and put over it the only cooking utensil she possessed, a small iron pot, full of water, saying that she must make some "tay."

"Tay!" repeated Tim Murtha,—"where did you get tay?" But the rare luxury was quickly forgotten in the surprise of seeing his little girl laid out in a white shroud, a neat cap on her head, and a snowy sheet covering the bed, whilst two mould candles were burning in brass candlesticks on the stool hard by.

The father was evidently pleased; his pale, emaciated cheek was flushed with joy, and a light seldom seen there, shone in his sunken eyes.

"What do you think o' that?" said the fairy-woman, looking up in his face with very natural exultation.

"Well, I declare that's great," said Tim. "Where in the world did you get all the things?"

"It's no matter to you where I got them"—

"Where *would* she get them, why?" said Ned Murtha, doubtless with a good intention, "barrin' from Mrs. Esmond—the ould lady."

Both Pierce and the vanithee tried to stop Ned's tongue by signs; but all in vain, Ned would have his say. The effect on Tim was terrible. His face was livid in a moment, and his whole frame trembled with passion.

"Is it true what he says?" said he, turning to the old woman with forced calmness; "did you get these things out o' *that* house?"

"Why, then, I did—God reward her that gave them!"

"An' you went to *his* wife to beg a shroud for *my* child, that he was the manes of starvin' to death, an' her mother too?"

"Well, I did; why, an' who else 'id I go to, barrin' young Mrs. Esmond, an' she's too far away?"

"Take them every stitch off of her!"

"The Lord save us, Tim! are you out o' your mind?"

"Take them off, I say!"

"I wouldn't do it for all Mr. Esmond's worth! Is it to go strip the dead you'd have me?"

"I'll do it, then!" and, dashing away with maniac strength even the powerful arm of Jerry Pierce extended to prevent him, he tore the sheet off the bed, and, what was still more awful, the shroud off the body, and even the little cap off the poor dead child. The candlesticks he hurled to the floor, regardless of the mischief that might possibly follow, then told the old woman to stop her screeching and light the resin candle, and put the old "duds" again on Nelly. "An' only for fear o' settin' the place on fire I'd make a bonfire of them things," said he; "but mind the first thing you do in the mornin' is to take them back where you got them, an' tell what you seen me doin' now!"

"Oh, you unnatural man, you!" cried the vanithee; "that was worse than all! You're a haythen, so you are, an' a Turk, an' you'll never have a day's luck as long as you live! The curse o' God 'ill come down on you hot an' heavy for that black deed! See there! you have frightened Ned and Jerry out o' the house, an' no wondher!"

It was true enough; when the men saw that he was not to be prevented from carrying out his fell design, they both rushed from the room and from the cabin, fearing to look on such a sight of horror. But Tim Martha only smiled a ghastly smile, and said, "Let them go!—do as I bid you!" And the vanithee was fain to obey him without further parley.

CHAPTER XIII.

A SUNDAY EVENING AT ESMOND HALL.

The young May moon was shedding her mild radiance into the spacious parlour, or rather saloon, in Esmond Hall, where the family were assembled one fair Sabbath evening with nearly the same party of friends as we first saw together there on Hallow-eve night some six or seven months before. Uncle Harry and his wife and Aunt Winifred had dined at the Hall, and Moran, and the Hennessys, and the O'Gradys, having all dropped in during the afternoon, had willingly accepted Mrs. Esmond's invitation to remain for the evening. Harriet Markham was there too; indeed, she made it a rule to spend part of every day with Mrs. Esmond, whose grief, never violent or demonstrative, had now assumed the form of gentle melancholy, which those who knew her best expected to continue during her life. It was touching to see the meek, uncomplaining sadness that marked her look and voice and manner, yet she seldom or never recurred to the subject of her loss, and when the kind friends around strove to cheer and amuse her, she smiled her appreciation of their kindly efforts. But it was easy to see that sorrow had set its seal on her whole nature, mind and heart and all, and, as it were, dried up the well-springs of life and hope and joy. Yet she loved to have her friends around her, and listened with apparent interest to all they had to say.

The day was fading into night, and the moonbeams mingled faint and fair with the light of parting day, gradually dispelling the shadows of the twilight and ushering in the starry hours. Harriet Markham and Mary Hennessy had been giving an account of their meeting on the Rock some months before on St. Bridget's Day, and the lively fancy of the young ladies had vividly portrayed, to the great amusement of the company, the meeting of two extremes in Bryan and Mr. Goodchild. The gentlemen laughed heartily at Bryan's caustic replies to the bland, smooth chaplain.

"That was very good," said Moran; "but not quite so good as the same gentleman's encounter with the fairy-woman."

"How was that?" said Maurice Hennessy.

"Why, did none of you hear of it?" No, none of them had.

"Well, it seems the old dame manifested a touch of humanity some three weeks since, when somebody's child died in her vicinity under circumstances of great misery. She came down from her perch late at night to beg what was necessary for laying out the corpse."

"I remember the night well," said Aunt Martha; "it was the child of that poor man Tim Murtha that was dead, and she died of misery and want, as the old woman told me."

"Nonsense, Martha!" said her husband angrily. "I think you ought to know that Murtha better than to believe all you hear of his destitution. He's a lazy, good-for-nothing vagabond, that's what he is! If he were not, would he take the bag on his shoulder and go begging from door to door, as I hear he does? If I happen to get my eyes on him, upon my honour I'll hand him over to the police as a vagrant!"

"Shame, shame, Harry!" said his wife. "Do not, for pity's sake, talk so wildly! Why, to hear you, one would think you were the greatest tyrant in the whole country!"

"And, begging your pardon, madam, what do *I* care what one thinks?"

"Well, well, Mrs. Esmond, don't mind," cried Moran; "pray continue. What more were you going to say?"

"Oh, nothing, Mr. Moran, nothing—only that the old woman came to our house one evening late, as you say, and, telling me what had happened, asked me for a sheet and a shroud in which to lay out the poor child."

Here her husband started angrily to his feet. "And you gave them, of course?"

"Certainly I did. Would you have me refuse such a petition?"

"Then, madam, you did what you had no *right* to do, knowing the feelings with which we are all regarded by those wretched creatures. I forbade you before to give anything whatever to these people, and I think I had a right to expect that my command would have been obeyed."

"Not where Christian charity is concerned, Harry,—assuredly not; you know yourself as well as I do that neither you nor any one else has a right to command anything contrary to the law of God and the law of nature."

"Why, Aunt Martha," said Hennessy, adopting the common appellation by which she was known in the Esmond family, "I gave you credit for more penetration than I see you have. Now, don't you see that Uncle Harry is only joking?"

"Joking?" repeated the old man, with his wonted vehemence when excited,—"joking, did you say, Hennessy? A pretty subject for joking, truly! Now, my wife knows as well as I do how much cause we all have to love these wretched people, who, after all their hypocritical lamentations for our murdered Harry, will not give up his murderer to justice!"

"Stop, stop, for God's sake!" cried Dr. O'Grady; "see what you have done now!" and, following the direction of his finger, all eyes were turned on young Mrs. Esmond, who had fallen back fainting in her chair.

"I don't care," said the harsh old man; "she'll get over her hysterics. But I tell you all, over and over again, that if the people about here weren't as bloodthirsty as himself, Jerry Pierce would be long ago in the hands of justice."

The ladies would fain have persuaded him to retire, fearing the effect that the very sight of him might have on Mrs. Esmond when she began to recover, but not one inch would the old Trojan move.

"Humph!" said he; "one would think I had Medusa's head on my shoulders! Henny is not such a puling baby as to be frightened at my old phiz."

"Oh, you shocking man!" cried Aunt Winifred, as she knelt in front of the death-like figure of the young hostess, holding a bottle of sal-volatile to her nose, while Mary Hennessy and Mrs. O'Grady rubbed her temples and hands with Eau de Cologne,—"oh, you very shocking bad man! You grow worse and worse every day! You'll be the death of us all—*as you were of poor Harry!*" she added, letting her voice fall a very little.

"What's that you say, Winny?"

"She says, my dear," said his wife, with an admonitory glance at her sister-in-law,—"she says we had better all keep quiet till Henny recovers."

"She does, eh?—why doesn't she keep quiet herself, then, by way of good example?"

The doctors thought it the better way to have Mrs. Esmond removed to her own room till such time as she had thoroughly recovered, naturally fearing the effect of Uncle Harry's harsh and careless brusquerie. In a few minutes the ladies all returned, with the exception of Mary Hennessy, bearing Mrs. Esmond's compliments to the gentlemen that she hoped to meet them all at tea, if they could only continue to pass the intervening time agreeably.

"In that case, Moran," said Hennessy, "let us hear how the fairy-woman served Parson Goodchild. Did she cast her spell on that portly person?"

"You shall hear. It so happened that on the night to which reference has been made, the reverend gentleman, being 'homeward bound' from the rector's, where he had been dining, was riding along at a brisk pace towards the Castle, his mind probably full of the tales of blood and murder he had heard from the sapient rector and his guests, who were always sure to be the truest of 'true blue,'—in other words, staunch haters of Popery, and pillars of the new Reformation established some years before by the far-famed Lady Farnham on the double basis of blankets and fat bacon. As young Douglas says in the play—

Yon moon which rose last night round as my shield,
Had not yet filled her horn, when by her light

stepped forth, from the shadow of the tall white-thorn hedge, *not*

A band of fierce barbarians from the hills,

but a decrepit old hag wrapped and hooded in a red cloak. The horse was a little startled, perhaps so was his rider, but he managed to keep the animal in subjection, and was fain to continue his way. Such, it appeared, was not the intention of the ancient dame, who, suddenly extending her stick towards him, croaked out the remarkable words—

"'Stop, I command you!'

"All aghast and bewildered, the chaplain stopped, wondering much what was to follow. Perhaps he had some misgivings that he had before him a robber in disguise.

"'My good old woman,' said he, 'what is your purpose? What do you want?'

"'I want some money for creatures that's a'most dead with hunger and want.'

"'Oh, certainly,' quoth the chaplain, much relieved; 'it is at all times a pleasant duty to relieve the wants of our fellow-creatures;' and out of his vest-pocket he took a silver sixpence, and handed it to the old woman, saying with a smile that he probably thought worth another sixpence at least—

"'Now go, my poor old woman, and provide what is needful for your suffering friends or relatives. I rejoice in the opportunity you have given me this night of alleviating, in some measure, the sorrows of the poor.' He pulled the reins and was moving on, when the hag hobbled after him and again commanded him to stop, which he did, as it were, mechanically.

"'An' is this what you're goin' to give me, after all the talk?' said she, looking up in his face.

"'My good old woman, that is really all the small change I have got.'

"'Why, then, the curse o' Cromwell on you, you ould stall-fed bullock! isn't it great good that 'id do any one?' cried the dame, much excited. 'Keep it, an' make much of it—I'd scorn to take it!' and she flung the coin up in his face.

"'Old woman,' said the person, surprised out of his bland acquiescence, 'how dare you thus insult a minister of the gospel?'

"A scornful laugh cackled in the hag's throat. 'Minister o' the gospel, inagh! You mane the Divil's gospel, if there is such a thing! You talkin' of relievin' the poor! I'll go bail it's not much one of you 'ill give to the poor, barrin' yees want to buy their sowls like cattle, at so much a head! then you'd find *small change*, an' large change too! Oh, you set of schamin' vagabonds! it's little pace or comfort there ever was in the country since the first of yez came into it! Go your ways now, an' may God give you the worth of your *charity* here an' hereafter!'

"The biting sarcasm with which these words were uttered is beyond my power to convey, but the chaplain felt it keenly, I can tell you, and his feelings are easier imagined than described when he heard the hoarse, asthmatic laugh with which the crone greeted his departure as she stood in the middle of the road looking after him. She was not long alone in her merriment, for a person who happened to come within earshot during the colloquy, but had purposely kept out of sight, just then stepped out on the road, and, slapping the victorious emulator of Biddy Moriarty approvingly on the back, laughed right heartily at the parson's defeat, and gave the rough but good-hearted old dame a trifle of change that proved a more acceptable offering than that of the extra-generous and more than charitable churchman."

"And the person?"

"The person, Maurice, was Phil Moran, your humble servant to command."

"And pray how came you there?"

"I have half a mind not to answer you, my good fellow, but on second thoughts I will, being duly mindful of the maternal legacy of Mother Eve to her daughters, some of whom I have the honour to address. Know, then, that I, like the Rev. Mr. Goodchild, was on my return from a dinner party, and having but a short distance to go, and the weather being fine, both went and came on foot. I had Sam Elliott with me till he turned off at his own avenue, and while I stood a few moments admiring the fine effect of the moonbeams falling through the arching branches of the trees that lined the short avenue, I heard the clatter of a horse's feet coming up the road; it proved to be the portly chaplain; and so it was that I, being myself in the shade of the oaks that guard the Elliott gate, saw and heard what I have had the honour and happiness of relating for the entertainment of this worshipful company. Now, Miss Markham, what do you think of my old woman as compared with your old man?"

Harriet, like all the others, had been much amused by Moran's droll description of "the encounter," as he called it.

"Really, Mr. Moran," she said, laughing, "your old woman beats my old man hollow, and I think between the two they have given our worthy chaplain a thorough understanding of what it is to 'play with edged tools.' Had she only the traditional blanket instead of a red cloak, your dame, as you describe her, might very possibly be the identical *old woman* who, once upon a time, was 'going to sweep the cobwebs off the sky.'"

"If she didn't sweep the cobwebs off the sky," laughed Dr. Hennessy, "I'm entirely of opinion that she swept them off Goodchild's brain. Upon my honour, she must have knocked his wits into a cocked hat. Excuse the vulgarism, ladies, but the fact is, vulgarisms are confoundedly convenient at times to a fellow like me, whose thoughts are often gone a-woolgathering just when he wants to use them."

"If I had my will," said Mr. Esmond, "I'd make short work of that same fairy-woman, as they call her. I'd have her sent to Botany Bay or fairy-land—I would! It's positively a disgrace to the country to tolerate such old baldames as she in their nefarious practices—trading on the besotted prejudices and blind credulity of the people. I wish I had only been in Goodchild's place; I'd have whipped her within an inch of her life, the ill-conditioned hag!"

Before any one had time to answer this characteristic speech, a request was sent up from Mulligan that his honour, Mr. Esmond, would be pleased to step out to the stables to see the poor roan that had something the matter with her, the creature! and the farrier was there, and he'd like to speak to his honour about the beast before he went. Thereupon Mr. Esmond hurried off in much anxiety for the health and safety of poor Harry's favourite saddle-horse, which was, of course, highly prized by all the family. His wife took the opportunity of his absence to express her fear that sooner or later something bad would come of his tyrannical treatment of the poor, and his harsh, overbearing manner.

"Now, I am going to tell you all," she said, lowering her voice, "what I would not dare to tell him, knowing that it would but exasperate him the more against these miserable creatures. You heard how he blamed me for giving those things to that old woman for the laying-out of Tim Murtha's child,—well, he little knows, and I trust he will never know, that the man tore that shroud and that sheet from off his dead child when he learned who it was that gave them!"

Exclamations of horror were heard on every side, and the ladies all, but especially Mrs. O'Grady and Aunt Winifred, spoke loud in execration of the unnatural deed.

"But how did you come to know this, my dear Mrs. Esmond?" inquired Harriet Markham. "Or have you reason to believe that it really did occur?"

"I cannot possibly doubt it," was the reply, "seeing that the old woman brought back the things I had given her next day, and told me what had taken place. You may be sure I was dreadfully frightened, and, indeed, I cannot get the thoughts of it out of my mind ever since. It was so very awful, and gives one such an idea of the man's ferocity—I am sure, sure that the man who did that is capable of any atrocity."

"If it were that horrible Pierce, now, that did it, one would not be so much surprised," said Aunt Winifred, "but I really didn't think there were two such human fiends to be found in all Tipperary. Oh dear! what is going to become of us if such men are prowling at large?—no one's life will be safe, after a while."

"Bless me!" sighed Mrs. O'Grady; "who would have thought that the doom foreshown on Hallow-eve night would have fallen with such crushing weight, and so very soon?"

"Doom, indeed!" repeated her husband. "Now, do you mean to say, Mrs. O'Grady, that you really were, or are, so foolish as to put faith in those childish superstitions practised by the young on Hallow-eve, or any other eve? If you do, you're more of a fool than I ever took you to be."

"Well, Doctor, I really wonder at you to talk so," rejoined the wife, "after seeing what we have all seen since that memorable night."

"Memorable fiddlestick! Would you have us believe, now, that it was because poor Harry Esmond put his hand in the plate of clay that night that he was killed?"

"Not because, Edward,—oh, of course not *because* of his doing so,—but you cannot deny that it looked very much like a warning of what was to happen."

"I do deny it, Mrs. O'Grady; for if it was a warning for Harry, it was also one for Mary Hennessy, and what harm has come to her?"

"Humph!" said Maurice Hennessy, turning from a window where he and Moran had been standing in earnest conversation. "I'd be much obliged to you, ma'am," addressing Mrs. O'Grady, "if you'd keep those dreary notions to yourself. Now, to my knowledge, your gloomy suggestions on that same Hallow-eve night rankled so in poor Mrs. Esmond's mind that she felt miserably depressed at times from that night forth—to an extent, indeed, that injured her health considerably, the more so as she tried to conceal what she now believes to have been a pre-sentiment."

"Dear me, Dr. Hennessy, what a thing for you to say!" said Mrs. O'Grady, averting her head with a slight shudder, while her husband clapped his hands and cried, "Hear, hear! bravo, Hennessy!"

"Now, I must request, my dear Mrs. O'Grady," went on Maurice, "that you never mention that silly affair again, for if Mary be once put in mind of it, there is no knowing but she might begin to fancy herself 'doomed,' and take on to moping and pining, which might eventually accomplish your fairy warning—or what shall I call it?"

"Why, my dear Doctor," exclaimed Mrs. O'Grady very innocently, "you needn't be the least afraid of Mary pining away on that account, for I give you my word, I've been trying ever since Harry's death to convince her that we had a forewarning of it that night, and if you'll believe me, she only laughs at me."

"Well, well!" cried Hennessy, more annoyed than he cared to show; "after that, I need say no more. That beats Banagher, and Banagher beats—we know who."

Dr. O'Grady and Moran laughed heartily at the blank amazement visible on Hennessy's face, and the former gentleman subsequently told him, with as much gravity as he could assume, that there was more than that in his "little wifie" for the taking out. "If you press her a little," said he, "you would be apt to find out that there isn't a thing occurs to herself or any one she knows, of which she hasn't had warning one way or another. Do you know, it often occurs to me that she must have some sort of telegraphic communication with the other world. It was only the other day, when I was sent for to Father Maguire below, for a bad cold he got, that she told me she knew something was going to happen to poor Father Maguire, and that she was sure he'd never leave his bed."

"Well!" said more than one of the listeners, with ludicrous anxiety.

"Well, a hot bath and a good active cathartic falsified Mrs. O'Grady's prediction, and placed my reverend friend on his legs as stout and staunch as ever. I'm afraid the telegraph wire was broken that time—eh, Susan?"

The laugh that followed drove Mrs. O'Grady fairly from the room. She made her exit in double-quick time, on the pretence that she was going to see how Mrs. Esmond was.

"Well, now," said Aunt Winifred, raising her eyebrows very high, and straightening her long back to the most perfect perpendicular possible,—"well, now, you needn't laugh so much, after all, about Mrs. O'Grady's 'warnings.' I tell you there are warnings given, and I've had them myself before our dreadful misfortune came upon us."

"Is it possible, Miss Esmond?" said Harriet, with assumed earnestness, while the others exchanged looks and smiles.

"Yes, indeed, my dear, it is both possible and true. For many nights before poor dear Harry's death I heard a drop falling—falling—just outside my room door. And then the death-watch—why, I used to hear it night after night at my bed-head just as plain as if my watch were there, which it was not, you know, for I always leave it in the watchstand on the toilet-able."

"Well, that is really astonishing," said Harriet, endeavouring to keep from smiling, Aunt Winifred's predominating acid being now too well known in the circle to permit any jocose liberties in her regard. The gentlemen suddenly remembered that Uncle Harry was in the stables, and thought they would go seek him there, as the tea-bell had just rung, and Mrs. Esmond and the other ladies were descending the stairs, Mary Hennessy's pleasant voice being heard in a tone of playful remonstrance.

The gentlemen had not yet returned from the stables when Dr. O'Grady was summoned to a patient some miles away towards Killenaule, and having to go home for something he required, Mrs. O'Grady preferred going with him, feeling probably a little sore from the wound that had been inflicted on her oracular dignity.

Very sad and very pale was Mrs. Esmond when she took her place that evening at the tea-table, but, looking round on the kind, dear friends whose faces expressed the sympathy they did not choose to speak, she smiled and made an effort to appear cheerful, that the shadow of her grief might not fall on them.

Uncle Harry was unusually silent during the earlier part of the meal, and at last the young men began to rally him on his taciturnity.

"May I venture to ask what are you thinking of, Mr. Esmond?" said Hennessy; "the advance on fat cattle, or the next presentment before the Grand Jury—eh?"

"Or the chances of getting the 'bang-beggars' banished to parts unknown?" said Moran, looking with sly meaning first at Uncle Harry, then at his wife.

"The bang-beggars?" repeated the doctor, catching the expression of Moran's face; "why, what should Mr. Esmond have to do with them?"

"Oh, we know that ourselves," replied the lawyer; "don't we, Aunt Martha?" Mrs. Esmond smiled her acquiescence, but her husband was in no humour for smiling.

"Now, I tell you what it is, Phil Moran," said he, setting his cup down in the saucer with a force that much endangered the safety of that particular piece of Mrs. Esmond's fine old Dresden, "I'd thank you to crack your jokes on proper subjects, and *that* is not one, whatever you may think to the contrary. I consider it a very serious business—very serious indeed, involving, as it does, the very lives of the landowners of this country."

"Not a doubt of it, Mr. Esmond, not a doubt of it," said Moran very gravely, "and for that very reason I naturally supposed you might be occupied in devising ways and means to get rid of a fraternity so dangerous to the community."

"You were mistaken, then," said Uncle Harry gruffly; "I was just thinking of poor Henny here."

"Of me, uncle? And, pray, what were you thinking of me?"

"Why, I was just thinking that you will never have peace or rest in your mind until that wretch Pierce has paid the penalty of his crime."

Every eye except Mrs. Esmond's was turned reproachfully on the harsh old man, and a murmur of surprise and indignation ran round the table. Mrs. Esmond started as if an adder had stung her,—her face was pale and red by turns, and the tears gushed to her eyes.

"Mr. Esmond," said she, her voice and her lips trembling,—"Mr. Esmond, I know not what I have done that you should inflict so cruel a punishment upon me as to tear open so rudely and so unnecessarily the yet unhealed wound in my poor heart. God forgive you—God forgive you!"

"Well, upon my word, Mrs. Harry Esmond junior," said the old man, with a raised voice and an angry look, "I didn't expect to hear you talk so. I see you are all just the same at bottom, let the top be ever so smooth and smiling. There's a touch of the tiger in every mother's daughter of you!"

"For shame, Harry—for shame!" cried his wife.

"That's right, Harry!" echoed his sister; "give us all a specimen of your politeness. Show how amiable you can be when you like!"

"Mr. Esmond," said the young widow, addressing him slowly and distinctly, "what you have said I think it my duty to answer, and I will, though it tear my heart-strings asunder. Know, then, that I do not desire to have the—the guilty person brought to justice."

"You do not?"

"No—God forbid that I should! I pray every day that he may escape the penalty of his crime, as you say, for the sacrifice of *his* life would not give me back what the grave has taken from me. Let him live and repent. God will deal with him in His own wise way, and in His own good time. Vengeance is His, not mine." She rose, and, taking Mary's offered arm, passed from the room. Tea was just over.

The carriage came just then for Miss Markham, and the rest of the company did not long remain. Before they left the dressing-room, however, the young lady of the mansion had heard from Aunt Martha the strange and pitiful story of Tim Murtha's misery and his gloomy desperation.

"And where is the unfortunate man now?" she asked, with tender sympathy.

"That I cannot tell you, my dear," said Aunt Martha, as she drew her sable boa around her neck and took up the capricious muff of the same costly fur. "He and his family were in the hut of that old fairy-woman, as they call her, when the child died,—so she told me when she came herself to ask the sheet and things,—but it is quite impossible to say where such poor wanderers are to be found at any particular time. They are hardly ever two nights in the same place, you know; for if they get one night's lodging for God's sake, they think it enough in one house, and travel on next day till nightfall brings them to some hospitable door, perhaps miles away from their shelter of the night before."

"Then you think, my dear aunt, that there would be little use in trying to find this poor man out? Indeed, I feel very anxious about him and his family—their case seems so very hard."

"It is hard, Henrietta, very hard; for the wretched man has, as I am informed, never entirely recovered the effects of the long illness following on his fall. They say he is a most pitiable object, and I would be most happy to do what I could for him and his poor children, but, you see, he will accept no assistance from me, and your uncle, on the other hand, will not allow me to give it."

"Poor miserable creatures!" sighed the gentle mourner; "their lot on earth is surely a hard one. God help the poor!"

"My poor Henrietta," said her aunt, as she kissed her at parting, "in all your own sore affliction your heart is not closed against the sorrows of others. And yet there are those who would be scandalised to hear of your expressing sympathy for any of these unfortunate people."

"Say no more of that, my dearest aunt," was the earnest reply; "why should I blame all for the fault of one? I cannot, and I will not, be scandalised who may! Good-night, dear aunt; may God bless and protect you from every danger!"

CHAPTER XIV.

MISS MARKHAM'S STORY.

A week or two after that evening at Esmond Hall, Harriet Markham sat by the bow-window of a summer-parlour in Effingham Castle, looking out with pensive eyes on the richly variegated landscape presented by the fine old park, with its hill and dale, and wood and water, for a fair lake slumbered in its "bosom of shade," visible from that end of the Castle where Harriet sat.

> The scene was more beautiful far to the eye
> Than if day in its pride had arrayed it,

and, as she watched the blue mist curling upward from the lake in delicate forms of beauty, her graceful fancy fashioned them into naiads and fays, the guardian spirits of the silvery waters. Then her thoughts began to wander back into the past, and the shadowy forms of other years crowded around, mingling with the mists of eve, their voices whispering, as it were, in the low soft zephyr that so gently murmured by, stirring the leaves on the branches outside as with the breath of life. Notwithstanding her flight into the realms of fancy, Harriet was not alone; the Earl and Mr. Goodchild were playing chess at the farther end of the room, and near by sat Mrs. Pakenham, a large, handsome woman of very mature years, and slightly overdressed, watching the game with much apparent interest. The little girls had made their curtseys some time before and retired with their nurse, who was an older sister of Celia Mulquin—this *en parenthèse*.

"Take care, my lord," said Mrs. Pakenham, who, being a cousin-german of Lord Effingham, had kindly taken charge of his splendid *ménage* since the death of the Countess some two years before,—"take care, my lord! there goes your knight!—you have need to look after that castle! What were you thinking of that time?"

"That is easy told," said Lord Effingham; "I was thinking of an air I heard that poor maniac sing on our return from the Rock last spring. Do you remember it, Miss Markham?"

"Excuse me, my lord," said Harriet, with a start and a blush; "I—I did not hear what you said."

The Earl repeated his question, and then hummed the first part of the air. It was "Shule Aroon."

"It were strange indeed, my lord," said Harriet, smiling, "if I did not remember *that*. It was one of the airs that oftenest soothed my infant slumbers."

"I know not why it is," said Lord Effingham, "but ever since it seems to haunt me like a voice from the world of spirits. It is, indeed, a fine old air. Do you know the words, Miss Markham?"

"I know one set of words, my lord, but perhaps not the best, for there are several versions of 'Shule Agra' and 'Shule Aroon,' —as it is indiscriminately called,—sung here in Munster; most of them are in Irish, and can hardly be rendered into good English so as to preserve the exceeding beauty and simplicity of the original. The words I have are a sort of free translation, the *refrain* being still sung in the old musical language of the Gael."

"You would oblige me much by singing the song for us," said the Earl, whereupon the Honourable Mrs. Pakenham drew up her portly form in loftiest state, and looked the contempt for Irish music which she cared not at that moment to express in words.

Miss Markham bowed her acquiescence. Mr. Goodchild rubbed his fat white hands, and smiled and nodded, and asked if he should not have the honour of fetching the guitar.

"No, no, Mr. Goodchild—many thanks for your politeness," said Harriet, laughing at the odd association of ideas; "the guitar and my old song would make strange discordant melody together—to borrow a *bull* for the occasion. Here is the song, my lord." And she sang with all the sweetness and simplicity of the true ballad style—

> "Oh, have you seen my Norah Fay!
> She's left me all the sad long day,
> Alone to sing a weary lay;
> Go dhi mo vourneen, slaun;
> Shule, shule, shule aroon;
> Shule go sochir agus shule go cune,
> Shule go theiv dorris agus eilig lume.
> As' go dhi mo vourneen slaun.
>
> You'll know her by her raven hair,
> Her deep blue eye, her forehead fair,
> Her step and laugh that banish care;
> As' go dhi mo vourneen slaun.
>
> In form you may her semblance find,
> But none like her, of womankind,
> If you can see her heart and mind;
> As' go dhi mo vourneen slaun.
>
> Oh, bring to me my Norah Fay,
> For hours are days when she's away;
> The sun looks dark, and sweet birds say,
> Go dhi mo vourneen shaun," etc.[1]

"Mercy on me, what a barbarous tongue!" said Mrs. Pakenham. "How in the world can you articulate such harsh, guttural sounds?"

"Just as easily as I do the improved Saxon which now forms our vernacular. You think the Gaelic a 'barbarous tongue,' my dear Mrs. Pakenham, and yet that 'barbarous tongue,' which ought to be still the vernacular of the Irish people, was once the language of a highly-civilised nation, spoken alike by king and chief, and warrior-knight and noble lady. The bards of Erin in the long-past ages moulded it into forms of rarest beauty, and men who were great lights in their generation made it the vehicle of their thoughts and their lofty inspirations."

"Dear me! I should not have thought so," said Mrs. Pakenham, with an extra assumption of dignity, "but I suppose you know best, Miss Markham. How stands the game, my lord?"

"Oh, the battle is fought and won—for once Mr. Goodchild has carried the day. Miss Markham, you were kind enough to

---

[1] The above is Mr. and Mrs. Hall's translation of one version of "Shule Aroon." Of the Irish chorus I have elsewhere given a translation.

promise to tell us the story of Mad Mabel. Suppose you told it now to while away the hours?"

"With much pleasure, my lord," Harriet replied, "and the more so, as Lady Ann and Lady Emma are not present; for, although they have frequently reminded me of it, I have purposely refrained from gratifying their curiosity, as the story is not exactly one that would benefit them to hear. The tragical scenes I am about to describe as briefly as I can are, alas! but too common in this unhappy country, and are to some extent, perhaps, Irish, owing not so much to the natural ferocity of the people as the unsatisfactory relations between landlord and tenant."

"Why, Miss Markham," said Mrs. Pakenham, opening her eyes to their fullest extent, "you don't mean to say you are going to entertain us with 'a tale of Irish peasant life,' do you?"

"I would not, on any account, think of doing so, Mrs. Pakenham," said Harriet, "were it not Lord Effingham's wish to hear it. So, with your permission and Mr. Goodchild's, I will proceed at once, promising, at the same time, for your consolation, to make the story as short as possible."

"Miss Markham is very good," said bland Mr. Goodchild, and he folded his plump hands athwart his goodly paunch with an air of meek resignation that was altogether impressive. The Honourable Mrs. Pakenham took up a Chinese fan that lay on a spider-table near, and commenced fanning herself with great force and admirable dexterity.

"Your lordship has doubtless heard," said Harriet, "of the murder of Mr. Chadwick? I believe almost every one has heard of it, either at the time it occurred or since." Lord Effingham replied that he had not only heard of the murder, but had known Mr. Chadwick, who had been for a short time a sort of under-agent on his Irish estates, before he got promoted to that situation which subsequently cost him his life.

"Then your lordship probably knows what manner of man he was, and how little calculated to win either love or respect from the people over whom he was placed in 'brief authority.'"

"It was precisely on account of his excessive harshness, amounting at times almost to brutality, that I was finally obliged to supersede him in his office," replied the Earl. "I had heard so many complaints of his tyrannical treatment of the tenantry that I could not possibly allow him to continue it longer."

"Well, my lord, there is reason to fear that his more recent employer cared little how he treated the tenants provided only he squeezed the money out of them. He appears, indeed, to have had a *carte blanche*, as most Irish agents have, in regard to the means to be employed for that end. And yet it is said in the neighbourhood, by way, I suppose, of giving the devil his due, that Mr. Chadwick was not so excessively severe in exacting the payment of rent as many others who are permitted to live on in their heartless oppression of the poor; but somehow his manner of dealing with the tenants and the peasantry in general was most insulting; he neither understood nor cared to understand the peculiar sympathies or antipathies of the people amongst whom he lived, and was, therefore, continually treading on their corns, as the vulgar phrase goes, taking no pains at any time to conceal his contempt for them, and though fully conscious that he was an object of hatred to them, taking every opportunity of openly breathing defiance. He was a man of large, unwieldy proportions, as your lordship doubtless remembers, and I have been told that on some occasions, when he had a large number of the peasantry around him, he would say in a scoffing tone, as he rubbed down his huge frontal, puffing the while like a juvenile whale, 'You see I'm growing fatter and fatter every day. I'm thriving on your curses, I believe.' Then the rustic dissemblers around would glance furtively at each other, and force a laugh, and say, 'Your honour is mighty pleasant, so you are, an' fond of crackin' your jokes—more power to you, sir, for that same.' But deep in their hearts were rankling the imprecations that fell on them from his foul tongue, and the bitter mockery and contempt wherewith he treated them on all occasions."

"Upon my honour, I do not wonder at his treating them so," said Mrs. Pakenham, all at once renewing the fanning process which she had perhaps unconsciously suspended. "I really think they deserve no better."

The Earl cast one of his black looks on his stately kinswoman, and she was silent. Harriet resumed, with a heightened colour—

"There is no knowing how long this might have gone on,

had not Mr. Chadwick commenced building a police-barracks at Rath Cannon, adjacent to Holy Cross Abbey, and only a short distance from Thurles. He was in the habit of boasting in all companies, and even to the people themselves, that he was the man to keep the Bloody Tips in order, and that he was going to have a police-station at Rath Cannon for the very purpose of watching them. Now this, in the peculiar state of the country, and for reasons known to themselves, was just what the peasantry least wished for, and, recognising in this new move yet another and more convincing proof of Mr. Chadwick's hatred of them, and, moreover, an open defiance of them, they accepted the challenge, and swore to each other, in their secret meetings, that *Chadwick must die.*"

"What a horrible set of wretches!" cried Mrs. Pakenham, now fully absorbed in the narrative. "What fiends incarnate they must be, and what a cowardly set, moreover, to conspire for the murder of one man!"

"My very dear Mrs. Pakenham," said the chaplain, "if you knew this unhappy country better, you would wonder at no act of baseness or cruelty on the part of the people—especially here in Tipperary."

"You are scarcely just to this 'unhappy country,' Mr. Goodchild," said Harriet, looking at him in a way that made him feel rather small, as the phrase goes; "even as regards Tipperary, your assertion is by far too general and sweeping."

Thereupon the good man began to justify himself. "I protest, Miss Markham," said he, with intense earnestness, "I did not mean to censure the people—the Romanists, namely, of this most miserable country"—

At this the Earl smiled, and Harriet laughed. "Why, my dear good sir," said she, "you are making matters worse instead of better. Just allow me, pray, to continue my story, and I will take your explanation for granted."

"Permit me to ask one preliminary question, Miss Markham," said Lord Effingham: "how can you account for the widespread conspiracy entered into by the peasantry for the execution of their diabolical purpose?"

"Very easily, my lord. By the simple fact that the conspiracy already existed in the form of a secret organisation, having revenge for one of its principal objects. They called it, and probably believed it, *justice*—acting on the assumption, not always unfounded, that there was no justice for them in the law-courts of the land; that the oppressors—excuse me the harsh word, my lord, I do but borrow it from *their* phraseology—that the oppressors had the *law* in their own hands, and that they had to look for justice to themselves alone. There was a time when this was true to the very letter, but the misfortune of the people is that they do not see how times have changed in the country, that a more enlightened spirit is abroad amongst the gentry, and that justice is now to be found on the bench—that, in fact, the partisan magistrate of a former age is now almost the exception to the general rule, and is frowned down by the majority of his brethren on the bench. However, old prejudices, long and fondly cherished, are not easily eradicated from the minds of the illiterate, and, moreover, there are always some designing knaves interested in their perpetration, so it is that many of our poor people are led blindfold into these dangerous societies formed amongst them for what they consider self-defence. Many, too, who are naturally peaceable and well-disposed, are actually forced, by the most dreadful threats, to join these associations, against their own honest convictions, and against the positive and most solemn prohibition of their Church."

"It is truly a lamentable state of things," said the Earl, "and the worst of it is, that legislation has no power to reach the evil."

"None whatever, my lord. Human legislation will have little effect amongst Irishmen, who set Divine legislation at defiance. Where the efforts of religion fail to make them wiser or better men, no human power can do it. However, as I had the honour of telling your lordship, it was in the midnight assemblies of these misguided men that the death of Mr. Chadwick was resolved upon. The only difficulty was then to find executioners for their horrid resolve. For some days this was a difficulty, for Mr. Chadwick was known to have his house well provided with arms, and, moreover, to carry arms on his person wherever he went. It was the old story of the cat and the bell. Things did not long remain in that state, however, for before the grand meeting of the secret conspirators one night, in a wild gorge of the Keeper Mountains, appeared a stalwart young fellow, Patrick Grace by name, who enjoyed the reputation of being an avenger of wrong and the sworn foe of the tyrannical landlords. Without any sort of hesitation he declared his willingness to undertake the execution of the dread sentence pronounced on Mr. Chadwick, provided he were left to do it in his own way and at his own time. Of course his proposal was eagerly accepted, for, though young in years, Patrick Grace was strong in courage and in resolution. He had so many times proved his prowess in one way or another against the landlords that he was looked upon as a champion of the people's rights. A rustic Don Quixote he was, ready to do and dare all things for 'the cause.' A deplorable instance he was, too, of that perverted sense of justice which I have endeavoured to describe. What made him still more popular amongst the people was his remarkable personal beauty, accompanied by great sprightliness of manner, and that whole-souled generosity which, above all other qualities, finds its way to the Irish heart. Such was Patrick Grace when he presented himself to execute the popular vengeance on Mr. Chadwick—the admiration of the women and the envy of the men in his own class, and the pride and boast of all. But though the rustic Adonis danced with all the pretty girls, and applied 'the blarney' with skill and effect, he had already made his choice from amongst them, and, as the old ballad says—

Placed his affections on a comely young dame,

And like that same 'comely young dame,' sung by her enamoured swain under the poetical title of the 'Rose of Ardee,' and therein familiar to every rustic singer in many parts of fair Ireland, the object of Patrick Grace's love was

Straight, tall, and handsome in every degree;

in fact, just the one to catch and fix the affections of a 'Roving Bachelor,'[1] if they ever were to be caught or fixed. She was an orphan, and lived as a servant in the house of a comfortable farmer, where she was treated, as is usual amongst that class here in Ireland, as one of the family. Grace was a son of the

[1] Miss Markham here had reference to the name of one of the liveliest and most popular dance-tunes ever "screwed" on an Irish fiddle.

family, and during the pleasant evenings that followed the days of toil, the youth and the maiden, thrown together in the heart-opening sunshine of rustic merriment, found themselves, they scarcely knew how or why, bound together by the tenderest bonds of loyal and true affection. And if ever the course of true love did bid fair to run smooth, it was for Patrick Grace and this rustic beauty, who was soon his betrothed bride, their marriage being only deferred till a mud-wall cabin was put up to shelter their household gods."

"Dear me, Miss Markham," said Mrs. Pakenham, yawning wearily, "what a very tiresome story!"

"I cannot agree with you, *ma belle cousine*," said Lord Effingham; "I find it extremely interesting. Pray proceed, Miss Markham."

"It has a peculiar interest for me," said the grave chaplain, "from the insight it gives into the atrocious immorality of the Romish system."

"I am not aware that it does give any such insight," observed Miss Markham. "I have shown, on the contrary, that the 'Romish system,' as you say, so far from encouraging men in these secret combinations and lawless courses, is at all times engaged combating their evil passions, and endeavouring with all its might to suppress those occult associations which are ruinous to the faith and morals of any people, but doubly so to a Catholic people, because they withdraw them from the saving influence of religion, and from the life-giving sacraments of the Church, in which they are not allowed to participate. Do I make the matter intelligible to your lordship? I see Mr. Goodchild is in the condition of those who, being 'convinced against their will, are of the same opinion still.'"

The Earl bowed affirmatively, and smiled at the keen sarcasm, which Mr. Goodchild, luckily for himself, did not seem to understand, probably in blissful ignorance of the gist of the old adage quoted by Harriet.

"Pray go on with your story," said the somewhat petulant Mrs. Pakenham; "supper will soon be on the table."

"Well, Patrick Grace was, of course, loudly applauded, and his proposal eagerly accepted, by the secret conclave, few of whose members would have cared to risk their precious lives as he did for the common good,"

"And did he do it, Miss Markham?" exclaimed Mrs. Pakenham in a state of breathless anxiety. "Did he do that wicked act?"

"He did," said Harriet, her voice sinking beneath the weight of horror and of shame,—"he did; he promised to kill the obnoxious agent, and *he kept his word.*"

There was silence for a moment, and then Harriet resumed, as by an effort—

"The young betrothed of Patrick Grace knew nothing of what was going on; fearing, perhaps, her importunate entreaties not to imbrue his hands in blood, or run the risk of losing his own life to do the will of others, he would not venture to see her till after the deed was done, and then, he expected that, so far from blaming what he considered his heroic and patriotic act, she would be the first to applaud his self-devotion."

"But where—when—how did he accomplish the awful deed?" cried Mrs. Pakenham.

"He probably waylaid the unfortunate gentleman in some lonely spot under cover of the night," suggested Mr. Goodchild.

"He did no such thing, reverend sir. If you will have the goodness to listen, you shall hear what he did. One day, when the great broad sun was shining overhead, Mr. Chadwick was superintending the erection of the constabulary-barracks before mentioned, talking in his loud, domineering way to the men employed on the work, and little dreaming that his last hour had come, when the daring youth who had undertaken the execution of the fearful sentence secretly pronounced upon him, walked deliberately up, with a pistol in his hand, and shot him with so sure an aim that he fell dead to the ground."

A groan of horror escaped from the lips of Mrs. Pakenham —she could not speak; the chaplain was little less agitated. Lord Effingham alone preserved his composure.

"What!" he asked, "in the presence of the workmen?"

"Even so, my lord, and of the passers-by, relying, doubtless, on the hatred wherewith Mr. Chadwick was regarded by all the surrounding peasantry, and fully as much, perhaps, on the secret organisation which underlay the whole strata of society. He very naturally thought that no one would venture to give evidence against him for fear of their terrible revenge. And, indeed, it seemed at first as though he reckoned not without his host, for he walked away after doing the deed unmolested by any one. One man only, a mason who was standing by Mr. Chadwick's side at the fatal moment, exclaimed, perhaps involuntarily, 'God forgive you, Patrick Grace!' But Grace little heeded the words, his conscience being perfectly at rest with regard to the nature of the deed he had just perpetrated, and no thought of personal danger from the recognition ever entering his mind."

"What a frightful perversion of mind!" said the Earl.

"And especially of the Irish mind. If your lordship only knew as I know the intensity of horror wherewith the Irish, perhaps more than any other people, regard the commission of murder, you could then understand, in some degree, how great must be the provocation, how fierce the excitement that closes their hearts to pity."

"Well, well," said Mrs. Pakenham, with an impatient gesture, "we can dispense with all that. But what came of it? —did the horrid wretch escape? Did no one give evidence against him?"

"That is just what I am going to relate," said Harriet, with a quiet smile, and she resumed as follows: "As may be supposed, Grace, having no fear of being brought to trial, took no pains either to conceal himself or deny the commission of a crime which he considered as an act of retributive justice. The news of the tragic event spread like wildfire through the country, and when the veil of darkness covered the earth, the conspirators came together in their secret haunts to meet their emissary and congratulate him and themselves on his successful attempt to rid them of their detested enemy. When asked if he thought any one had seen him doing the deed, he answered carelessly, 'Why, then, to be sure, didn't all the men that were workin' on the buildin' see me? But what of that—sure, I knew before I went every one that was in it, an' they're all the right sort. Philip Mara was standin' right alongside the ould chap when I paid my respects to him, an' more by token he said, "God forgive you, Patrick Grace!" when he seen Chadwick fallin'.' So far all was considered safe, and Patrick Grace was the idol of the hour, and enjoyed for the time, in his own limited sphere, all the glory of a conqueror. Short indeed was his unhallowed triumph. Early next day he was arrested on the deposition of

Philip Mara, and whilst he and his fellow-conspirators cursed the traitor, as they chose to call him, and breathed the most terrible threats against him and his, they little knew what an agonised struggle the worthy mason had undergone before he decided on giving information in the case. Mara was an upright, honest, right-thinking man, with intelligence somewhat in advance of his class, and, above all, a deep sense of his obligations as a Christian, which would not permit him to keep so atrocious a crime secret. And so it was that, trampling under foot all the suggestions of fear and prudence, and most probably encouraged by the advice of his venerable pastor, the brave man did what he considered his bounden duty, and gave information to the nearest magistrate concerning the murder of Mr. Chadwick. The storm of indignation that burst forth amongst the peasantry on hearing of what they considered Mara's treachery is beyond all conception. Those who were, like himself, under the strong influence of religion, secretly applauded his self-devotedness, and prayed that God and the Blessed Virgin might save him from the deadly vengeance of 'the boys' who held the whole population in terror. But these kindly sympathisers, being the most orderly and virtuous portion of the community, naturally shrank from incurring their enmity by any public expression of their sentiments; whereas the friends and upholders of the imprisoned Grace were loud and vociferous in their denunciations of the 'Informer,' as they chose to call him. Indeed, there would have been little chance of Grace's conviction on poor Philip Mara's testimony had he been left at large, but the Government had prudently provided for his safety by keeping him in safe quarters under a strong guard till the time came for the trial, viz. the summer assizes, then not far distant. Fear and terror then took possession of the friends of Grace, lashed to fury by the consciousness of their inability to save him ; but amid all the raging storm of public and private excitement, which his family largely shared, there was one gentle heart that uttered no loud complaint, but pined away in sad, heart-wearing anxiety, with scarce one gleam of hope to keep the life-current flowing. That one was the betrothed bride of Patrick Grace. And when at last the dreaded day came, and the unhappy culprit stood at the bar, in the pride of youth and manly beauty, firm and undaunted as though the shadow of the gibbet fell not athwart him, it was hard to look on him and believe him guilty of so heinous a crime, so cold blooded a murder. His 'sweetheart,' as they would say themselves, was not present, being kept away from the court by her friends almost by main force, and the fact of her being absent from the family group, whose presence his keen eye soon detected, was an inexpressible relief to the doomed prisoner, though the sight of her, as his heart whispered, would have been to him as dew to the parched flower. Yet he was glad—oh, how very glad !— that she was not there to see him a manacled felon at the bar, charged with a fearful crime which he well knew was about to be proved home against him. And it *was* proved home, and notwithstanding all the professional skill of the eminent lawyers engaged for the defence, and the audible sobs and groans and piteous entreaties for mercy, which all the exertions of the police could not silence in the body of the court, the awful sentence of death was pronounced on Patrick Grace, unanimously found guilty of the murder of Mr. Chadwick. Then the fiery spirit of revenge burst forth from the ashy lips of the yet undismayed prisoner, and he said, when permission was given him to speak, '*Before a twelvemonth passes I'll have revenge in my grave.*' Many a heart echoed those fatal words that day, and swore that so it should be. The sentence was that the prisoner should be hung by the neck till dead, on the very spot where his crime had been committed. And so they reared the dismal gibbet within sight of the grand old pile beneath whose ruined walls the royal O'Brien who raised it to the honour of God sleeps in peace, 'his warfare o'er,'—and much warfare did King Donald wage, for he was a man of might in his generation, and a thorn, moreover, in Strongbow's side. It was a strange scene,—the noble ruins and the sculptured tombs, and the forgotten graves of the dead of other years,—and the rich level fields heavy with the unreaped grain, and green in the freshness of Irish verdure,—and the seething, surging, heaving multitude topping ditches and walls and trees and every spot that could give a view of the doleful spectacle,—and high over all the dreadful apparatus that was to launch into eternity the pride of Tipperary peasants. The place immediately round the gallows was occupied by a large body of constabulary, their bayonets glittering in the sun, and their dark green uniform strongly contrasted with the many-hued frieze coats of the country-people in the crowd outside their serried circle. Much anxiety was felt amongst the people generally as to whether Grace would die penitent or impenitent; the good hoped the former; the bad, and especially his brethren of the secret society, the latter, for they would consider it a triumph for the enemy and an indelible disgrace to them if he 'gave in' at the last moment and 'didn't die like a man.' Fortunately for his own eternal welfare, young Grace had been brought to a sense of his condition before God, and when he appeared on the gallows with the priest by his side,—

While breathless silence chained the lips, and touched the hearts of all,—

he spoke in a clear, firm, manly voice, and expressed his heartfelt sorrow for the awful crime which he was now to expiate with his life, asking God's pardon, and the pardon of all good Christians, and, moreover, warning all who heard him to beware of the evil course which had brought him to that untimely and ignominious end. This was a stunning blow to his late associates, but to his nearest and dearest, and to all pious Christians, it was both joy and triumph—the triumph of religion over irreligion and impiety. But just as the young man ceased to speak, and the priest withdrew from the lapboard, one wild scream of heart-piercing anguish rose from the outskirts of the crowd, then a shriek of maniac laughter, and people were seen to carry away a fair young girl, whose wild gestures and wilder cries, mingled with strange fits of laughter, told too plainly that there, indeed, was 'a mind o'erthrown.' It is hardly necessary to say that this unhappy young creature was the affianced bride of Patrick Grace."

" But how did she come to be present at such a moment? Surely her friends might have anticipated such a result."

" It is probable that they did, my lord, for they had kept her at home under a close watch, but by some means she eluded their vigilance and arrived just at the fatal moment."

" And she is "—

" Mad Mabel. You may judge what her beauty must once have been when you see how much of it still remains."

" Poor thing!" said Lord Effingham in a tone of sincere

compassion,—"poor thing, what a hard fate is hers!—a young and a loving heart so early blighted!"

"It was very sad," sighed Mr. Goodchild,—"very sad indeed!" and he refreshed himself with a pinch of snuff.

"It was worse than sad," said Mrs. Pakenham, rising, "it was horrible; and I'm sure I don't know how you could sit to hear it out, my lord. I hope, Miss Markham, when you next undertake to tell us a story, it will be of a more entertaining kind. Now let us go to supper."

"But what about the promised revenge?" said the Earl to Harriet, as he gave his arm to the elder lady, who was looking her loftiest at the moment.

"That is a tale in itself, my lord; and one more tragical even than this. It would be the death of Mrs. Pakenham to hear it."

"Pray do not tell it, then," said the chaplain, as he offered his arm, with a very low bow, and they all proceeded to the supper-room.

CHAPTER XV.

MIDSUMMER-EVE ON THE ROCK OF CASHEL.

IT was Midsummer-eve, and the sun of the longest day had just sunk beneath the western horizon; star after star came out in the blue heavens above, and fire after fire dotted the broad plain below, as if a brighter reflection of the pale light shed down from the glorious canopy hung on high. These were the bonfires which on St. John's Eve make all Ireland glad and bright, the young uproarious in their harmless mirth as they danced in merry circles round "the bonfire," and the old sad amid the festal joys as they talk to each other of "Auld Lang Syne,"

And the summer days when they were young,

——young and blithe and light-hearted as those who have now taken their places around the Midsummer-eve fires, just as those Christian fires in honour of St. John, and symbolising the light of Christianity, have replaced the ancient "fires of Boal" lit on the same charmed eve on the hills and in the valleys of Ireland, where the sons and daughters of the land once reverenced in those "sacred fires" the image of their most potent god, even the great Bel.

Half sad, half gay was the chat wherewith our old friend Bryan Cullenan and his friend Shaun the piper beguiled the tranquil hour as they sat together under the shattered arch of what was once the grand portal of the cathedral. The noises of the old borough and of all the merry dancers at the fires round the base of the Rock came softened to the ears of the two old men, and the soothing influence of the hour brought that ineffable calm to their hearts which only the contented, trusting, simple Christian can experience here below. Earlier in the evening it had been Shaun's intention to visit some of the bonfires, with a lucrative object in view, but, as time wore on, and he and Bryan exchanged reminiscences of their boyish days, and of friends long dead, and joys long vanished, Shaun gave up the notion of going to the bonfires: "For," said he, "it wouldn't be worth my while, maybe, for all I'd make, to be trampin' round from one to another, an' that's what I'd have to do to make anything at all! So if I'd do *with* it, I'll do *without* it, an' any way I'm not badly off at the present time, thanks be to God Almighty! Now, only it 'id be drawin' them all about us from below, I'd give you a tune or two that 'id warm your poor ould heart."

"Oh, not here, Shaun agra, not here," said Bryan in a deprecating tone; "why, you don't know who'd be listenin' to you!" And he dropped his voice almost to a whisper, and cast a furtive glance around.

"An' what do *I* care who'd be listenin' to me?" said merry-hearted, fearless Shaun. "There isn't one buried on the Rock o' Cashel, I'll go bail, that wouldn't have a *gra* for the ould piper that never did man or mortial any harm, but makes pleasure an' innocent divarsion wherever he goes. You needn't be squeezin' my arm, now, Bryan; for I'm sure there never was priest or friar, or bishop aither, on Irish ground—barrin' them big buddaghs of English bishops, an' who cares about *them?*—that hadn't an ear an' a heart for the ould ancient music."

"Athen, Shaun, will you howld your whisht?" said Bryan in a low troubled voice. "I'll tell you, there's some o' them round us now! You're bringin' them out o' their graves with your foolish talk."

This staggered Shaun a little. "Wisha, Bryan," he whispered, "how do you know that? Do you see anything?" And he began rolling his sightless eyes around as though they too could penetrate the deep recesses of the ruins.

Bryan made no answer; his eyes, wide distended, were following a dark figure that had glided out from the farther end of the palace, across the little open space towards the south transept of the cathedral, close to which stands the pillar-tower. The old man held his breath to listen, but no sound could he distinguish within or around the buildings save the dull flapping of the bat's wing and the light breeze rustling in the ivy on the walls.

"Is there anything wrong wid you, Bryney?" whispered Shaun anxiously.

"Well—no," hesitated Bryan in the same low tone; "but, some way or another, Shaun, ever sence the poor young master came to his end in the way he did, I feel as if there was somethin' over me; an' there's times when I'm a little daunted to be out afther nightfall, barrin' I'm up here on the Rock."

"Wisha, Bryan, it isn't afeard of his ghost you'd be?" said Shaun in a tone of anxious inquiry that had fear at the bottom of it.

"No, it isn't himself I'd be so much afeard of seein' as his *murderer!*" The last word was whispered in Shaun's ear, and it made the piper shiver all over. "I think I'd never get over the sight of him now, for I seen him onst sence he done the deed, an' I wasn't the betther of it for many's the day afther."

"You seen him onst, Bryan?—no, but did you?"

"As plain as I see you now, an' as close to me, too, in a manner. Christ save us! what's that?" A cold, heavy hand was laid on the old man's shoulder, and, starting up, he saw a tall dark figure close by his side, the eyes looking down on him from under a cap or hat that seemed to his excited fancy of wonderful shape, and one, moreover, that "would fit Finn MacCoul,"—at least, so thought Bryan. It was, or appeared to be, precisely the same figure that had glided through the evening shadows a little before, and, moreover, if Bryan were not much mistaken, he had seen it, or something like it, more than once of late flitting far off behind the pillars, or under the arches, when the night shadows began to fall, or the moon's pale ray lay cold and ghastly on the place of death.

"In the name o' God what are you?" said Bryan, starting up from under the stony hand, every hair on his head beginning to stand on end. "Spake, I command you, in the name o' the Father, Son, and Holy Ghost."

Instead of answering, the figure glided away as noiselessly as it came; but Bryan, anxious for the honour of the Rock, where a ghost had never crossed his path till these latter days, and determined to sift the matter to the bottom, so as to ascertain what manner of spirit it was that made bold to show itself in that holy place, hastened after the apparition with all the speed he could make.

"For God's sake, Bryan, who are you talkin' to?" cried Shaun, forgetting his caution in his increasing apprehensions. "Bryney, I say, Bryney!" raising his voice still higher; "athen, why don't you answer me?" All was silent, and, as the echo of his own voice died away amongst the ruins, a chilling sense of loneliness fell like a pall on Shaun's heart and mind. "I vow to God he's gone!" said he, after feeling with his hand in the place where he knew Bryan had been sitting; "it's a trick he's playin' on me, an' nothing else. Wisha, who'd think Bryney the Rock had so much fun in him? Well, he can't frighten me, that's one comfort, an' to let him see that, I'll give him a tune—it'll pass the time bravely, an' keep up one's heart a bit till my ould chap comes back, for afther all it is a lonesome place, an' that's God's truth. Here goes, now."

And so saying, Shaun blew his chanter, and struck up "The Dusty Miller" with a hearty goodwill, and a lusty vigour that brought out the merriest tones in his bag, and made his own heart as light as a feather.

"I'm thinkin' that'll chase the ghosts, anyhow," quoth Shaun, warming more and more at the exhilarating sound of his own music. "Now we'll give them 'Haste to the Wedding!'" and no sooner said than done. "Well, it's a folly to talk," said he, "there's a power o' fun in these same ould pipes o' mine. Hoogh! Shaun, your sowl! it's a pity you'd ever die!"

His music and his self-laudation came to an end together, when Bryan rushed up breathless, and, seizing the chanter with no gentle hand, pulled it from between his fingers, saying, "Are you mad, Shaun? or what's comin' over you, at all, to go playin' up your jigs an' reels among the dead on the Rock o Cashel! Didn't I tell you not to do it?"

"You did, an' then you goes off wid yourself an' laves me here all alone wid my pipes, an' sure, what could I do but make them spake to keep me company? If I done any harm, it's you's to blame. I didn't expect you to do the like, Bryan Cullenan, an' you my sister Mary's sponsor, God rest her sow. in glory—och, Am-en this night!"

"I couldn't help it, Shaun," said Bryan, his voice trembling with some new and strange emotion.

"You couldn't help it?—athen, how is that, Bryney?" said Shaun in his natural tone of easy good-humour; anger or vexation was but a ripple on the surface of his tranquil mind. "An' now I think of it, didn't I hear you talkin' to some one there a while ago?"

"In coorse you did," said Bryan as composedly as he could; "an' if you were anywhere convaynient, many's the time you'd hear me talkin' when there's ne'er a one but myself."

"I know that," replied Shaun; "but there's two ways of talkin', an' more, too, if it goes to that. Come now, Bryan, tell the truth, didn't you see or hear something that time?"

"Wisha, the ne'er a thing worse than myself," returned Bryan evasively; "maybe it was them weary bats I was talkin' to, for they do be flyin' about me here in the dusk when I'm at my night-prayers, or maybe sittin' thinkin' of one thing or another—sometimes they'll come flappin' their wings in my very face, the mischievous craythurs, that you'd think it was makin' game o' me they wor. But hadn't we best be gettin' down off the Rock, Shaun agra? It must be gettin' late, for I see most o' the fires are dyin' out."

Shaun assented in a tone of abstraction very unusual with him. He was not satisfied with Bryan's explanation, and wondered much that his old friend would have any reserve with him. "Howsomever," said he to himself as the two descended the steep road from the old palace to the gate, "it's like he does it for the best—maybe it's afeard of scarin' me he is, on account o' me bein' out so often afther nightfall." The bare supposition was more than sufficient to clear Shaun's sunny old brow of the light cloud that had settled on it, and so! Richard was himself again.

"In coorse you'll come home with me," said Bryan, as having locked the gate, he took hold of Shaun's arm.

"No, no," cried Shaun hastily; "I'm obleeged to you all the same, Bryan, but I'd sooner go somewhere else."

"Why, then, what's that for?"

"Och," replied Shaun evasively, "sure, I know you haven't any room to spare."

"There's room enough for you, anyhow," said Bryan somewhat testily; "but if you don't want to come, you can't say but you were asked."

Now Shaun had a reason for declining the offer which he could not, or would not, tell Bryan, yet he felt that some reason he ought to give, and he was casting about in his simple mind what he had best say. All at once a voice spoke near him, almost at his elbow.

"I thought you weren't comin' down the night—it's a wondher you did, aither."

Shaun uttered an exclamation of terror, and came near dropping his pipes in his fright.

"Why, Shaun, what ails you, man?" said Bryan soothingly. "Sure, it's only poor Cauth that came up the road to see if I was comin'."

"I know—I know," stammered Shaun, gasping for breath, "but it took a start out o' me to meet *her* in this lonesome place—I mane—I mane—to meet any one at all of a suddent that way." The shudder that was creeping through Shaun's sturdy frame was not lost on either of his hearers.

A kind of nondescript sound, neither laugh nor cry, but something between the two, was heard to escape from Cauth's lips, and, drawing closer around her the skirt of her drugget gown which she had turned up over her head, she muttered some unintelligible words, and hurried away towards the cottage.

"Is she gone?" whispered Shaun.

"She is, avick; but what in the world come over you that time?—sure, it isn't afeard o' Cauth you'd be?"

"Well, I dunna how it is, Bryan; of coorse I'm not afeard of anybody, leastways her, but then it's aisy takin' a start out of a poor dark crathur like me."

"But where are you goin' to lodge the night?" inquired Bryan, himself no little disturbed by what had passed.

"At Johnny Farrell's there below, if you land me to the door, for God's sake."

"It's myself 'ill do that, Shaun, if you didn't ask me at all," said Bryan, and they walked on in silence for some five minutes, when he spoke again: "Shaun," said he, "there's something about Cauth that's mighty quare: *you* know more about her than *I* do—I see that—an' I'd be very thankful to you if you'd tell me what and who she is."

"It wouldn't do you any good if I did," replied Shaun quickly. "But I'll tell you what I'll do," and he laughed good-humouredly; "I will tell you what I know about Cauth if you'll tell me what you seen and heard this night on the Rock above?"

"Well," said Bryan evasively, "sure, I seen, for one thing, the best hand at 'The Swaggerin' Jig' in all Tipperary, an' the pipes he has that can't be bate any more than himself; an' as for hearin', why, upon my credit, Shaun, I heard what I never expected to hear on the Rock o' Cashel if I lived to the age of Mathusalem,—an' what no one ever heard there before, *I'll go bail,*—that's 'Bobbin' Joan' an' 'Haste to the Wedding.' I'll warrant you, it 'ill be all over the town the morrow that music was heard on the Rock the night, an' they'll be all full sure it was nothing earthly that was in it."

"An' there was *something* there that wasn't earthly," put in Shaun. "Now, wasn't there, Bryney?—yis or no, like a man!"

"Well, not that *I* seen or heard."

"Bryney," said Shaun, lowering his voice to a whisper, "take care, now, what you say—did you, or did you not, see young Mr. Esmond's ghost?"

"Mr. Esmond's ghost?" said Bryan, with a start; "why, what in the world put that in your head?"

"Well, but *did* you see him?"

"Did *you* see him?" retorted Bryan. "Now, you seen him jist as much as I did, an' that's God's own truth. Here we're at Johnny Farrell's now—but stop a minnit, Shaun!—now 'on't you tell me afore we part what you know about Cauth? I declare I'm beginnin' to be a little daunted myself on account of the quare ways she has. Maybe it isn't safe to have her in the house—eh, Shaun?"

"Pooh, pooh, Bryan! don't be makin' a fool of yourself—she'll not hurt *you!*"

"But did she ever hurt *any one?*"

"Wisha, Bryney the Rock, you foolish ould man, you! do you think it's *murdher* any one she'd do? Not but what there's people that does worse"—

"Worse than murdher, Shaun? Why, what worse *could* they do?"

"Many a thing, Bryan—many a thing; though God forbid

I'd ever be the man to make light of *murther*, still I say there's as bad things done—ay, and worse, that there's no law for, aither! God be with you, Bryan, an' I wish you may never die, or nobody kill you, till you catch me again, afther dark, on the Rock o' Cashel!"

When Bryan entered his own cottage, he found his frugal supper awaiting his coming, consisting of some few potatoes, kept hot in the skillet beside the brush-fire, and a noggin of fresh buttermilk standing on the little table. Cauth was sitting on her "creepy," both her hands tightly clasped around her knees and her eyes fixed in moody thought on the faintly-flickering blaze emitted by the crackling brambles on the hearth. As Bryan entered, she broke into a somewhat angry apostrophe addressed to a harmless cricket who was warbling his merry solo in some crevice about the hearth.

"Wisha, weary on you for a one cricket! it's aisy seen you have little to trouble you, or you wouldn't be ever an' always deovin' my ears wid that sharp voice o' yours that goes through my very head!"

"Athen, Cauth," said Bryan, as he took his seat at the table, and, blessing himself, began his supper, "what harm does the poor cricket do you?—it's often I'd wish there was a cricket near me on the Rock above. I think it's great company to hear the weeny crathurs singin' their little song, divartin' themselves down among the ashes."

"Humph!" said Cauth, "I wouldn't doubt you. But never mind the cricket now—I've news for you the night."

"You have, now?—and what is it, aroon?"

"The young mistress was here the day, an' she wants me to go up the morrow to the big house, an' blamed me for not goin' this while back."

"Wisha, Cauth, are you in earnest?" said Bryan, laying down his noggin, his mouth and eyes wide open to catch the answer.

"Arrah, maybe it's jokin' I am!" said Cauth, with bitter irony. "I tell you she was here, an' that's all about it. But och, och! it's the sore change that's in her since I seen her last—she looks twenty years older, you'd think,—an' sure, sure, that's no wondher—didn't myself grow twenty—ay, thirty years older in one week?—oyeh! it's me knows what heavy grief can do!" and she shook her head drearily, her gaze still on the fire, or rather on vacancy.

"An' dear knows but *hers* was a heavy grief, Cauth. But wouldn't it be a quare thing, now, if there was them above ground that has as sore a heart about that same murder as she has, God bless her for ever!"

Cauth started from her reverie and gave Bryan a look that, as he afterwards said, "was as good as a *process*"—(a law term this, non-Irish reader?) "Well, Bryan, you do bate all, sometimes, wid the foolish words you say!—now, *who* could have as sore a heart for the loss of *him* as his own darlin' wife, that was the flower o' the world wid *him*, an' him the same wid her? Hut, tut, man! let nobody ever hear you say the likes o' that again! It's aisy seen you have no *gumption* in you, anyhow, or you *wouldn't* say it."

"Wull, now, see here, Cauth," said the old man meekly, "I know one that went to Lough Diar-og for the good of *his* sowl not many weeks ago, an' them not a drop's blood to him, aither. Now, what do you think o' that?"

"Wisha, what *could* I think, barrin' that them that did it must have had a great wish entirely for the poor master? Now, if it was one of his own a body wouldn't wondher, but a stranger to do it was past the common altogether. The Lord reward them, whoever they wor that done it, for sure it must be some holy pilgrim or another—maybe Barney Byrne?"

"No, it wasn't. Guess again."

"Well, maybe it was Susy Rooney?"

"No, it wasn't any pilgrim at all, but"—

"But who?"

"Why, *Jerry Pierce!*" and he lowered his voice to the lowest pitch.

"Jerry Pierce?" repeated Cauth, jumping fairly from her seat, and in so doing upsetting the skillet, whereupon the few potatoes remaining in it ran helter-skelter over the floor in all directions,—"Jerry Pierce?" and she crossed herself as Bryan had never seen her do before. "How dare you mention his name to me, the curse-o'-God villain? Him to go to the Island! I wondher he wasn't afeard o' bein' swallowed up in the lake! —sure, I'd be there many's the day ago myself, only for fear of vexin' the Lord more an' more, goin' among good Christians in that blessed an' holy place, where the best that goes has to walk barefoot all the time they're in it."

"Well, be that as it may, Cauth, what I tell you's true—with all the watch that's on him, that same man made his way to Lough Diarog,[1] with the intention I tould you."

"An' how did *you* know that?" asked Cauth sharply. "Did you see him?"

"It's no matter whether I did or not,—if I didn't see himself, I seen them that did."

"Bryan Cullenan," said the woman, her eyes flashing with a strange and lurid light, "you're not the man I took you for, or it isn't colloguin' you'd be with Mr. Esmond's murderer! I thought, if it was true to you, there was no one worse agin him than yourself. I vow to God, if I could only get wind of where he's to be found, I'd go myself an' give information to the magisthrates, though I wouldn't take a penny of the reward, but jist to put *him* in the way of gettin' what he desarves. Hangin' would be too good for the villain, an' I'd be glad to see him strung up like a dog the night before the morrow!"

"I wouldn't doubt you," said a deep voice from outside, speaking through a chink of the frail door,—"I wouldn't doubt you, *Kate Costelloe!* You're an old hand at that business,—but *you'll not hang Jerry Pierce!*"

The turbulent spirit of the dame was fairly overcome by this mysterious salutation; she sank breathless on a seat. Bryan lost not a moment in opening the door, muttering to himself as he did so, "Well, if *he's* a livin' man this night, that's his voice." Whoever it was, there was no one to be seen outside, though the moonlight was shining full on the road, revealing in all the distinctness of "garish day" the jagged outlines of the great Rock, the wall, and the overhanging ruins.

"He's not there, anyhow," said Bryan, coming back and addressing the old woman, who had by that time recovered her momentary faintness; "but whoever he was, he seems to know *you.*"

"He does," she replied doggedly.

"And is it thrue, then, that you're"—

[1] This is the way in which the word *Derg* in this name is always pronounced by the peasantry.

"Kate Costelloe!" she said, with a look and tone, as it were, of defiance.

Bryan was silent for a few moments, during which he sat looking thoughtfully down on the clay floor, the woman watching him with a sort of lynx-like scrutiny. At last he spoke, but without raising his eyes: "Why didn't you tell me before who you wor?"

"Don't you hear it time enough?"

"Well, that's true, but still"—

"But still you'd rayther have known before that you had Kate Costelloe on your flure? Well, that's a droll thing, too, for I thought there wasn't man or woman in Tipperary that 'id care to have my four bones undher the roof wid them."

This she said in a tone of bitter mockery, but all at once her sharp features assumed a softer expression, her pale lips quivered with a tremulous motion, and she said, as if to herself—

"An' sure, what wondher is it? I am a fearsome thing, an' there's no one more afeard o' me than I am myself—och, och!" And, laying her hands one over the other on her heart, she groaned heavily, "Och, och! but it 'id be the aise to me if this weary heart 'id break at onst; but it 'on't do that, for it's as hard as a stone—ha! ha!" and how dreary was her laugh, "sure, I needn't tell anybody that, for the world knows if I hadn't a hard, hard heart I'd never a' done what I did."

"Well, well, Cauth—or Kate, or whatsomever you are."

"Call me Cauth still, for fear of any one hearin' the other name—an' besides, I don't want to hear it myself—oh no, no!" she added, with sudden wildness, "anything but that—anything in the world wide but the one *they* used to call me." She covered her face with her hands and lapsed into stolid silence.

"Well, Cauth," began Bryan again after a long pause, "I know there's many a one wouldn't wish to have you next or nigh them, but—but "—he drew a long breath—"I see you're sorry for what you done, an'—an'—I'll not be hardar on a fellow-crathur than God Almighty is. But what brought you here at all?"

"Ay, that's the question," said Cauth, raising her face from between her hands, her eyes again flashing that angry fire. "You want to know what brought me here? I'll jist tell you then: I couldn't stay where I was, an' the people all knowin me, an' where I'd have a chance of seein' the ould man pinin' away, lonely an' lonesome, wid the staff gone from his ould age,—an' knowin' who took it—knowin' who took it !—ochone, ochone! wouldn't I thravel on my knees to Africa to get out of his way, an' to hide myself where nobody 'id know me?"

"And that's why you came to Cashel all the way?"

"An' what else 'id bring me? I thought that nobody 'id know me here, but I see I was mistaken—an' sure, I might ha' known that I couldn't hide myself,—no matter where I'd go I'd be found out, an' the shame taken out o' me. O Lord! O Lord! is there no place where the sinner can be at rest? Ay, there's one place—*one place*," she added solemnly,—" one place where the broken heart is at rest, an' shame an' grief an' trouble are never felt any more—that place is the grave—the quiet grave under the green sod; but sure, we must wait for that rest till God plases—we can't cut short the life that God gave us; no matter how miserable it is, we must live it out till our time comes!—an' *we will, too,*—we'll fight the battle out, come what will, an' bear the burthen to the last." There was a hectic flush on her cheek and a bright light in her eyes as she raised them to heaven, and Bryan thought as he watched her that the very features changed before him, and the face was not that of old Cauth, but another and a fairer. It was the strong spirit of faith that shone there triumphant over despair.

"Cauth," said Bryan, "don't fear that you'll ever want a home while *I* have one; it's a poor one, to be sure, but you're as welcome in it as the flowers of May."

"An' you'll promise me that you'll never tell who I am— unless I give you lave?"

"I will, Cauth. There's my hand on it."

"God bless you, Bryan—God bless you!" said Cauth, with touching fervour; "it's a comfort to know that there's one creature on the earth that doesn't hate poor Kate Costellos."

Here a loud, sharp knocking at the door cut short any further conversation. Cauth started up, alarmed; but Bryan, calm as ever, telling her not to be afraid, went toward the door and asked who was there.

"It's me—don't be botherin' me with your questions, but let me in."

The voice was that of a female, and Bryan opened the door without further parley. An aged crone hobbled in, and it was with no very pleasant feeling that Bryan discovered under the hood of her red cloak the fairy-woman. By an involuntary movement Cauth retreated, as she thought, out of sight, into a dark corner. Not unseen she went, however, for the uncouth visitor, striking her stick on the ground, called out in a tone of the sternest authority, "Come out here, Kate Costelloe, an' put some milk in this can for me. Come out, I say; where's the use o' you hidin' from me?"

The woman came forth at a snail's pace, and took the tin vessel which the other held out, trembling the while like an aspen leaf. "Well, I'll give you all I have," she faltered out, "but that isn't much. There it is, now, an' much good may it do you."

"I don't want it to do me good," was the sharp reply; "it isn't for me it is, at all, but for Tim Murtha, that's down with the faver."

"Tim Murtha!" cried Bryan. "The Lord save us, honest woman, is it in earnest you are?"

"If you come up to my fine elegant house on Gallows Hill above, you'll soon see whether I'm jokin' or not. I tell you the man took bad this mornin' from the fair dint o' hunger an' misery—not but that he'd ha' got enough to keep life in himself and the childer, but somehow he couldn't bring himself to go out and ask it, barrin' of an odd time afther night, and though I was willin' to share the last bit I had wid him an' the poor motherless childer he has, all I could get wasn't enough to give four of us a mole a day, so it's starvin' we all wor, for Tim wouldn't let me go ask the good bit an' sup where I knew I'd get plenty if I went."

"An' is he very bad?" said Bryan anxiously.

"Not as bad as he will be, but he's bad enough, an' it's my opinion he will never stand on green grass,—but I must hurry back with the milk to make whey for him. My blessin' an' the blessin' o' God be in the place o' what you gave me."

And away she stumped with her knotty stick, leaving Bryan and Cauth full of compassion for the misfortunes of poor Tim Murtha.

CHAPTER XVI.

SUNSET ON THE ROCK, AND PHIL MORAN'S STORY.

The first July sun was sinking behind the western rim of the mountains that gird the Golden Vale, when the Effingham carriage was again in waiting at the foot of the Rock of Cashel, whilst a liveried groom led a handsome saddle-horse to and fro, the noble animal nowise content, it would seem, with the restraint imposed on his light and agile limbs. On the Rock above, the Earl, Mrs. Pakenham, Miss Markham and the children, with a widowed sister of Lord Effingham, recently arrived from England, were listening with more or less attention to some of Bryan's old-world legends. It was partly to show the antiquities on the Rock to Lady Pemberton, the Earl's sister, that the party were there on that occasion, and partly because Lord Effingham wished to pay the place another visit before he left for England, which he proposed doing in a few days. It so happened that, whilst Bryan was entertaining the party with his curious descriptions and quaint reminiscences of persons and things, another party came to claim his services as guide, and in the new-comers Harriet recognised with pleasure the two Mrs. Esmonds, Mary Hennessy, and Bella Le Poer, with Uncle Harry and Attorney Moran as escort. Miss Markham at once excused herself to her own party, and joined the others in their exploration of the ruins, which she soon understood was proposed at this particular time for the special benefit of young Mrs. Esmond, with a view to divert her thoughts even for a while from the dreary circle to which they were now so long circumscribed.

"Bryan," said Miss Markham, smiling, "you can continue to give your undivided attention to Lord Effingham and the ladies—I will endeavour to supply your place to that party just arrived, who are my particular friends."

"But who are they, Miss Markham?" inquired Bryan anxiously, as he put up his hand to shade his failing eyes from the slanting beams of the fervid sun.

"Oh, it's the Esmonds, Bryan, and Miss Hennessy and Miss Le Poer, and Mr. Moran. You know some of them know the Rock almost as well as yourself, so between us we shall manage to do the honours to those who are not so familiar with the ruins."

So saying, away she went, and after her tripped the two little girls, never so happy as in her company.

For some time the two parties moved in different directions over the Rock, but in the Hall of the Minstrels in the old palace they chanced to meet, and as Lord Effingham was already acquainted with Miss Hennessy and Miss Le Poer,—the latter of whom he took care to present to his sister and Mrs. Pakenham as a cousin of Lady Blessington,—a general introduction followed, and the interchange of courteous but distant civilities being duly gone through, the company proceeded together to examine what yet remained to be seen, forming themselves naturally into such groups as taste or sympathy dictated. For some time the Earl, with Lady Pemberton on one arm and Mrs. Pakenham on the other, accompanied Mr. Esmond, leaving the other ladies to the frank good offices of Phil Moran, who, for some cause probably known to himself, was in extra good-humour that evening, and more than ever disposed to make himself generally agreeable. Finding that Mr. Esmond, with all his first show of *brusquerie*, was really a gentleman and a man of some parts, not by any means unacquainted with the ways of *their* world, the two stately dowagers began after a while to unbend somewhat in his regard, and at length condescended to accept his careless invitation to go back and look at some of the sculptures in Cormac's Chapel which seemed to have escaped their aristocratic attention.

By some chance Harriet found herself alone, gazing with delight on the glorious expanse of country that stretched around and beneath her. Eastward, gently sloping from the town upwards, lay Gallows Hill, and Summer Hill, and green

Killough, while farther to the east rose the lordly Slievenamon, and beyond it, closing in the far perspective, the undulating and softly rounded hills of Kilkenny reposed in their summer freshness, tinged with the faint flush of the warm sunset. Far to the north lay the Slievebloom Mountains, and nearer the shaggy outlines of the Devil's Bit Hills, their wild valleys resting in shade; from these the eye passed on to the Keeper Mountains, which look down on Limerick vales, and thence wandered afar to the Clare highlands beyond the upper Shannon; westward the lofty hills that cross the country from the Lower Shannon stretched away north to King's County, and as if springing from them in the far south the Castle Oliver Mountains, with the magnificent Galtees standing in front of them on the great champaign country nearer to the Rock of Cashel. Dim and far were some of these mountain ranges, yet in the clear atmosphere of this summer eve, with the rich rays shining down on them, their outlines were clearly visible to Harriet's practised eye. Nearer, in a southerly direction, and more distinctly revealed, were portions of the Knockmeledown and the Monavoilagh mountains, and then back to the base of the Rock the admiring gaze wandered over the luxuriant plains of Tipperary, with all their wealth of wood and water, fruit and blossom, dotted with towns and hamlets, with here and there spacious demesnes encircling lordly mansions, such as Effingham Castle and the picturesque dwellings of the gentry. And bright through these lovely scenes wandered the silvery Suir, winding its way to the distant ocean. It was but a moment and the eye took in all this wondrous panorama of richest bloom and stateliest grandeur and most luxuriant beauty, and a pensive shade stole over Harriet's thoughtful face as she prepared to rejoin her companions. She was arrested by Lord Effingham's voice speaking near her, so near that she started, seeing which the Earl smiled, though his smile was scarce perceptible.

"What a scene for a painter's eye!" said he, glancing over the splendid panorama.

"It is, indeed, my lord, a fair scene for painter or for poet," Harriet replied; "yet I was just thinking of what an Irish poet has sung of the mournful associations that sadden our loveliest scenes," and she repeated that verse of Moore's—

> "Then if, while scenes so grand,
> So beautiful, shine before thee,
> Pride for thine own dear land
> Should haply be stealing o'er thee,
> Oh, let grief come first,
> O'er pride itself victorious—
> Thinking how man hath cursed
> What God has made so glorious."

"Truly it is a fair land," said the Earl thoughtfully, "and a fertile land too,—strange that misery should be the lot of multitudes of its people."

"To you, Lord Effingham," said Harriet, with an earnestness of look and tone that surprised her auditor,—"to *you*, I should think the causes, or rather the cause, of this so strange anomaly *might* be plainly manifest; but"—she blushed, smiled at her own thought, and said in a tone of assumed levity—"but here I am talking in a way that must give your lordship a poor opinion of my modesty—to say the least of it. But the truth is, my lord, that I *am* somewhat of an enthusiast in my love of this native land of mine, once so great, now so fallen—so rich in memories, so rare in beauty, so pitiable in misfortune."

"I can understand your enthusiasm," said Lord Effingham; "perhaps were I, like you, of Irish birth and Irish *breeding*, I might feel somewhat as you do."

Harriet was silent a moment; but, as though feeling the silence awkward, she hastily resumed, in a somewhat subdued tone—

"There, in the vale below us, is Hore Abbey, once a famous Dominican establishment, and a dependency of the great Abbey of Cashel, the two houses being connected, it is said, by a subterraneous passage; some miles beyond lies Holy Cross, perhaps one of the most beautiful ecclesiastical ruins in the empire, built by Donogh O'Brien, the warlike King of Munster, for monks of the Cistercian order; and beyond that again, away to the northward, on the confines of the King's County, lies storied Toomavara, where of old the Knights Templars had a preceptory, the ruins of which are now barely visible. Alas! the soil of Ireland is covered,

> From the centre all round to the sea,

with remains of ancient greatness, attesting her historic fame."

Lord Effingham's answer, whatever it might have been, was prevented by the approach of Mr. Esmond and the elder ladies, obsequiously followed by Bryan.

"We were looking for you, Effingham," said Lady Pemberton in her cold, listless tone.

"But Lord Effingham was not looking for us," pointedly said the Honourable Mrs. Pakenham.

"Certainly not, Mrs. Thomasine Pakenham," said the Earl very composedly. "I was well entertained by Miss Markham's account of the antiquities scattered over the wide plain before us. And I was about to observe, when you came up, what a pity it is that this fine county of Tipperary, with all its beauty and fertility, and wealth of old renown, should yet rest under the black cloud of murder and assassination."

"Very true, my lord, very true," cordially assented Mr. Esmond.

"And poverty, my lord," subjoined Moran, who had just come up with his party in time to hear the Earl's observation. "Mr. Esmond can tell you that the greatest plague of Tipperary is beggarmen—tall strapping fellows who patrol the country by night and by day with bag on back and murderous designs in heart."

"Pshaw! nonsense!" said Mr. Esmond. "Don't mind Moran, my lord; he is always midway between jest and earnest."

"Well, but you won't pretend to deny, will you, that you have been waging a sort of crusade against the men of the bag and staff ever since a memorable night when one of them—saved your life?"

"And another wanted to take it. Well, I don't deny it Phil—I mean Mr. Moran; you know I never deny the truth But with all my crusade, as you call it, and the active exertion of the entire magistracy of the county, we have never been able to catch that atrocious criminal, Jerry Pierce."

"No, but you caught a brace of beggarmen, and committed them as vagrants—that was doing something *pro bono publico*."

Lord Effingham, who had been listening attentively to this characteristic dialogue, now asked Mr. Esmond how it happened that the murderer of his nephew had so long eluded the pursuit of the law. As he spoke, his eye fell on old Bryan, who had thrust his face amongst the group with a look of intense anxiety on his shrivelled features. After satisfying himself that his niece was not within hearing,—a fact which Lord Effingham had ascertained before putting the question,—

"Oh, that's easily understood, my lord," replied Uncle Harry; "it's all owing to the d———d conspiracy—I beg your pardon, ladies—that exists amongst the peasantry. A conspiracy for purposes of assassination, and also for purposes of concealment. See how things went at the time of Mr. Chadwick's murder."

"Yet there was found a man, one of themselves," said Moran, "to give honest testimony against the murderer at all risks to himself."

"Humph! and see what came of it! Hadn't Philip Mara to be sent out of the country after the trial?—and you know yourself, Phil Moran, how it ended with his family."

"*Apropos* to Philip Mara," said Lord Effingham, "Miss Markham some weeks since gave us an interesting account of that tragical affair in which he played so prominent a part, but she intimated, if I remember right, that the tragedy did not end with the execution of the unhappy Grace."

The three young ladies were at this time exploring with Mrs. Esmond amongst the ruins. A shade fell on Moran's face as he replied—

"Alas! yes, my lord, that was but the second act in a bloody four-act tragedy, the effects of which are still felt in the country like the last throes of an earthquake. The first act was the murder of Chadwick—the second, the hanging of Grace."

"And the others?"

"It would, perhaps, trespass too much on your lordship's patience were I to tell."

"I should like to hear it," said the Earl, "if Mrs. Pakenham and you, Caroline,"—to his sister,—"have no objection."

"Certainly *I* have none," said Lady Pemberton, with a sort of incipient attempt at animation; "I should like, of all things, to hear an Irish story."

"And when you *have* heard it, my lady, you'll never want to hear another Irish story, I can tell you that," said Mr. Esmond, as he walked away to join the younger ladies.

"Is the gentleman angry?" said Lady Pemberton, looking after him with a look of languid surprise.

"Not at all, madam," said Moran very gravely; "on the contrary, he is particularly amiable just now." The court lady raised her eyebrows—perhaps shrugged her shoulders a very little à la Française, and, seating herself on a prostrate pillar, prepared to listen to the "Irish story," to which Mrs. Pakenham could not in politeness object, so she took a seat beside her cousin.

"The story is not long," said Moran, "otherwise I would not consent to inflict it on this company," and he bowed slightly, "under these circumstances. But, to commence my story where I infer from what your lordship said that Miss Markham ended hers, at the execution, namely, of young Grace :- the feeling of execration wherewith Mara, the informer, as they called him, was regarded by the great majority of the country-people can be best understood by the fearful revenge planned and executed under the auspices of the same dangerous association which had authorised the death of the unfortunate Mr. Chadwick. Enraged that Philip Mara had been sent by the Government beyond seas, where their power could not reach him, they resolved that he should still suffer in his nearest and dearest, and swore a terrible revenge against his three brothers, who were all, like himself, masons by trade, and, moreover, engaged as he had been in the erection of the fatal barracks at Rath Cannon. Quietly and sternly did these dark conspirators proceed to the execution of their fell purpose. The Maras were all decent, respectable men, and men, moreover, who, being under the saving influence of religion, kept themselves carefully aloof from the demoralising influence of the secret organisation, which like a mighty serpent had wound itself round and over the bone and sinew of the country, the stalwart labouring classes, crushing within them every higher and nobler instinct, and changing with its poisonous breath the best feelings of their nature into bitterness and gall. United they were amongst themselves, as all Christian families—and, indeed, most *Irish* families—ever are, and were always happiest when together; so it was that the three brothers, with a young apprentice of theirs, were returning from their work one fine evening in the early autumn, little thinking of the doom that was impending over them, when, from a place of concealment where the gang had lain in wait since early morning, eight well-armed men darted on them. Quick as lightning the Maras fled, and from their perfect knowledge of the neighbourhood two of them managed to escape the murderous attack, as did also the apprentice; the third brother, Daniel, frightened and bewildered, instead of trusting to his heels and his ingenuity, like his brothers, took refuge in the house of a widow close by, and the murderers, forcing their way after him, killed him without remorse or pity, laughing to scorn his piteous entreaties. It may be that the delay occasioned by the murder of the unfortunate Daniel facilitated the escape of his two brothers, who succeeded in getting away from the country."

"What an awful state of affairs!" said Lord Effingham; while the ladies held up their hands and averted their heads in horror. Still, they wished to "hear it out," especially Lady Pemberton.

"You may well believe," resumed Moran, "that the news of this barbarous murder, even less justifiable than that of Mr. Chadwick, because wholly unprovoked on the part of the victim, threw the whole country into a state of the most violent excitement; proclamations were issued, offering rewards, —even a sum of two thousand pounds was offered for any information that might lead to the apprehension and conviction of the murderers,—still, no one came forward to claim the reward."—

"Why, that is precisely the case now with regard to the murder of Mr. Esmond," said Lord Effingham, with some sternness. "You say no tangible evidence has yet been obtained to throw light on that revolting crime, and, for aught we know, the murderer may be prowling round the neighbourhood in wait for some other opportunity of popping a landlord. I see plainly that the people do connive with these wretched criminals, and make common cause with them; how could they, otherwise, elude the vigilance of the police, and baffle the power of the law?"

"In the case of Mara, my lord, the non-detection of the criminals for so long a time is easily accounted for, as the misguided people made it a point of honour to conceal those whom they looked upon as the champions of the people's cause and the ministers of popular justice; but as regards the murder of Mr. Esmond the case is widely different, and I know the perpetrator of that crime is as much abhorred by the peasantry as by any class in the community. The feeling against him is strong and universal, and I can nohow account for the delay in his apprehension, except it be that he has managed to leave the country. Now, however, that the Solicitor-General has come down to investigate the affair, something may be done to bring the assassin to justice, if he be still within reach of its arm."

The sun was just setting, and his last rays fell at the moment on the mullioned window of the cathedral, where a man's face was distinctly visible to the Earl and Mr. Moran, shaded by the peak of a cap, yet still broadly marked with an expression of mingled cunning and drollery that would have delighted Hogarth. The vision was but momentary, and the exclamation that hovered on the lips of the two who alone saw it was suppressed by a mutual glance of admonition. The Earl was surprised—the attorney more than surprised ; but, fearing the effect on the ladies, they made no remark, and Moran resumed his story, just as Mr. Esmond and the ladies made their appearance once more, attended by Bryan.

"There is no knowing," said Moran, "how long the murderers might have escaped were it not that a young fellow named Fitzgerald, a well-known leader of 'the boys,' being taken up for highway robbery, in order to save his life, forfeited to the law, turned State's evidence, and gave such information relative to the murder of Daniel Mara—in which, it appeared, he had been a principal actor—that several persons were at once arrested, either as principals or accessaries to that awful deed. The first brought to trial were two men named Walsh and Lacy, the latter a remarkably handsome and intelligent young man, well dressed and altogether respectable in appearance, with nothing in his aspect to indicate the evil qualities that had led him to the commission of such a crime. The case, as stated for the Crown by the Solicitor-General, disclosed some facts that evidently startled the prisoners. It was shown that these men, with some others, had been brought from a distance, by the friends and relatives of Grace, to do the deed, and that it was to have been done a week earlier, but for some cause which kept the unconscious Maras at home from their work that day, and thus compelled their assassins to await their opportunity for some days longer. It appeared that, on the following Sunday, the entire band of conspirators met at the house of a farmer named Jack Keogh, in the immediate vicinity of the barracks, and were there hospitably entertained, a female relative of Keogh's, who was also his housekeeper, waiting on them at table. Early next day they all proceeded to a woody hill called 'The Grove,' which overlooked the new barracks, and where arms had been secreted ready for use. Whilst lying there, waiting for the time when the doomed brothers would leave off work, refreshments were brought them by the same woman who had waited on them the previous day at Jack Keogh's. Now, amongst the party secreted there with such murderous intent were the two sons of Keogh, both of them fine young men in the bloom of life, the prop and stay of their old father and the pride of his heart. One of them in particular, John, the elder of the two, was a man of powerful frame and unusually tall stature, with a placid, good-natured look and comely, well-formed features. Though not so neat or trim as his brother, who was of much smaller proportions, John Keogh was a man to be signalled out in a fair or market as a fine specimen

> Of that bold peasantry—a nation's pride,
> Which, once destroyed, can never be supplied.

Well, these two brothers had been arrested, with many others, for the murder of Daniel Mara, and the main point now was to procure sufficient evidence to convict them all. It is true Fitzgerald swore quite enough to hang them, and another of the band, named Ryan, had also turned King's evidence, but both being informers, or, as the people call them, 'stags,' there was still a hope cherished by the prisoners and their friends that some other evidence than theirs would be required where so many lives were at stake. It was, therefore, with a sort of dogged indifference that the prisoners in the dock, Walsh and Lacy, appeared to listen to the elaborate statement of the learned counsel for the Crown, and his recapitulation of the evidence which the two 'informers' were to give. All at once, however, Mr. Doherty paused an instant, and then, turning towards the dock, held up his hand and mentioned a name—the name of another witness—it was that of the housekeeper and relative of Jack Keogh who had brought food and drink to the murderers whilst they lay in wait for their victims, and who had heard all their plans on the previous day at Keogh's house. The mention of her name had a terrible effect on the prisoners, and, indeed, on all the country-people present, her position in the Keogh family being well known, her intimate acquaintance with all the circumstances preceding and succeeding the murder, made her a most formidable witness; whilst at the thought of her going against her people—for, of course, the evidence that criminated Walsh and Lacy involved the conviction of the young Keoghs and many others—'curses, not loud, but deep,' were heard on every side, mingled with expressions of pity for the prisoners. It was here 'Oh, vo, vo! they're done for now, anyhow!' there it was 'Well, well! afther that who'll thrust any one?' 'Their own flesh and blood! oh, wirra, wirra!' Still, it was hoped, and all but believed, that Kate Costelloe would not do so foul a deed, and this hope buoyed up the prisoners and their numerous friends amongst the audience, even whilst the two informers and other witnesses of minor details gave their sworn testimony. At last came the moment when *Kate Costelloe* was called, and instantly a dead silence fell on the court;—the bench—the bar—the dock—the hall—all remained in speechless, breathless suspense, for all alike felt that in all probability the issue of the trial—the fate, not only of the prisoners in the dock, but of all who were yet to be placed in it, including, of course, the two Keoghs—all depended on the evidence of this woman. As the moments passed slowly away, and the death-like hush continued unbroken, and no Kate Costelloe appeared, the hopes of the prisoners and their friends rose higher and higher; all eyes were eagerly turned on the door by which the witnesses were introduced, and the intensity of suspense was becoming painful even to those least concerned in the issue— when, all at once, the fatal door opened, and a small female figure, closely veiled, was seen to enter, carried, as it were, by two persons, who supported her on either side—she was evidently unable to support herself. A groan of fierce execration burst from the crowd in the body of the court-house—the glow of hope died away on the faces of the prisoners, and they stood looking down with ghastly eyes on the diminutive

SUNSET ON THE ROCK. 215

creature that was being placed on the table with their life
resting on her word. Never did stranger apparition burst on a
court of justice or occupy a witness-table. So struck, indeed,
were even the officials themselves, that for some moments no
effort was made to elicit the woman's testimony, and she
stood there, a veiled, muffled figure, far below the ordinary
stature of woman, her hands, which alone were visible, white
and clammy and rigid as those of a corpse, and no motion in
her frame except once that a visible shudder shook her whole
body—such a shudder as accompanies and precedes the parting
of soul and body. At length the veil was removed from her
face, and such a face as that was! I am sure no one that saw
it then will ever forget it. The features might once have been
fair to look upon, but they were then almost hideous in their
ghastliness—the closed eyes sunk far into their sockets, the
lips drawn apart in livid paleness, and scarcely a breath of life
stirring the pulses of the corpse-like frame: as the head rested
on the shoulder, a mass of long black hair fell in wild disorder
from under the bonnet or hood, adding to the wanness of the
face and the ghastliness of the appalling figure. It was some
time before the wretched creature could be brought to answer
the questions put to her, and then only when water had been
sprinkled several times on her face and applied to her parched
lips. When she did speak, her voice was scarcely audible, and it
was only by a single word at a time, and that at intervals perhaps
of some moments' length, that she was got over the first preliminary statements, and on at last to the scene in The Grove, when
she brought refreshments to the party waiting there. But when
she was asked to identify Walsh—the first of the prisoners—
and the wand was placed in her hand for that purpose, she
seemed to relapse into her former death-like torpor; the same
process had to be gone through to revive her, and some began
to hope that she could not identify Walsh, having never seen
him except on that one occasion. At the agonised request of
the prisoners, a number of others were brought from the gaol
and placed in the dock,[1] so as to give them at least a chance.

[1] In Sheil's *Sketches of the Irish Bar* (edited by Dr. Shelton M'Kenzie)
there is a very interesting account of this famous trial. Speaking of the
introduction of these prisoners, the author says : "It was now four o'clock
in the morning ; the candles were almost wasted to their sockets, and a

Then was the witness again called upon to identify the prisoner Walsh."

The whole party on the Rock had now gathered round the narrator; every face expressed more or less interest, though to some of the listeners the story was not altogether new. When Moran paused, as if to take breath, Mrs. Pakenham and Lady Pemberton simultaneously exclaimed, "Well, and did she do it?"

"She did, after another terrific struggle with herself that was visible to all the court. Just as she was placing the rod on the head of Walsh, a female voice in the court called out, 'Oh, Kate!' and the cry seemed to act on the miserable creature like an electric shock. Still, she did her awful duty, and was borne from the table and from the court more dead than alive. Walsh and Lacy were accordingly convicted, and in a day or two after the two Keoghs were placed at the bar, and Kate Costalloe was called and brought forward as the last and best witness for the prosecution. People thought that although Kate had been terrified into giving testimony against the other prisoners, she would never be either forced or persuaded into swearing away the lives of her own relatives, with their venerable old father sitting near the dock, full in her sight. She did it, nevertheless, and, strange to say, with more firmness than she had before manifested. With all her faculties plainly on the alert, and a quick, sharp intelligence in her eyes and in all her features, she gave her evidence clearly and methodically, and deliberately placed the fatal rod on the heads of the two

dim and uncertain light was diffused through the court. Haggardness sat upon the spectators, and yet no weariness or exhaustion appeared; the frightful interest of the scene preserved the mind from fatigue. The dock was crowded with malefactors, and, brought as they were in order that guilt of all kinds should be confused and blended, they exhibited a most singular spectacle. This assemblage of human beings laden with chains was, perhaps, more melancholy from the contrast which they presented between their condition and their aspect. Even the pale light which glimmered through the court did not prevent their cheeks from looking ruddy and healthful. They had been awakened in their lonely cells in order to be produced, and, as they were not aware of the object of arraying them together, there was some surprise mixed with fear in their looks. I could not help whispering to myself as I surveyed them, 'What a noble and fine race of men are here, and how much have they to answer for who, by degrading, have demoralised such a people!'"

young men, which was the more remarkable that whispers had been afloat, even in the court-house, that there was between her and the elder of the brothers a tie stronger than blood—a love that was the growth of years."

"Love?" cried several of the ladies in a breath,—"love! Impossible! How could *she* love the man whose life she swore away?"

"She did love him, then!" spoke a little woman who had joined the group a few minutes before, her presence unnoticed in the absorbing interest of the story,—"if ever woman loved man, Kate Costelloe loved John Keogh."

Every eye was instantly turned on the speaker, but her features were concealed by the deep hood of her grey cloak drawn closely over her face; one was there who could have told who she was, but he remained silent—as did most of the party gazing on the strange figure before them. At last Moran and Mr. Esmond spoke together—

"How did it happen, then, that she swore against him, if she loved him as you say?"

"God knows that—and she knew it—and John Keogh knew it too! But it's no business of yours, and if you take my advice you'll say no more about it, any of you. Go home wid yourselves, and don't be draggin' the dead out o' their graves for no raison in life only to make fools o' yourselves, talkin' of what you know nothin' about. Get away wid you, now, out o' this, or maybe there's some o' you'll get what'll not be for the good o' their health before they're much oulder."

There was no use trying to reason with a creature who was set down by all present as insane. The two parties had, moreover, seen all they could possibly see for that time; they therefore retired from the Rock, leaving the supposed maniac to share its solitude with Bryan, who, as usual, conducted them to the gate with bows and thanks for the several gratuities given him. Any questions they might have been disposed to ask concerning the hag in the cloak were prevented by the continued presence of that interesting person, who followed them to the very gate, laughing occasionally in a hoarse inward way that confirmed in every mind the conviction of her insanity, and made some of the ladies no little anxious to have the gate between her and them. The gentlemen exchanged looks and smiles amongst themselves, but said nothing to renew the subject of Moran's story, as they exchanged their parting compliments at the gate, and the two parties went their several ways.

CHAPTER XVII.

INNER LIFE IN EFFINGHAM CASTLE.

In the drawing-room at Effingham Castle the conversation that evening turned principally on the wild and gloomy tale heard on the Rock—a tale so illustrative of the darkest phases of Tipperary life. Mr. Goodchild was already in possession of the facts, but he took occasion to expatiate in his own smooth and unctuous way on the deplorable state of a country where such things could be done under cover of a system—where murder was as familiar to the people as the air they breathed, and human life of no account whatever. "The people," said he, "are all leagued together for the worst of purposes—the overthrow of the landed proprietary—*extermination* is their object, and I am of opinion that nothing less will content them than the death of every landlord in the country. Truly, it is an awful state of things."

Harriet smiled, and bent her head over a volume of engravings that lay open on the table before her. Lord Effingham said with his usual coldness, amounting almost to austerity of manner—

"Do you not think, Mr. Goodchild, that the landlords themselves may be in some measure to blame?"

"Not to any great extent, my lord,—oh, certainly not; witness the murder of Mr. Esmond, who was considered one of the very best landlords in Tipperary."

"Yes, but that was an exceptional case; the rule is, as I understand, that those landlords who have been murdered were all more or less obnoxious to the people for their oppressive exactions and their harsh treatment of their tenantry."

"But surely, my lord, that does not justify murder—even

admitting it were just as your lordship seems to have been informed ?"

"*Nothing* justifies murder," said Lord Effingham, with stern emphasis ; "but it strikes me, Mr. Goodchild, that the very league which you say exists to an alarming extent amongst the peasantry goes to prove that there must be some radical fault on the part of those who have immediate authority over them, and I think it is well worth considering what chain of circumstances it is that has so hardened the hearts of these people, and perverted a nature not in itself wicked or furocious —how it happens, in short, that the peasantry of Tipperary, so warm-hearted, so susceptible of kindness, so keenly alive to justice or injustice, have become so bloodthirsty as it would seem they are—so ready to take life themselves, so prone to sympathise with others whose hands are red with the blood of their fellow-men."

The chaplain took out his box and refreshed his nasal organ with a pinch of snuff, shook his reverend head, and declared that "he had never viewed the matter in that light,—had never given much attention to the history of Ireland,—but he *thought* the cause of all these evils was undoubtedly to be found in the pernicious and soul-debasing doctrines of Rome, to which those unhappy people were so incurably addicted."

"For shame, Mr. Goodchild !" said Harriet Markham, her eyes flashing with the contempt and indignation she could not help feeling. "How often have I explained to you that it is not because of their *Romish* belief, but in despite of it, that the Catholic peasantry of this and other countries do at times take the law into their own hands ? Were they not addicted to the *doctrines* of which you speak, you may take my word for it that [such bloody acts of revenge would be ten to one—ay, twenty to one what they now are."

"My dear Miss Markham," said the chaplain, with his most insinuating smile, "I have an insuperable aversion to contradicting a lady, but really—ah !—really "—

"My dear Mr. Goodchild," put in Harriet, by way of filling up his hesitating pause, "I know there are many persons who are afflicted with a dreadful obliquity of vision in matters Irish or Catholic. If such be your case, I regret it exceedingly, and will charitably suppose that you never even heard of the mighty and incessant struggle everywhere going on between—between the Catholic Church and all manner of secret organisations, from Freemasonry to Ribbonism, and all between."

"What a dreadful country to live in!" said Lady Pemberton to her brother. "I wonder how Lady Jane will like it?"

"Like it, indeed?" cried Mrs. Pakenham, with a toss of her stately head. "I wonder did Lady Jane ever like anything beyond herself?"

"I should hope she did," quietly and somewhat sarcastically said Lady Pemberton, with a glance at the Earl, who, however, appeared to take no notice. The next moment he turned his keen, piercing eyes on Miss Markham, and said rather abruptly—

"What a singular old woman that was who broke in so unseasonably on Mr. Moran's narrative! Do you know anything of her?"

"I am not sure that I do, my lord, but I rather suspect. For the present, however, I may not say more."

"An old woman?" exclaimed the chaplain,—"what old woman?"

"Not *your* old woman, Mr. Goodchild," said Harriet, with a meaning smile,—"at least, I think not."

The ladies looked surprised, but the chaplain looked astounded, and blushed like a very schoolgirl under Harriet's mischievous glance.

"Mr. Goodchild's old woman?" said Mrs. Pakenham, laughing,—"and pray who may *she* be?"

"*Not* one of the weird 'sisters three,' madam,

'Who met Macbeth
Upon the heath,'

but probably an Irish kinswoman of theirs on whom our worthy chaplain has been experimentalizing of late—shooting her *with a silver bullet*, I believe,—or how was it, Mr. Goodchild?"

"I protest, Miss Markham," stammered the chaplain, his professional gravity entirely at fault,—"I protest—I do not understand the allusion."

"Oh, fie, Mr. Goodchild! fie, fie!" and Harriet raised her finger admonishingly and smiled archly. "You do not mean to deny that *you* met somebody 'on the heath'—well, not exactly 'on the heath,' but—somewhere between this and the globe-house?"

The chaplain looked more and more confused, the ladies more and more delighted at what they saw was a good joke, and more and more urgent with Miss Markham to let them into the secret. Just at that moment Lord Effingham rose, and, saying he had letters to write, withdrew. Harriet glanced timidly up as he passed her, and was not surprised to see a deeper cloud than usual on his brow and a sterner look in his dark, proud eyes.

Half an hour after, Harriet having gone to her own apartment for a book, chanced to pass the library, the door of which was ajar, and by the dim, subdued light from a study-lamp at the farther end of the spacious room, she saw Lord Effingham sitting at a table, his thoughtful brow resting on his hand and a look of care and weariness impressed on every feature. Harriet stopped involuntarily, with the thought uppermost in her mind, "Neither rank nor riches give immunity from care." It so happened that Lord Effingham raised his eyes at the moment, and looked towards the door just as Harriet was gliding away. Rising hastily, he came to the door, and said, "Miss Markham, will you have the goodness to favour me with a few moments' conversation?"

"Certainly, my lord," said Harriet, with an effort to assume a composure which she did not feel, her mind being full of the idea that the Earl was not pleased with the freedom she took in rallying his chaplain, with a still more painful fear natural to a delicate mind that her having passed at that particular moment might be construed into prying curiosity; in short, she felt troubled and unhappy, and her face—ever the index of her thoughts—told all too plainly what was passing within. She saw that her discomposure was not unnoticed, and that very consciousness increased it considerably. The Earl regarded her a moment with a smile so sad that she could have wept under its strange and softening influence, but she mastered her emotion and looked up with as calm a mien as she could command.

"My lord," she began, with some hesitation, "you will pardon me if I say that I thought you seemed somewhat displeased by my thoughtless *badinage* in relation to worthy Mr. Goodchild." An involuntary smile flitted over her face as she spoke the name, but, casting her eyes down with a demure expression, she stood awaiting the answer. It was longer delayed than she expected, and, looking up in some surprise, she found Lord Effingham regarding her with the same mournful smile.

"Witchcraft!" he muttered in a tone that was not meant for her ear, yet she heard the words distinctly,—"witchcraft! Ay, there is witchcraft that even silver bullets cannot reach. Miss Markham," he said in his usual voice and manner of cold impassiveness,—"Miss Markham, you were much mistaken in supposing that I resented your—your playful attack on my reverend friend—which I considered perfectly fair. Were I disposed for *badinage*, I might perhaps say that he was more to be envied than commiserated under such an attack." Miss Markham smiled, and acknowledged the courtly compliment by a slight inclination. "But," continued his lordship, "that was far from being the subject on which I wished to speak with you—you are probably aware of the object of my approaching visit to England?"

"I cannot say I am, my lord," said Harriet after a pause, during which she ran over in her mind certain words that had fallen from Lady Pemberton and Mrs. Pakenham, together with certain preparations going on around the Castle.

"I wonder at that," said the Earl, "knowing how difficult it is for ladies to keep secrets. You must know, then, Miss Markham, what perhaps you should have known before, as a valued friend rather than the mere preceptress of my children," —Miss Markham bowed somewhat haughtily,—"in a word, I am about to fulfil a matrimonial engagement, entered into some months since, with the daughter of an English marquis."

"The *Lady June*, I presume, whose name I heard this evening for the first time?"

"The same," said Lord Effingham, with a scarcely perceptible tremor in his voice.

"Your lordship does me honour," said Miss Markham, looking up with a gracious smile,—"an honour for which I feel deeply grateful—believe me, I do." She was about leaving the room when the Earl's voice arrested her steps, and she returned to where he stood.

"I have yet another word to say,"—he paused, then hastily added, "I wish to know, Miss Markham, whether you will still remain with us—that is, with my little girls?"

"I see no reason why I should not, my lord," said Harriet proudly; "my position in the Earl of Effingham's family will be in no degree changed, I should think, by the advent of a *Countess of Effingham*," and she smiled with an archness that well became her. "Unless, indeed," she added quickly, "her ladyship may object to having the young daughters of the house of Cartwright educated by a Catholic. In that case, my lord," she said, with much earnestness, "I will rely on the friendship you do me the honour to profess for me to give me timely notice."

"Rely," said Lord Effingham, with more warmth than was usual to him, "on all that I can do at any time to shield you from aught that would in any degree compromise your dignity— your self-respect. I know the innate nobleness of your mind, and rest assured, Miss Markham, it shall never be subjected to any trial under my roof."

"I thank you, my lord," said Harriet, her voice slightly tremulous; "you give the best proof of your good opinion in entrusting me with the education of your dear children, and it shall be my ceaseless endeavour to form their minds to the best of my poor ability, and make them such as I *know* you would wish to have them. In that way, at least, I can repay your lordship's kindness to—a penniless orphan whom fate has thrown *almost* on your bounty!" The last words were spoken with that peculiar archness which gave such a charm at times to Harriet's speaking features, and, bowing with the grace which marked her every action, she was leaving the room when on the threshold she encountered Mrs. Pakenham and Lady Pemberton.

"Dear me!" said the former lady, with a sudden change of countenance; "we were not aware that your lordship was *engaged*—that is, we thought you were writing letters, and came to ask if you would spare time to join us at supper. I see Miss Markham has been beforehand with us."

"You are mistaken, madam," said Harriet coldly; "I can lay claim to no such amiable intention. I was merely passing the library on my way upstairs for a book I wanted, when Lord Effingham, seeing me pass, requested to speak with me on a matter of business, and I stepped in."

"And I," said the Earl, "owe you an apology, Miss Mark-

ham, for I just now recollect that I had not the politeness to
offer you a seat. The business on which I wished to speak
with Miss Markham affects us all, I should hope. I was
desirous of ascertaining, before any further changes take place
here, whether we might count on the continuance of her in-
valuable services in regard to Ann and Emma."

Lady Pemberton, who much resembled her brother in
character and disposition, and also in appearance, turned at
once to Harriet and said, with a courteous smile, "Surely Miss
Markham would not think of leaving her young charges at
a time when, perhaps, they most need her kind and judicious
care?"

"That was precisely what induced me to ask her, Caroline,"
said Lord Effingham.

"Well, it is very true," said Mrs. Pakenham, a little
maliciously, Harriet thought; "with all her beauty and sprightly
grace, I fear dear Lady Jane is not *exactly* the type of a good
stepmother."

"Excuse me, Thomasine," said Lord Effingham in his
coldest and sternest accents, "I cannot permit such an inference
to be drawn from what I have said. Your remark is altogether
superfluous, and entirely irrelevant to our purpose. I asked
Miss Markham a simple question, and she gave me a simple
and direct answer—I am glad to say, in the affirmative."

"Well, well," said Mrs. Pakenham a little testily, "now
that the matter is arranged to general satisfaction, I presume
your lordship will honour us with your presence during the
remainder of the evening—and in the first place, to supper?"

Harriet heard no more, for she quietly made her escape, and
took refuge in her own apartment, there to muse in silence
and alone on what she had heard and seen during the last
quarter of an hour, for no longer time had passed since she left
the drawing-room. Short as the time was, and unimportant
what had occurred, she somewhat felt as though a page had
been written in her life's record, and a strange feeling was
knocking at her heart, but of what kind she cared not to
examine. Was she humbled or exalted in her own estimation?
Was her peace more or less than it was an hour before? These
were questions that she did not trouble herself to answer, but,
smoothing as she best might the fair surface of her sweet face,

she descended to the drawing-room, just in time to bring up the rear of the party on their way to supper. She had ascertained on her way down that the little girls were already in bed and locked in the blissful unconsciousness of childish slumbers.

The conversation during supper was lively and animated, and Harriet Markham was the gayest of all. Still, it could not have escaped an observant eye, if any such were on her, that her cheek was paler even than usual, and her eyes burning with an inward fire. No one seemed to notice anything unusual in her tone or manner, though all felt the ineffable charm that hung around her. Lord Ellingham, indeed, took little notice of anything; silent and abstracted, though condescendingly polite as usual, he seemed occupied with serious thought, and took little part in the conversation. He complained of a headache and retired early. As Harriet caught his parting glance, she said to herself, "There is a load of care on that proud, cold heart—there is sorrow in the troubled depths of those deep eyes. Does *he* feel—even he?"

The remainder of the evening passed away without anything particular; but Harriet learned for the first time that Lady Pemberton was to remain at the Castle during the Earl's absence, to preside over the general preparations, and also to receive the young Countess on her arrival. The little party broke up early, and Harriet Markham, with an exquisite sense of relief, locked the door of her spacious and elegant apartment, and threw herself in an arm-chair near the one large window of a boudoir connected with her chamber which commanded a prospect of that mingled wildness and beauty that most impress a lofty, imaginative mind. The curtains were as yet undrawn, and the lady-moon shed her heart-soothing light into the small apartment, so graceful in its furniture and decoration, so meet for the inner home—the retreat, as it were, of a being so *solitary* in her heart's life as Harriet Markham. So she lay in that delicious sense of *rest*, and the no less delicious sense of solitude—of loneliness—which casts its spell over the world-weary heart and the tired brain when the deep hush of the solemn night is around, and the noisy, frothy, hollow, heartless world shuts its bleating mouths for a while, leaving the deep heart to commune with its own thoughts, to indulge for a space its earnest longings, to drink in the beauty of earth and heaven, and commune with the dead of other years, or the loved and far removed.

Such are the moments happily described by the sweetest of modern poets—

> When lost in the future the soul wanders on,
> And all of this life but its sweetness is gone.

And Harriet Markham felt the charm of the hour and the scene, and her soul was upraised to that heaven which the eye of faith can see afar off through the blue ether of the midnight sky—for it was verging on midnight. All at once a footstep sounded on the verandah beneath her window—a light but measured step, and Harriet's heart beat—not with fear—as she bent her head to listen, and furthermore raised the window just enough to admit a sound from without. The measured footfall continued—to and fro—now broken and irregular, now firm and distinct, like that of a sentinel on duty. Occasionally there came to the ear of the lonely watcher another sound, like that she might have heard in dreams—it was a voice, deep, full, yet subdued, humming as if for no listening ear, but the singer's own heart. Oh, how eagerly did Harriet listen to catch the low but musical tones, and an inexplicable feeling of delight enwrapped her senses as she recognised the air, and the words too—

> "Oh, bring to me my Norah Fey,
> Hours are days when she's away."

The voice ceased, but oh, the passionate yearning that was in the rich, soft tones! Never had Harriet heard the charm of "Shule Aroon" brought out with such effect, and she listened with all the intensity of her heart to hear the sweet sounds again. Softly she murmured to herself—

> "Oh, not more welcome the fairy numbers
> Of music fall on the sleeper's ear,
> When half awaking from fearful slumbers,
> He thinks the full choir of heaven is near."

"Who can it be?" was the next thought. "That was no rustic—oh no, no! Then who can be within the Castle grounds at this lone hour?"

Then came from below the sound as of a deep, thrilling voice speaking in an audible whisper, and to Harriet's excited fancy it sounded almost close to her ear.

"O night! what anguish do you shroud full often!—O moon! what sights you witness in your unclouded path through yon glorious heavens!—O heart! throbbing, bursting heart! why not break and be at rest?"

Why was it that, unknowing who the speaker was, Harriet Markham bowed her head on the window-ledge and wept tears that seemed to flow from her inmost heart? A strange, weird thing is human nature, and a stranger thing is the human heart! As an Eolian harp to the voices of the wind, so does the heart respond to the yet more variable tones of human feeling, human sympathy, human suffering. Long did the slow and measured tread break the stillness of the night, and by some strange fascination Harriet remained with her head resting against the window till the sound ceased, and the earth below was silent as the glittering stars above. Then, alone with the night, her mind and heart gradually resumed their usual tone, and, gazing upwards on the "spangled heavens," that "shining frame," which, in the language of the poet,

Their great Creator's praise proclaim,

her thoughts assumed the form of meditation, and in the contemplation of things divine she speedily lost sight of the thorns and briars that strew the path to those eternal mansions where joy ineffable for ever reigns. Calmly and hopefully she knelt to perform the last sweet exercise of the Christian's day, and having offered her heart to the God who made it, and to Mary the Mother of faithful souls, she resigned herself to sleep—the tranquil sleep of an untroubled conscience.

During the days that intervened between that night and Lord Effingham's departure, his lordship spent the greater part of his time in his study, a small and very pleasant room adjacent to the library, and opening on the verandah already mentioned. A solitary ride in the afternoons alone broke the monotony of his seclusion, yet when the family assembled at table there was no perceptible difference in his manner, always calm and cold and self-possessed, at times a little abstracted, but never discourteous to those around.

On the day before that fixed on for his departure, he approached the bow-window in the sitting-room, where Harriet occupied her favourite seat, her fingers engaged on some one of those pretty trifles the use whereof would puzzle any of those "lords of creation" whom "men we call," while her eyes wandered ever and anon to the graceful scene of woodland beauty spread out in fair array before the window, and nearer, where her young pupils were amusing themselves with hoop and skipping-rope on the smooth sward outside.

"Miss Markham," said the Earl, so suddenly that she started, and, blushing, looked up in surprise,—"Miss Markham, there was one trifling incident of our last visit to the Rock which I forgot to mention since, though I have thought of it many times. But why that look of surprise?" he added, with a smile of peculiar expression. "Does my voice grate so harshly on your ear?"

"Not at all, my lord," said Harriet, recovering her composure, and smiling pleasantly; "but—but—I did not think your lordship was so near, and I was just completing the erection of a superb *château en Espagne*."—

"Indeed? It were worth something to know what manner of edifice that was which so graceful a fancy piled in airy space."

"Architectural details are seldom interesting, my lord. But may I venture to ask what was the incident to which your lordship referred just now?"

Lord Effingham mentioned the face which he and Mr. Moran had both seen at a window of the old cathedral, adding that he could not help associating it in his mind with the singular apparition of the old woman in the cloak. "What is your opinion, Miss Markham?"

Harriet mused a moment before she replied in a thoughtful, hesitating tone, "That there is some mystery about both these appearances, my lord, I have not the smallest doubt, but what they indicate—especially the face which showed itself so suddenly, and so suddenly vanished, in such a place—is more than I can imagine,—perhaps it were even unwise to say it if I could."

"It is a strange country," was the Earl's remark, as he turned to Lady Pemberton, who was reading at another window in the room, and asked if she would ride out with him before dinner— a proposal which she smilingly accepted, then left the room to don her hat and habit. She was quickly followed by Lord Effingham, and in a few moments Harriet heard their horses' feet prancing away over the gravelled surface of the avenue. Rising, she went to a window and stood a moment looking after them, till their stately figures were hidden from her view by a turn in the road, then, muttering to herself some inarticulate words, she went upstairs, and having tied on a broad-leaved straw hat, went out to join the children at their play.

At length the day came for Lord Effingham to leave for England, and, after taking a tender and kind farewell of his children, his sister, and Mrs. Pakenham, he shook hands with Mr. Goodchild and Miss Markham with about the same degree of cordiality, and stepped into the carriage that was to convey him to Dublin.

It was early morning, and Harriet retired to her own apartment to spend in commune with her own thoughts the hour that yet remained to her before entering on the duties of the schoolroom. The first object that met her eye was a little bunch of pansies, freshly gathered, their rich petals moist with the dew of the morning; they stood in a small crystal vase, but taking them up to inhale their fragrance, wondering at the same time what kind hand had gathered for her those flowers to memory dear, she all at once perceived a scrap of paper twisted round their delicate stems; with a trembling hand she took it off, and, carefully smoothing it out, found these lines written on its fair surface—

>   I have sweet thoughts of thee!
> They come around me like the voice of song;
> They come like birds that to the South belong,
> And wear a gayer wing and brighter crest
> Than those that on the roof-tree build their nest,
> They come more tender, beautiful, and bright
> Than any thoughts that *others* can excite;
> They tell me gentle tales of thee and thine,
> Of gems of truth that in thy spirit shine,
> Of goodness, purity, and holy zeal,
> That can for others earnest pity feel;
> Of all things beautiful in soul and heart—
> And *such* they tell me ever that thou art.

"The voice of the *pansy*," murmured Harriet, with a proud and happy smile, her pale cheek flushing with a crimson glow; yet when she descended to the schoolroom the flush was gone, cheek and brow were paler than ever, and her eyes were red and swollen, as if with much weeping.

CHAPTER XVIII.

KATE COSTELLOR.

A DAY or two after Lord Effingham's departure, Harriet Markham and Mary Hennessy, walking out to enjoy the cool freshness of the evening, so grateful after the excessive heat of one of the hottest of the dog-days, stopped at Bryan's cottage, where Cauth sat knitting by the door, as usual. It was not the first time that either had been there, and the old woman seemed glad to see them. Hastily bringing forward the only two seats besides her own that the cottage afforded, she wiped them carefully with her apron, and invited the young ladies to sit down, adding, "It's not often we see the likes o' you here, an' sure, it's the great honour entirely ye do me."

"Cauth," said Miss Markham, after the young ladies had exchanged significant glances,—"Cauth, I hope you understand that Miss Hennessy and I wish you well, and take a great interest in both you and Bryan?"

"Wisha, then, it's myself knows it well," said Cauth, "an' good raison I have, too, for it's ever the kind, soft word ye both had for me, not to spake of the help ye gave me many's the time when, only for ye, I could hardly have the bit or sup before that poor simple ould man that 'id starve to death afore he'd go out to ask it, on account of the forgetful way he has wid him."

"Well, then," resumed the young lady, "you will not suspect us of being actuated only by prying curiosity when we come to ask you a few questions about yourself?"

"About me?" cried Cauth, dropping her knitting and turning on them with a face as pale as ashes. "Ah, then, Miss Markham—ladies dear!—what questions would ye be puttin' to me?—God help me!"

Both young ladies applied themselves to reassure her, and told her that they came to her purely as friends, and that whatever she told them would be kept an inviolable secret unless she gave them permission to divulge it at any time, or to any person.

"Well, an' what—what do you want to know?" she exclaimed in a husky voice, and with a sort of desperate resolution.

Before answering, Harriet rose and closed the door, at which Cauth nodded assent.

"Cauth," said Miss Markham, her voice more deep and solemn than usual, though perhaps she knew it not herself,— "Cauth, was it you that broke in on Mr. Moran's story a few days ago on the Rock? Now answer me truly, as you hope for mercy hereafter."

"There's no gettin' over that," said Cauth gloomily, as if to herself; "when you ask me that way, I can't deny the thruth. It was me, Miss Markham, and who else *would* it be?"

"I thought so, and so did Miss Hennessy, but we never breathed a word of our suspicions to any one,—that is," she added, after a pause, recollecting what she had said to Lord Effingham,—"that is, to any one who knows you even now, or in any way that could make you known. Now, having told us so much, you will not, I think, refuse to tell us more? Are you, or are you not, *Kate Costelloe?*"

At the sound of the name the unhappy woman dropped her head between her knees as suddenly as if she was shot through the brain, one heart-piercing groan escaped her, and then all was silent for a few moments, during which she might have been supposed dead were it not for the quivering motion perceptible in all her members, and the quick, irregular breathing that denoted her inward agony.

At last she slowly raised her head, and, fixing her heavy, bloodshot eyes on her interrogator, said, "I see there's no use in hidin' it any longer,—the earth or the say 'on't hide *murder*— an' sure, that was murder—the worst of murder! I *am* Kate Costelloe!" and, as if relieved to get over the confession, and feeling herself a freer woman, she sat up erect in her seat and looked the young ladies alternately in the face,—"I am *Kate Costelloe.* Is that all you want to know?"

"We want to know nothing that you do not want to tell us," said Harriet, "but"—

"But you'd wish to know why I did it, an' all about it," broke in Kate, with that keenness of perception which belonged to her strange character. She laughed—a low, inward laugh, as it were in scorn, fixing her eyes moodily on the ground the while, and the young ladies began to fear that her next move would be to open the door and bid them walk out. They were mistaken, for she looked up with a milder expression, and said in a voice low and mournful—

"There's not many livin' I'll tell it to, Miss Markham; but I'll tell it to you, an' Miss Mary, bekase I know you have the heart to feel even for me, bad as I am—an' sure, sure, but I'm bad enough! Ask me any question you like an' I'll answer you, no matter what it is."

"Tell us, then," said Mary Hennessy, seeing that Harriet shrank from putting the question, "what was the motive that induced you to give testimony against your own friends and relatives?"

"Friends and relatives?" repeated Kate, with strong and disdainful emphasis. "God help your wit, child!—that wasn't the worst of it, though it was bad enough, too. That wasn't what tore the heart out o' me, an' left me ever since without e'er a heart, at all."

"What was it, then?" whispered Harriet, awed by the intensity of passion that breathed in every lineament of the withered face before her.

"What was it?—ha! ha! ha!—what was it?" And, thrusting out her head till her face almost touched that of Harriet,—though both young ladies drew back instinctively,—she said in a low, hissing whisper, "It was the love that was in my heart for John Krogh!"

"You loved him?" exclaimed both her hearers in the same subdued tone,—"you loved him, yet you hung him—and his brother too?"

The woman drew back, raised her head to the highest, and flashed a look of fierce intelligence into the eyes of her astonished hearers. "Ay, I hung him; but I couldn't help it— it was his own fault. I didn't want to hang e'er a one—e'er a one, at all—an' them, leastways; but he took it out o' me—he dared me to do it!" Slowly she arose from her seat, and stood looking down at her silent and, as it were, spellbound auditors, with the eye and mien of a pythoness. "Ay, he dared me to do it—and I did it,"—her voice sank to a hoarse whisper,—"but I wouldn't have done it, even for that, only he taunted me with —with—no matter what, but I knew it was his sin and shame as well as mine—an' I knew how many bitter tears I cried many's the night an' many's the day for that same misfortune that came over me—an' then I thought of all the promises he had made, an' broke them all—an' how I forgave him everything, everything, everything, bekase I loved him—an' how I kept my shame an' my sorrow locked up in my own heart, an' never said a hard word of him even to his own father, ever an' always hopin' for the best; but when he said that word to me, before he was taken, when I tould him that I had his life, an' Patrick's life, in my hands, an' asked him wouldn't he put the marriage-ring on my finger—when he said *that word* to me, back again, an' made as little o' me as if I was the dirt undher his feet,—then," she almost shrieked, throwing up her arms like a maniac, —" then—*then* the love went out o' my heart, an' I said to my-self, though I didn't say it to him, 'If you had fifty lives, they're not worth a sthraw—*the gallows is your doom!*' That was the last sight of him I ever got, till I seen him in the dock, an' then I made him shiver with the one look I gave him when I put the rod on his head—ha! he looked at me then with such a pitiful look in his eyes, all as one as if he said, 'Kate, is it you that swears my life away?' But I didn't care for his looks then,—that time was past,—an' I did what was in my mind to do, an' in my heart, an' showed him what I could do when I was put to it, though he thought I'd never bring myself to do it. Och! och! och! sure, it was no wondher he'd think it, for he knew how I loved him!—*fareer gar*, he did!" and, breaking into a passionate flood of tears, she sank heavily on her seat, burying her face in her hands.

Harriet and Mary exchanged glances—they dared not speak, fearing another outburst of passion from the unhappy woman; they would gladly have effected their retreat, but they could not bring themselves to leave the poor creature without a word of consolation, so they sat patiently and silently awaiting the moment when the calm would follow the storm, in order to say some words of kindness and encouragement before they left the unfortunate victim of passion to the companionship of her own dreary thoughts. They rose, nevertheless, and the motion, slight as it was, brought Kate back to consciousness.

"I see you're for goin', ladies," said she, rising too; "an' sure, it's glad you'll be, I know myself, to get me out o' your sight. The Lord in heaven forgive me!"—she raised her clasped hands and swollen eyes to heaven,—"the Lord in heaven forgive me! sure, it's thinkin' of my poor sowl I ought to be, an' askin' pardon night an' day on my bare knees for all the harm I have done. Och, then, ladies dear, isn't it a poor thing an' a misfortunate thing to forget God?—for, sure, when we do once there's no tellin' what we'll come to,—them that 'id tell me onst that I'd ever do what I done, or be the thing I am this night, oyeh! but it's me that 'id give little ear to them."

"But, Kate"—

"Call me Cauth, if it's plaisin' to you, miss. I'd wish to forget, if I could, that I ever was Kate Costelloe."

"Well, then, Cauth, what was it brought you to this part of the country, for I know the sad events to which we have been referring took place in another part of the county?"

"Why, then, I'll jist tell you that, as if I was at the priest's knee this minnit. I couldn't bear to live where I knew everybody hated the ground I walked on. Besides that, *the ould man was there*—the lonesome ould man, that never raised his head afther hearin' the sentence, but went about like a wanderin' sperit among the good Christians that had the heart to pity him. The sight o' me would a' kilt him entirely, so I left the place altogether, and came where I thought nobody 'id know me. But sure," she added, "there wasn't even that comfort for me,—I'm as well known here as the town-pump, God help me!—an' if I happen to say a sharp word to any one, it's nothing but 'Kate Costelloe' here an' 'Kate Costelloe' there wid them all round, till I'd sooner be dead than livin'—if it wasn't for my poor sowl!"

"Speaking of that," said Mary Hennessy, "does the Dean or Father Sheehan know who you are?—have you been to your duty since you came here?"

"Well, to tell you the truth, miss, I was not. Many's the time I got ready to go, but somehow or another, the shame always got the better o' me, an' though I knew well enough it was the Evil Spirit that was keepin' me back, I couldn't bring myself to go."

Suddenly the latch was raised, the door was flung open, and in the aperture stood, leaning on her staff, an old woman in a red cloak, whom Harriet recognised at once as the original of Moran's graphic sketch of the Reverend Mr. Goodchild's courteous friend of argentine notoriety. Peering up into the faces of the two young ladies, as she stood resting both hands on her staff, her little black eyes began to twinkle with a brighter meaning.

"Ho! ho!" she croaked. "I came here to invite Kate Costalloe up to my place—and a nice place it is, too,"—she paused, and the pause was filled up by a despairing groan from Kate,—"not that I expected much from her, for, like myself, she isn't much the betther of all the bad she has done in her time,—but here's two grand ladies—one of them from the lord's Castle beyant, no less, an' the other Dr. Hennessy's purty sister—an' the world knows that's what she is, only not so pale or so grand-lookin' that way as the other—bekase why, the ould-quality blood isn't in her—the blood of the Markhams that were great people onst, an' even in my own memory." These latter clauses of the speech were spoken in an undertone, and by way of soliloquy, though they reached every ear within hearing, as the acrid dame probably intended they should. "Come now, ladies,"—and she pointed with her stick over her shoulder,—"come and see the fine sight I have at home for the quality. Come, when I bid you!" she added in a tone of authority; "I *want* ye up above there at my castle, an' I know there's naither o' ye'll be sorry for comin' when you get up."

"My good woman," said Mary Hennessy, after exchanging some whispered words with Harriet, "we have no objection to go with you, if we can really do you or any one else a service. But we should like to know where, or for what purpose, you would have us go."

"Ah, then, where would you be takin' them to?" said Cauth in a confidential whisper.

"To the house above, to tell their fortunes," was the short, ironical answer. "Now, don't be keepin' me here, I tell ye, but come along this minnit,—do ye think it's for harmin' ye I'd be?"

"I think ye'd best go," whispered Cauth. "She has odd ways wid her by times, but *her bark is worse than her bite*—she'll do ye no harm, I'll go bail."

This and their own reflections decided the young ladies to follow the crone, who was already hobbling down the road, nothing doubting, it appeared, that they would comply with her singular mandate. Cauth stood at the door looking after them till they had all three disappeared at a turn of the road; she turned then, and looked up at the Rock, wondering whether Bryan would come down to his supper, yet hardly expecting that he would, the night being so rarely beautiful.

"Well, to be sure, but it's the quare life he leads," said she to herself, "scrapin', an' sweepin', an' patchin' up ould walls all day long, an' every day of the week, jist as if he was paid for it,—which he isn't, an' never will be—in this world, anyhow, let it be as it may with the other. Och, och! see what it is to have a good conscience!—it's aisy seen that poor Bryan never harmed the livin', or he'd be more afeard o' the dead. Now there's me, an' barrin' it was in broad daylight, an' plenty o' company to the fore, I darn't set my foot up there among the graves and tombstones, an' the ould crazy walls that's in it—nor I *wouldn't*, if they gave me the best estate in Tipperary. Ochone! it's the dismal place to spend one's nights an' days in. But sure, afther all, didn't I hear Father Riordan—God be good to him!—tellin' on the althar one Sunday, many's the year ago, about St. Anthony, how he went an' lived among the tombs, jist to be away from the livin' altogether, and wash his hands of the dirty, wicked world. An' all the fine ould hermits his reverence used to tell us about, when we were larnin' the Catechise in the chapel—ould ancient men with great long beards, that went away to the desert to live all alone with God, or in caves in the rocks, or mountains. Well, it's a folly to talk, but I think our Bryney is jist as good a hermit as any of them, barrin' that he hasn't the beard. I'm sure he prays as much as e'er a one o' them, an' even the odd night that he's in his bed, don't I hear him, when he thinks I'm asleep, prayin' for the sowls in purgatory, an' for the convarsion o' sinners?—an' sure, myself begins to cry when I hear that, thinkin' that I'm the greatest sinner goin'. But whisht! who's that?"

She had just perceived a female figure, with a shawl drawn

closely around her head, moving stealthily in the shadow of the
Rock, on the opposite side of the road, moving in the direction
of the gate leading to the sacred enclosure. The motions of the
person, whoever it might be, were so cautious, so stealthy, that
it was quite clear to any observer that there was, there must be,
some strong motive for concealment, and Cauth stood leaning
forward, peering with her keen dark eyes into the deep gloom
after the object of her curiosity. Moved by some unaccountable impulse, she at last followed her with the same stealthy
pace ; on and on moved the silent and muffled figure, on and on
moved Cauth after her, as if impelled by invisible agency, till
the gate had opened and closed a second time, with a few
moments' intermission, and both were within the sacred precincts,
gliding up the steep ascent to the once stately portal of the
cathedral. Here Cauth's courage failed her ; she remembered
her soliloquy of a few moments before, and all the terrors of
superstition, heightened by the fears of a troubled conscience,
came back with overwhelming force. Frightened even at her
own boldness, she stood in harrowing uncertainty as to what
she had best do ; advance she dared not, and retreat was little
less formidable,—if she could only reach Bryan, but God
knows where Bryan was, as she said to herself, and to raise her
voice on the Rock of Cashel, with the dead all around her, was
something not to be thought of. Timidly and fearfully she
glanced around, almost certain that some shape of horror would
present itself to her aching eyes. In her terror she had half
forgotten the immediate object of her almost involuntary
intrusion on the lone place of death ; she had vanished from
her view round an angle of the palace wall, but all at once she
caught sight of her again, crossing the broad strip of moonlight
to the hall of the vicars-choral, then gliding along by the wall
of the cathedral—

   Where buttress and buttress alternately
   Seemed framed of ebon and ivory,

as the light figure flitted past them. Cauth watched her with
fear-distended eyes, the cold sweat oozing from every pore of
her body, and her tongue, as it were, glued to her burning
palate. All at once another figure appeared on the scene, and
to Cauth's inexpressible relief it proved to be Bryan. Somewhat encouraged by the sight of another living creature, and

that, too, the good old guardian of the ruins, she drew back a little farther into the shade, where she could see what passed, herself remaining unseen; for she began to suspect, seeing Bryan and the supposed ghost approaching each other, that it might after all be a creature of flesh and blood like herself. Then came distinctly to her ear the following colloquy:—

"Why, an' is this yourself, Celia? What in the world brings you here, my poor girl, at this time o' night?"

"I wanted to see *him*," was the reply in a low, earnest whisper that only half reached Cauth's ear.

"*Him?*—why, who do you mane?"

"Nonsense, Bryan! you know well enough. He's here now —I know he is—an' I *must* see him! For God's sake, Bryan, don't be keepin' me!" And the voice spoke louder, in increasing agitation.

Before Bryan could answer, a man's arm was stretched out from one of "the broken arches, black in night," that yawned close beside them, and, catching the female by the arm, whispered a word that arrested the scream on her pallid lips. Then Bryan and the young woman entered the arch, and Cauth managed to get so near them, creeping along in the black shadow of the walls, that she could hear their low, cautious tones as they all three conversed in whispers.

"Jerry," said the girl, her voice trembling with eagerness, "for the love of God get down to the vaults or somewhere; the peelers is out lookin' for you, with that stag, M'Gowan"—

"Well, an' what if they are? Weren't they often out before, an' they didn't catch me yit?"

"Ay! but, M'Gowan!—an' you know there's some great Crown-lawyer or another down from Dublin."

"So I hear."

"So you hear?—an' is that the way you're takin' it, an' me 'most frikened out o' my wits? If you heard about the Counsellor, maybe you didn't hear what M'Gowan swore?"

"No. What *did* he swear?"

"That you were hidin' somewheres about the Rock."

"There now, Jerry, didn't I tell you that?" said Bryan anxiously. "I knew it 'id be found out at last that you were here, an' now I'll have the whole country again' me for harbourin'—for harbourin'"—

"A murderer," put in the other, with some bitterness,—"out with it, Bryan, like a man!"

"Well, it's an ugly word to say, anyway, but you know what I mane—an' the raisons, too, that made me give in to you,—but what will the people say? Vo! vo! myself an' the Rock's disgraced for ever."

"Never mind, Bryan," said the other man quickly; "you done it for the best, you know yourself, an' God knows it, an' I know it too, Bryan, an' it's hard if we don't clear you an' the Rock between us three. Never mind, Bryan; you stood my friend when I most needed one, an' you'll not be sorry for it. Go home now, Celia astore, an' make your mind aisy —with God's help an' Bryan Cullanan's they'll not catch me this time aither; I could hide here for a month, if all the peelers an' the army from here to Clonmel was afther me, barrin' they'd blow up the Rock entirely. There's so many vau'ts an' places that nobody knows anything about, barrin' Bryan an' myself, that got into the knowledge of them this while back. So go home, darlin', an' don't be frettin'; if M'Gowan an' the peelers comes here afther me, there'll be the greatest game of hide-an'-go-seek that ever was played about Cashel town, or Rock aither."

"Oh, oh, oh! the Lord save us!" and Celia began wringing her hands. "Arrah, Jerry, what's comin' over you, at all? Is it losin' your senses you are, to be talkin' that-a-way? Och wirra, wirra! what'll I do, at all?"

"Why, you foolish girl, it's *you* that's losin' your wits. I tell you I'm no more mad than I ever was in all my life. Go home now, when I bid you, but take care would anybody see you goin' down from here at this hour o' the night. But that's true. Tell me before you go, did you hear since mornin' how poor Tim Murtha is?"

"Well, no, Jerry, I didn't hear. God help him for one misfortunate man, but it's him has the hard times of it one way an' another, an' a harmless poor crathur he ever an' always was."

"True for you, Celia. I suppose, now, you're thinkin', only you don't wish to say it, that it's strange how God afflicts the innocent, and lets the wicked escape—at any rate, for a while? Come now, can't I guess well?"

The girl was silent and a little confused, seeing which Jerry laughed a low, bitter laugh. "I knew it," he said, "but still I don't wondher at it—amn't I odious before God an' man, an' how could I expect any one to excuse me, or to feel for me? Go home now, an' God be with you!" So saying, he plunged into the inner darkness, and Celia saw him no more. She was turning to address some agitated words to Bryan, when from out the same darkness came a melancholy voice, singing—

> "Out of Lady Nancy's there grew a red rose,
> And out of Lord Lovell's a briar—iar—iar—
> And out of Lord Lovell's a briar."

"Lord bless us, who's that?" cried Celia, staring into the thick gloom.

"Why, don't you know the voice?" said Bryan.

Before Celia answered, out glided a ghostly figure wrapped in what appeared to be a sheet—a winding-sheet it was to Celia's affrighted fancy. But lo, a look at the face, only partially visible under the shroud-like covering, reassured poor Celia; for it was Mad Mabel, who went on quite unconcerned with a snatch from another old ballad, no less quaint and sad than the other—

> "My father married me to a knight,
> My stepmother owed me at a cruel spite—
> She sent three robbers that very night,
> They robbed my bower, and slew my knight."

"Celia Mulquin, I want to tell you a saycret!" and she put her head close to that of the shrinking girl. "I'm goin' to bring Petticoat Loose to friken them all here—husht! I'm thinkin' she's in there now,"—peering curiously into the ruined aisles, where the moonbeams were now falling in silver sheen.

> Through slender shafts of shapely stone,
> By foliage tracery combined.

"Didn't you hear something? But maybe it isn't her—hush —h-t!"—holding up the attenuated finger of one hand, while the other held the ghostly drapery under her chin,—"husht! maybe it's *Patrick* that's in it, or Walsh, or Lacy, or one o' the Keoghs."

A wild scream of horror suddenly broke the awful stillness of the dreary place, and whilst all the three, even Mabel, were struck dumb with amazement, not to say fear, Cauth emerged from the shade of a buttress, and joined the group, catching old Bryan by the arm with convulsive energy, and a force that made his frail body quiver.

Before any one had time to speak, she was drawing Bryan towards the gate with a strength which he could not resist, at the same time urging the others to follow.

"Come on, now, I tell you," she cried, in great excitement; "let us all get out o' this before worse comes of it. Celia Mulquin, it's you I may thank for all this."

"Me, Cauth? Why, dear bless me! what did *I* do?"

"You know well enough what you did—an' more's the shame an' the disgrace for a dacent girl like you to be runnin' afther a murdherer—ay, an' the worst of murdherers, too! I wouldn't b'lieve it, Celia, no, not if it was sworn to me on all the books that ever was shut an' opened, that you'd be havin' anything to say to that unlucky vagabone, Jerry Pierce".—

"Whisht, whisht, Cauth! somebody 'ill hear you."

"No, I'll *not* whisht, Bryan Cullenan, an' I tell you it's a sin and shame for ye both to be keepin' him from the gallows where he ought to be many's the day ago. If God spares me till the morrow mornin' I'll go before a magistrate, an' I'll go bail I'll put them in the way of catchin' him."

"God forgive you, honest woman!" said poor Celia, as they stopped for Bryan to lock the gate.

"I'm not an honest woman!" said Cauth fiercely, "but I'm a thankful woman, an' I'll hang the murderer of Mr. Esmond if it cost me my life."

"God in heaven forgive you!" said Celia again, and she burst into tears.

"Never mind her, Celia," said Bryan soothingly; "she only wants to frighten you. Doesn't she know, an' don't *you* know too, that Jerry Pierce is not fool enough to stay long in the same place? The country's wide, an' it's hard to say where he'll be the morrow night, or the morrow mornin' aither. So go your ways home, my poor girl! an' sure, it's my heart bleeds to see your father's child in sich sore trouble."

"Much about her trouble," said Cauth, as she entered the cabin, "what is it to Mrs. Esmond's?"

"Are you goin' to take Mabel home with you?" said Bryan, seeing that Celia had taken the poor maniac by the arm.

"In coorse I am, Bryan, if she'll only stay when I get her there."

"Poor Jerry Pierce!" muttered Mabel, as they went off together; "she'll hang him, I know well, an' then myself and Celia 'ill be walkin,' walkin' till the Day o' Judgment all alone—alone—alone!"

CHAPTER XIX.

AN APPARITION AT ROSE LODGE.

It was no idle threat of Kate Costelloe's that she would give information to a magistrate of having seen Jerry Pierce on the Rock, and it was with great difficulty that Bryan could persuade her from going off at once to Rose Lodge with that amiable intention.

"Do you think," said she, "that *I'm* goin' to screen the villain that dipped his hands in the blood of the poor young master? If I did, wouldn't I be jist as bad as he is, an' worse, too, in a manner? Now, I tell you, Bryan, there's no use talkin' to me, an' it makes my blood boil, so it does, to hear *you* tryin' to excuse the bloodthirsty villain"——

"I'm not tryin' to excuse him—how could I?"

"Well, how came you to harbour him on the Rock above, as I see you did? Tell me that, now, you hard-hearted, ungrateful ould man, you?"

"God forgive you, Cauth aroon," said Bryan mildly, "for all the bad names you're callin' me! Sure, if the man did hide himself of a time on the Rock, it wasn't me that harboured him. Scores of people might hide in the crypts an' places away underground without me ever seein' or hearin' one o' them. An' another thing, I'll warrant you Jerry Pierce has more *gumpshin* in him than to go tell me or any one else what place he was hidin' in."

"Well, anyway, I hope it'll never come to Mrs. Esmond's ears that he *was* up there"——

"An', to be sure, it'll come to her ears if you go an' tell the ould gentleman. But, anyway, say your prayers an' go to bed, an' maybe you'll not be so hot on it in the mornin' as you are now. Pray to God to direct you!" He was going to add,

AN APPARITION AT ROSE LODGE.

"I think you ought to be the last woman to do such a thing, after all the misery you brought on yourself before," but, knowing by experience the probable effect of any such allusion, he prudently kept the thought to himself.

Next morning Cauth declared her intention of going to Rose Lodge, and all Bryan could obtain from her in the way of concession was a promise not to go till after nightfall.

"Very good," said he, "an' I'll go with you myself for company." So the matter rested between them for that day, and Bryan went up to the Rock, after swallowing a hasty breakfast.

We will now introduce the reader to the parlour of Rose Lodge on the evening of that same day. It was a pleasant room on the first floor; and the breath of flowers, the faint sweet perfume of the jessamine and the honeysuckle, was wafted in from the creeping plants trained around the windows, mingled with the rich odour of mignonette and wallflowers in tasteful green boxes on the sills. The evening sun was sinking, and the evening breeze was sighing amongst the leaves and flowers, giving a tremulous motion to their fantastic shadows within the room. Without, all was peace—within, trouble and unrest, for of those assembled in that handsome apartment perhaps not one at that feverish moment

Enjoyed and blessed the lovely hour.

There was the master of the house striding to and fro the room with that quick, irregular pace which denotes not thought, but passion. There was his wife watching him with anxious eyes; and Aunt Winifred, rigid as ever, but with more colour than usual on her cheek, while a certain twitching of the mouth and a tremulous motion of the eyelids denoted some inward emotion not very common with her. Opposite her, near one of the windows, sat young Mrs. Esmond, in her deep mourning robe and widow's cap, her eyes red with weeping, and her lips and cheeks colourless as those of a marble statue. Her tearful eyes were fixed on a half-length portrait of her husband which hung on the wall opposite, and gradually her look became abstracted, as her thoughts wandered back into the blessed past—the sunny years and days of "Long Ago." And Mary Hennessy was there, and Dean M'Dermot, the latter evidently trying to reason Mr. Esmond out of some desperate purpose.

How anxiously Aunt Martha kept glancing from one to the other, hoping, doubtless, from the friendly remonstrances of the good pastor what she could not dare to attempt herself. As yet his arguments appeared to have had but little effect.

"I tell you, Dean," said Mr. Esmond, stopping suddenly in his march, and planting himself before the priest, with his thumbs in his vest pockets,—"I tell you there's no use trying to persuade me from it! I know it's Matty there that put you on the scent, and it may be that she and you are both right, but I've made up my mind, and the Pope himself wouldn't persuade me from it. I'll go out this night, with M'Gowan and the police, come what will, and see if we don't trap the fellow"—

"But, Mr. Esmond"—

"Not a word, Dean, not a word,—begging your pardon, and meaning no disrespect, none whatever,—but I'm of opinion that if I had gone out myself now and then from the first, the villain would have been caught long ago. I know my duty, sir, and I mean to do it. Yes, sir, I mean to do it; for the blood of my murdered nephew cries to me from the ground, and sleep or rest I cannot take for thinking of him. Blood must have blood, and it is a crying shame that the hardened ruffian who so wantonly shed my poor Harry's should have so long escaped detection, and that at our very door, as people say —why, it makes me mad—yes, sir, mad—to think of it!"

"Well, but, my dear Harry"—began his wife; but he quickly stopped her.

"Silence, you, Matty,—one's enough at a time, you know."

"I was going to remind you," said Dean M'Dermot, "that we do not any of us wish you to desist from any lawful means of securing the arrest of the unhappy culprit—that is, if he be still in the country, which I doubt."

"In the name of God, then, Dean M'Dermot, tell me what you *do* wish ?" cried Mr. Esmond almost fiercely.

"I *have* told you, sir," was the calm but dignified answer; "I have endeavoured to prove to you that your going out with the police and this informer"—

"Informer ? What do you mean, sir ?"

"Well, we shall not quarrel about a word," said the Dean, smiling ; "I mean this new witness you have got. I have endeavoured to prove to you, I repeat, that your going out at the head of the party was by no means necessary, and might possibly be a very dangerous proceeding on your part."

"Oh, as for the danger," said the old man curtly, "that's my own affair. I'll attend to that. So, if you have no other reason to advance, I will bid you good-evening at once, as M'Gowan and Mr. Moran and some others are waiting in the office."

"Oh, Uncle Harry, Uncle Harry," said the young widow, speaking for the first time, "I beseech you, risk not your own life in perhaps a vain effort to arrest the—the"—— Sobs choked her voice—she could say no more.

"Let him go," said Miss Esmond, with bitter mockery,—"let him go,—of course he has his life well insured. He knows he has the good-will of the people, and probably thinks that if any danger did threaten him, some stalwart beggar would haply advance to the rescue."

"For mercy's sake, Winifred, don't speak so!" whispered her sister-in-law.

Just at that moment, and whilst Mr. Esmond was clearly meditating some savage retort on his sister, the door opened, and in walked Phil Moran, followed closely by just such a "stalwart beggar" as Miss Esmond's biting sarcasm had indicated.

Every one looked astonished, the more so as the man kept his caubeen on his head, as though he had been my Lord Kenmare himself.[1]

Moran anticipated the angry question that was coming in thunder from Uncle Harry's tongue. "Here is a man," said he, "Mr. Esmond, who wants to see you on business so important that it will not brook delay."

"And why the d———l don't you take him to the office? Don't you know well enough, Moran, that *this* is no place for business?"

"Well, to tell the truth, *I* didn't bring him here. He came into your office with that queer genius of a clerk of mine, Ned Murtha, whom I left in *my* office hard at work, and,

---

[1] There are few of our readers, it is presumed, who are not aware of the high privilege enjoyed from time immemorial by the Barons of Kenmare, that of remaining covered in the presence of royalty—the reward of some leal service rendered in the stormy days of old.

according to Ned's statement, he is prepared to give evidence against"——

"Against Jerry Pierce!" cried Mr. Esmond, coming eagerly forward. "Why, that's capital good news, upon my honour!" and he rubbed his hands fast and furiously. "We'll have no lack of evidence now. But tell me, honest man, why did you not come forward before if you knew anything about this wretched business? How did it happen, I say, that you kept the secret so long?"

"I'd keep it longer," was the gruff answer, "if it wasn't for the reward. I may as well tell you the thruth at onst."

"What a barefaced villain!" whispered Moran to Mary Hennessy, beside whom he somehow managed to find himself.

"There is something in his voice that I don't like," was the young lady's reply at the same time.

The younger Mrs. Esmond turned to the window to hide her tears, and perhaps still more to avoid seeing the man, whose presence was distasteful to her, she knew not why. Luckily for her purpose, Mad Mabel suddenly appeared outside, and, after glancing with the wild look of her unhappy class at each of the persons within the room, her eyes rested on the beggar-man, and she sang in her usual way——

> "One of my false comrades did me betray,
> And for one bare guinea swore my life away."

"Hush! hush!" said Mrs. Esmond in her sweet, gentle voice.

"Och! why wouldn't I sing, ma'am? Sure, it's 'The Croppy Boy,' you know——

> In New Geneva this young man died,
> And in Killeavin his body lies;
> All ye Roman Catholics that do pass by,
> Pray the Lord have mercy on the Croppy Boy!

Poor Patrick! sure, I pray for you, anyway—och! no, I don't —I can't pray now, at all—

> Five hundred pounds then they would lay down,
> For to see me walkin' through Wexford town.

Ah! the poor Croppy Boy! Sure, they hanged him, afther all, an' they'll hang Jerry Pierce, and what'll Celia do then?"

"Will you send her off out of that?" cried Mr. Esmond, stamping his foot in a towering passion.

"Don't be angry with me, Mr. Esmond," said Mabel, with a frightened look. "Sure, I didn't say I'd kill ould Esmond that night in the abbey—it was Tim Murtha, an'—an'"—

Here she was dragged away by a gardener, whom Mrs. Esmond had seen passing, and beckoned to approach for that purpose.

"Speak out, you, fellow!" said Mr. Esmond, his face somewhat paler than usual, and a visible tremor in his voice. "What's your name, in the first place? Confound you! why don't you answer me?—who are you?" and, in his eagerness to know, he caught hold of the man's coat by the collar and gave him a shake.

"Take your hand off my collar, Mr. Esmond," replied the man in a tone half fierce, half sullen, "then I'll tell you who I am." The hand was removed accordingly, and he moved a step or two back, then said in a loud, distinct tone—

"I'm JERRY PIERCE! I heard you were goin' out wid the peelers to take me, so I came to save you the trouble."

The sound of his familiar voice, evidently disguised before, and the mention of a name so hated by all, had the effect of an electric shock on all present. The Dean started to his feet, and opened his mouth to speak, but remained as if spellbound by the man's audacity. One simultaneous shriek burst from the ladies, and young Mrs. Esmond fainted away in her chair. As for Uncle Harry, stout and stubborn as he was, he reeled back some paces, till the Dean caught him by the arm; every drop of blood forsook his cheek, and his eyes rested with a wild and haggard stare on the face now exposed to view by the removal of the caubeen.

Before another word was spoken, the parlour door opened, and a servant appearing, said that the old man of the Rock, and a woman he had with him, wanted to see his honour on very particular business.

"Let them go to—Halifax!" cried Mr. Esmond, his rage concentrating on the unhappy man who stood so unblushingly before him.

"You'd best let them in," said Pierce coolly. "I b'lieve it's comin' to lodge information agin me the woman is—to let you know where you'll find Jerry Pierce."

"Silence!" roared Mr. Esmond, and he motioned to the servant to show Bryan and Cauth into the office.

"Why not have them in here, Harry?" said Miss Esmond.

"Ay, that's always the way with you women," snapped her brother; "you want to see and hear everything."

"Well, I confess," said Dean M'Dermot, "I was just going to make the same request; however, if you have any particular objection"—

"None in the world, Dean. Though I really cannot understand why any of you should wish to have these old people brought in, you shall be gratified by a sight of them. Show them in, Dick. Mr. Moran, have the goodness to send word to the barrack for Captain Dundas to send some men immediately."

"Well, if it's plasin' to your honour," said Pierce, twirling his hat between his hands and looking at it sheepishly, "I would wish to have the business settled as soon as convaynient—in regard to the reward that's promised for the takin' of Jerry Pierce."

The ladies, more than ever disgusted by the man's audacious hardihood, raised their hands and eyes in horror, and uttered exclamations of terror and amazement, with the exception of young Mrs. Esmond, who, having somewhat recovered, stood up, and, taking Mary Hennessy's arm, prepared to leave the room, carefully avoiding the sight of Pierce. Moran, as if forgetful of the important commission given him, stood motionless in his place; Uncle Harry, between rage and astonishment, found himself incapable of uttering a word; Dean M'Dermot stood with folded arms watching the unhappy criminal from between his half-closed eyelids with an undefined expression of intense interest. As Mrs. Esmond passed him with tottering steps, he calmly and quietly laid his hand on her arm and said in a significant tone—

"I think you had better remain."

"Oh, Dean, I cannot—I cannot!—it would kill me—indeed, indeed it would! Oh, my God!" and she burst into a passionate flood of tears, "to think of me being in the same room with the murderer of my darling, darling Harry!"

"But, sure, you're not, Mrs. Esmond dear!—sure, you're not

in the same room with him, at all!" It was Pierce himself
that spoke, and his voice was broken and tremulous.

"Oh, the murdherin' villain, hear to what he says!" cried
Cauth from the corner where she and Bryan had placed themselves,—"the murdherin' villain! Isn't it a wondher the earth
doesn't open an' swallow him up afther tellin' that black lie,
'n' his reverence to the fore, an' the poor mistress!"

"Silence!" cried again the stern voice of Mr. Esmond;
"leave the wretch to me."

"Well, but, your honour, Mr. Esmond," persisted Cauth,
"doesn't the whole counthry *know* he done the deed? An'
didn't I come here myself a purpose to let you know that I
seen him last night on the Rock above? An' wouldn't I a'
travelled every fut o' the road to Dublin an' back again, to
prove agin him, the unlucky vagabone?"

Mr. Esmond was turning fiercely on Bryan to ask how it
happened that Pierce came to be seen on the Rock, when he
and all present were struck dumb with amazement by the
sudden change that had come over his niece. From the
moment that Pierce spoke those strange words she had stood
as if transfixed, her soft hazel eyes dilating with wonder as
they penetrated farther and deeper into the soul of the supposed murderer of her husband, through the big bold eyes that
never quailed a moment under that searching glance, but
seemed rather to invite it.

There the two stood—face to face—immovable—mute as
statues——gazing into each other's eyes, whilst nor word nor
breath from any of the spectators broke the awful silence. At
last Mrs. Esmond drew a long sigh, like one recovering from a
swoon, her pale lips opened, and some broken, tremulous words
were faintly heard—

"Do you mean to say, Jerry Pierce, that *you* are not the
murderer of *my* husband?"

And Pierce answered with the same unshrinking confidence,
"I do, Mrs. Esmond—that's what I mane to say, an' I take God
to witness this blessed day,—an' sure, His beautiful bright sun
is goin' down there behind the mountains," he raised his arm
solemnly and held it aloft,—"that what I say is truth an' no lie!"

"Great God! is it possible?" cried Miss Esmond. "Dear!
dear!" said her sister-in-law. Mary Hennessy said nothing,

she was too much intent in watching the principal actors in the deeply-exciting scene. Moran rested his hand on the back of a chair, in a position to examine Pierce's countenance, himself partially hidden by the goodly bulk of Mr. Esmond. The latter stood trembling like an aspen leaf with the fierce passion that was brewing within him.

"Then you didn't murder him, Jerry Pierce?" said the widow in softening accents,—"you didn't murder your good master?"

"If you don't b'lieve me, ma'am," said Pierce, the tears choking his utterance, "ask his reverence there—I'll engage he doesn't misdoubt my word."

Almost involuntarily every eye was turned on the Dean, and Mrs. Esmond in particular fixed an anxious look on his benevolent face, where some deep emotion was setting every muscle in motion.

"I believe him, Mrs. Esmond," said the venerable man, with that calm dignity which never forsook him; "I believe in my heart he tells you what is true."

"*I* don't believe him, then," cried Mr. Esmond vehemently; "I'd as soon believe the father of lies, that was *a murderer from the beginning!*" His voice was hoarse, and his face livid with rage. "I tell you both he's an incarnate fiend, that same Jerry Pierce, and it's burned he ought to be—burned instead of hanged. But hanged he'll be, if there's law or justice in Tipperary! I'd—I'd hang him myself if there was no one else to do it. I would, by——" The oath that was on his foaming lips never passed them—it died away unspoken, beneath the stern glance of the Dean.

"Well, all *I* can say is this, Mr. Esmond," said Pierce in a firm, manly tone, "that if you knew but all, you'd be the last man alive to say that of Jerry Pierce."

"What do you mean, you villain?" thundered the enraged magistrate.

Here the elder Mrs. Esmond uttered an exclamation of surprise and looked significantly at Moran.

"I mane this, your honour—that only for poor Jerry Pierce, villain an' all as he is, you wouldn't be here now to call him so, but moulderin' away in the vault above, beside my poor dear master—God rest his soul in glory!"

"This is more of your atrocious lies!" cried Mr. Esmond, "Do you take me for a fool, you scoundrel?"

"Well, I don't, Mr. Esmond, bekase them that 'id buy your honour for a fool, 'id be apt to lie a long time out o' their money. Howsomever, you ought to remember me of all people, for if I hadn't been out on my thramp the night your horse wanted to put you an' the mistress in the quarry beyant, an' one that wasn't a horse, but a poor heart-broken man, had a pistol in his hand at *the limekiln*, I'm thinkin' it's little trouble the world 'id be to you now. An' listen hither, Mr. Esmond," he added slowly and emphatically, "*that pistol was the very one that shot your nephew*,—the light of heaven to his soul!—an' the same hand that pulled the trigger that black an' dismal night was goin' to pull it then, an' would, too, Mr. Esmond, only for the voice that said '*Remember!*' and that voice was Jerry Pierce's."

Various exclamations of astonishment escaped the listeners, the younger Mrs. Esmond alone remaining silent. She had sunk on a chair opposite Pierce, and sat with her hands clasped and her head bowed down beneath the crushing load of newly-revived sorrow.

"Do you hear that, Mrs. Esmond?" whispered Mary Hennessy. "You see it wasn't poor Pierce that did it, after all."

"I heard it, Mary, I heard it," she listlessly replied; "but it makes little difference to me who did it. Some one did it—that's certain."

For several moments Mr. Esmond and Jerry Pierce stood looking at each other in silence—the one with a look of blank amazement, in which a certain tinge of incredulity was strangely mingled—the other with the same unshrinking confidence with which he had before confronted the widowed wife of young Harry Esmond. The Dean and Moran exchanged significant glances, intimating to each other the prudence of keeping silent for the present.

When the old man spoke again his face was paler than its wont, and there was a husky tone in his voice, yet he laboured hard to keep up his usual sternness of voice and mien. "I know it doesn't hurt *you* much," said he, "to trump up a story"—

"Harry," said his wife, suddenly breaking silence, "he didn't trump up that story, anyhow,—he saved our lives that night, as true as he's standing there. I suspected as much the moment he came into the room in that costume, and I would know among a thousand the tone of the voice that uttered that word 'Remember!' for it has rung in my ears ever since, sleeping and waking."

"And who was he," resumed Mr. Esmond in the same half-incredulous tone, as if scarcely noticing the interruption,—" who was he that, according to your showing, would have made away with another of the Esmonds? You are not going to keep his secret, are you?"

There was a long pause, during which the heavy features of Jerry Pierce were convulsed as by some inward struggle. Every ear was strained to catch the answer, every eye was fixed on the man's face—even Henrietta Esmond had started into sudden animation as the important question reached her ear, and she leaned eagerly forward, with her very soul in her eyes. Moran and the Dean shifted their positions so as to get a fuller view of Pierce's countenance, but neither spoke.

Slowly at last spoke Jerry Pierce, and his lips and his cheeks were ashen white as he hissed out the name of *Tim Murtha*, then covered his face with his hands, as though to conceal the shame of that moment.

"Tim Murtha!" was repeated from mouth to mouth in tones of horror and disgust, while each one looked into their neighbour's face to read the effect of the announcement.

"Take care how you answer me, fellow!" said Mr. Esmond, speaking with difficulty, some strange emotion quivering in his frame; "are you sure—sure it was Tim Murtha?"

"As sure as I am that there's a God in heaven!" answered Pierce solemnly and reverently.

"Dean, or you, Moran, question him," said the old man in a choking voice. "I—I can't go on with it;" and he sat down beside his niece.

The Dean motioned to Moran to speak, for even he was more agitated than he cared to show. Moran bowed assent.

"Then we are to infer from what you say," said he, "that it was Tim Murtha who shot young Mr. Esmond?"

"Wisha! God pity him an' me, it was, sir!"—and the tears

came trickling from between the big, hard, sinewy fingers that still covered Pierce's agonised face.

Moran raised his hand gently to enjoin silence on the listeners.

"And what motive," said he, "induced *him* to perpetrate so foul a murder? What ill feeling could *he* have against Mr. Esmond?"

Here Mr. Esmond raised himself in his chair and fixed a look of searching scrutiny on Pierce. And Pierce, before he answered, turned a deprecating, almost a compassionate look on the old man.

"He had no motive, at all, in killin' *him*, Mr. Moran," he slowly replied, " nor no ill-will that ever man had,—an' he no more meant to kill him that night than he did to kill me or you."

"Great God! how was it, then?"

"He mistook him for another."

"Ha!" cried Miss Esmond, starting to her feet, "I knew it —I knew that no one ever meant to kill our darling Harry."

"Glory be to God!" cried Couth, advancing a step or two from her corner.

Still the widow stirred not, nor did Mr. Esmond.

"But how—how," said Moran, after an embarrassed pause,— "how did—such a mistake occur?"

Jerry Pierce avoided looking at Mr. Esmond, though he felt that his piercing glance was on him, reading his very soul.

"It was the horse he rode—an' the name he had—that caused *his* death—an' saved another!"

"Merciful Heaven!" cried Aunt Martha, as her own secret misgivings and the often-hinted suspicions of her sister-in-law were thus to the letter justified.

Moran came to a dead pause, turned a troubled, anxious look on Mr. Esmond, and seemed as if uncertain whether he ought to continue.

"Go on," said Mr. Esmond, rightly interpreting his hesitation.

"Pardon me, Mr. Esmond," said the kind-hearted lawyer, would it not be better to postpone the further hearing of this strange and mournful tale?"

"Go on I tell you," was the stern reply. "Ask him how

it happened. It will all be soon known to the whole country."

"You hear what Mr. Esmond says?" said Moran, addressing Pierce.

"I do, sir, an' if he wants to hear it I'll tell it, though I'd sooner not." But still he hesitated, looked askance at young Mrs. Esmond, wiped his eyes with the sleeve of his coat, coughed, looked again, then fairly burst out crying, and said as well as he could for the choking in his throat, "There's no use tryin' any more—I can't do it—an' the mistress to the fore!—I can't—it 'id kill her dead, so it would!"

Mrs. Esmond raised her head and looked at him with a ghastly smile, as she replied, "No fear of that, Pierce!—it is pretty hard to kill *me*!—and I must hear what—what *you* have to tell, one day or another, so in God's name tell it now while I am able to listen."

Here the tramp of marching men was heard outside; the parlour-door was opened stealthily, and the cadaverous visage of Ned Murtha made its appearance, followed by his lank body. He looked at no one, seemed to think of no one, but Jerry Pierce, who stood near the door, and to him he whispered in a tone of horror and alarm—

"The peelers, Jerry!—the peelers is without, an' Sargint Kellett!"

"Well, what o' that?" said Pierce, though his cheek blanched at the dreaded name. "Didn't I know they'd be takin' me, an' didn't I give myself up?"

"Sure I know, Jerry dear—I know; but—och, och! Lord help us!"

"Leave the room, sir!" cried Mr. Esmond sternly. "How dare you come in here unbidden?"

"Perhaps it were well to let him remain," suggested Moran; "we may want him."

"Humph! want him?" growled the surly old man, not in dissent, however. "Go on, you, Pierce!—Mr. Informer, I suppose we may call you now—giving up your associate in crime to save your own worthless life—eh?"

The evil spirit was coming back on him, and Pierce glared on him like a tiger preparing for a spring. Fire flashed from his eyes, and his face was suffused with a burning glow. Words sharp and bitter were on his lips, when young Mrs. Esmond rose, and, approaching him, to the surprise of all present, laid her hand on his arm.

"Pierce," said she, "there's something telling me that you have spoken truly denying the murder of my poor husband—if you were not accessory to it, tell us, I beseech you, what you know about it, and how you came to know it."

"I will, ma'am, as I have God to face, I'll tell you all about it," said Pierce, more firmly than before, as though braced up to greater hardihood by the wanton attack of Mr. Esmond. "I said before that it wasn't my poor master Tim Murtha meant to kill, but"—

"But his uncle?" put in Mr. Esmond, with a bitter sneer.

"You've jist guessed it, Mr. Esmond," said Pierce, turning on him almost fiercely; "it was *his uncle* an' nobody else. An' if the truth was known, maybe it was no great wonder. Anyhow, the whole country knew that Tim had it in for you, an' maybe more than Tim, for that matter."

"Villain! scoundrel!" cried Mr. Esmond, starting up in a rage.

"Take it aisy now, Mr. Esmond," said Pierce coolly, and with an impressive motion of his hand, "if you want to hear the story before I'm taken off to gaol. Don't be callin' people sich ugly names till you know whether they desarve it or not. I said every one knew that Tim had it in for you, an' I was tryin' all I could to put the evil thought out of his head, but jist as soon as I'd get him persuaded to lave it all in the hands o' God, Mr. Eamond here was sure to do something to stir up his blood worse than ever?"—

The old gentleman was again breaking in with a fierce objurgation, but the Dean, laying his hand on his arm, begged him to remain quiet, or that otherwise they might as well give up hopes of hearing the sad details.

"He never got right over that hurt," resumed Pierce, "an' so he wasn't able to work, an' there was nothing for it but to go out an' take to the road at onst, an' when himself an' the childer 'id be goin' their rounds he met Mr. Esmond of an odd time, an' though he never asked him for anything—he'd scorn to do it—still he always gave him the height of abuse, an' called him a 'lazy dog,' and all sich names, an' many's the time he threatened to horsewhip him, till at last he had the poor fellow 'most beside himself, an' he said the two o' them couldn't live any longer, that one o' them must die! Well, afther that, sure myself was night an' day on the watch for fear he'd have the misfortune to do it, and things wore round till that unlucky day that the poor master went to Rose Lodge"—

"Merciful Heaven!" cried young Mrs. Esmond; "he went at my urgent request to warn his uncle of the danger to which he was exposed."

"I know that, Mrs. Esmond. It was Cauth there that told you of it, and Cauth can tell you who told her, and put her up to tell you."

"Well, sure enough it was your four bones, Jerry Pierce," said Cauth, with a groan; "there's no denyin' that, anyhow!"

"An' I was watchin' Tim all that day," went on Jerry, "an' havin' others watchin' him too, both him and ould Mr. Esmond—ay, an' the young master too, for some way or another I had a fear over me about him, though I couldn't tell what it was for, or how it came. At last, when it was wearin' on near evenin' I made up my mind that I wouldn't stand it any longer, but I'd go to Tim an' get him to go with me, himself an' the childer, to some other part o' the counthry, where I'd work for them all, an' keep poor Tim out of the way of doing the bad that was in his heart to do."

"And that was the object of your leaving, Jerry?" said Mrs. Esmond in a tremulous voice.

"Surely it was, ma'am; but, as I said, there was something over me, and when I heard that the master—God rest him!—was goin' to Rose Lodge, well, do you know, but my flesh began to creep, an' I went out to Mulligan, an' says I to him, 'Tom, I'm afeard there's something bad goin' to happen;' an' Mulligan laughed at me, an' says he, 'I have to go in to give the bit of this bridle a rub, for it isn't as bright as I'd wish, an' do you be gettin' the roan saddled while I'm away, for you see the master's in a hurry.' 'I will,' says I, an' sure enough I tried to do it, but somehow I was so through-other in myself, an' my hands was tremblin' to that degree, that I couldn't get on as I'd wish, an' when Tom came in a great hurry to take out the roan, he was as mad as a March hare when he found I hadn't it done, an' I b'lieve it's angry enough the poor master was at havin' to wait so long. Well, he got off, anyhow, an' afther I went in an' said some words to the mistress before I'd go, I went off as fast as my legs 'id carry me towards the Lodge. Not a sight o' Tim could I see up or down, an' there I kep' walkin' backwards and forwards along the road near the Lodge, sometimes takin' to the fields for fear any one 'id notice me, till at last it came on night, and then says I to myself, '*He'll* not be goin' out the night, I'm thinkin', when he wasn't out before ; an' sure there's no danger of my master, anyhow,' so with that I was makin' the best o' my speed to Larry Mulquin's, where I had a little business o' my own, when, jist as I got to Mr. Elliott's gate"—

Here a singular interruption took place, the nature of which we will describe in our next chapter. At the window again appeared Mabel, chanting still the tragic fate of "The Croppy Boy"—

"Five hundred pounds then she would lay down,
For to see me walkin' through Wexford town.

Farewell, father, an' mother too,
Sister Mary, I have but you—

"Och, wirra! there's the peelers!" and, with an unearthly scream of terror, she fled like a lapwing.

CHAPTER XX.

WHO KILLED MR. ESMOND.

Jerry Pierce had just reached the most critical point of his narrative, as we have seen, when loud voices were heard in the hall, the door was flung open, and an old woman in a red cloak planted on the floor, first herself, then her staff, with angry determination, and a fierce exultation that was explained by the sheepish look of a servant in livery, who had been vainly endeavouring to keep the dame from entering the parlour.

"Be off wid yourself, now!" cried she, turning and shaking her stick at him; "you don't know what it is to anger me, but I'll make you know it afore you're many days oulder!—be off now, when I bid you!" and she slammed the door in his face, then turned again and faced the company, her two hands resting on her stick, and her keen old eyes peering sharply from under her deep hood.

"Where's Jerry Pierce?" said she. "I want Jerry Pierce."

"Here I am, vanithee," said Pierce, close beside her; "what's wrong wid you?"

"There's nothing wrong wid *me*," she said, drawing close to him, and looking up in his face with an undefinable expression of interest; "but there's everything wrong wid *you*, an' I come to stand your friend, bekase I know you want one. What are they all doin' here? And what's the pealers doin' there abroad? They didn't take you, did they?"

"No; but I took myself, vanithee—I gave myself up."

"God help you, then! for it's you was the foolish man to do it—you'll be sorry for it, mind I tell you, an' I often tould it to you before. But, *past counsel past grace*."

Here Mr. Esmond rang the bell furiously, and ordered the

servant who appeared to remove the woman immediately. Hearing that, she faced him like a lioness.

"No, nor you'll not remove me," she cried, mimicking his tone. "Here I am, an' here I'll be as long as he's in it," nodding sideways to Jerry Pierce. "When he goes I'll go, an' not till then."

"We shall see that. Tell Sergeant Kellett to send in some of his men."

This soon changed the woman's tone, and she addressed herself in piteous terms to those present. "Oh, Mrs. Esmond, you were always good to me—an' the poor young madam! Oh, ma'am dear, sure, you'll not be hard-hearted, anyhow!—'on't you put in a word for me? O Lord! here they're comin'! Father M'Dermot, I know you're not pleased with me, an' sure it's little wondher, God He knows; but I'm not so bad as they say, your reverence! Och, take pity on a poor ould crathur, an' don't let the peelers take me!—I want to stay wid Jerry here."

"But, my good woman," said the Dean kindly, but coldly, "what business have you here? This is no place for you, and you ought to know that."

"And sure I do know it, your reverence, sure I do know it well—but isn't it my own son that's here to the fore, an' the peelers abroad to take him for murder—though he's as innocent of it as the child unborn!"

"You his mother? You Jerry Pierce's mother?" was heard on every side, and no one appeared more surprised than Jerry himself, who was actually struck dumb with amazement, and stood looking at the woman with eyes wide distended.

The door opened, and Mr. Esmond made a sign to the two policemen who appeared to take the old woman from the room. Involuntarily Jerry Pierce put his great strong arm round her, and her piteous cry drew an earnest remonstrance from the ladies. Dean M'Dermot approached Mr. Esmond and whispered a request that the wretched creature might be suffered to remain, whilst Moran took it upon himself to dismiss the policemen, telling them to remain in the hall.

None of these movements escaped the keen eye of the vanithee, and as Moran passed her she whispered, without moving her head, "Come to my house this evening after dark, and I'll tell you something you'll be glad to hear." He turned in surprise to look at her, but she was looking another way.

"If you are to remain, then," said Mr. Esmond sternly, "mind you don't open your mouth to speak—if you do, out you go, and off to the black hole."

"Long life to your honour, I'll be as quiet as a mouse!"

Jerry Pierce was then ordered to resume his sad tale, which he did in these terms—

"I said I had just got to Mr. Elliott's gate, an' you all know what a dark place it is on account o' the big trees that spreads out over the road—well, something put it into my head to stop a little so as to take a look round, for the moon was jist beginnin' to rise, an' it was as purty a night as ever you seen. You'd wondher how any one could have murdher in their heart sich a night as that; but, ochone! the Divil cares little for purty nights or purty days! Well, anyhow, I was only a minnit or two standin' wid my back to one o' the gate-piers, when I hears a horse's foot comin' dashin' up the road from Ross Lodge, an' says I to myself, 'If the master's above ground now that's *him*,' an' sure enough it was, an' didn't my heart jump to my mouth when I seen him as plain as I see any of you now, an' sure enough he was goin' like the wind, 'most at a gallop"—

"My poor darling! my poor Harry!" sobbed Mrs. Esmond; "true enough you said it, '*Nine o'clock or never!*'" And she buried her face in her handkerchief. The other ladies were all in tears.

"Jist as he passed me," resumed Jerry, "I heard a voice among the trees sayin', 'There's the roan now, an' Harry Esmond—but stop, stop! it's young Harry!' The last words came too late—a shot was fired at the sound of the name—and before I could get out a word I heard my poor master sayin', 'My God! I'm killed!' and he fell sideways off the horse; but he didn't fall on the ground—I catched him in my arms!"

Here poor Jerry's voice failed him, and, after many ineffectual efforts to master his emotion, he burst into tears and cried as if his heart would break. No one spoke—the mighty grief of some, the deep sympathy of others, the compassion of others, kept all silent.

At last Pierce spoke again, after clearing his voice divers times—

"The horse galloped away towards the Hall, an' I sat down on the roadside and laid my poor master's head up again' my breast an' strove all I could to bring him to ; but sure, what could I do when death was there?—all I could do was to staunch the blood wid a bit of a handkercher I had,—an', indeed, I have that same handkercher away in a little box wid his blood on it, —the vanithee can tell you that,—an' I mane to keep it, too, though it's a poor keepsake, but it's all the keepsake poor Jerry Pierce has. Well, while I was sittin' there, afeard to lave him for fear there might still be a chance of him comin' to, who should start out to me but Tim Murtha, an' he says to me, ' Why, sure, sure, it isn't your master 'id be in it ?' an' says I to him, ' It's nobody else that's in it, God look down on his poor wife this night, an' the little weeny crathurs he left afther him ! —an' God forgive them that spilled his blood ! for it's the heavy curse I'm afeard 'll come down on them !' To tell God's truth, poor Tim was as much troubled as I was in a manner, an' he didn't attempt to deny that it was him done it, but all the satisfaction I could get out of him was that it was ould Harry Esmond he meant to shoot. 'But do you think he is dead ?' says he, leanin' over him. ' As dead as a door nail,' says I, 'God help us all this night !' 'Amen !' says he, 'amen ! an' sure, God He knows I'd sooner be lyin' there where he is this night, than to think I'd have the hard fortune to shoot *him*! But och, och ! it was all the fau't of that unlucky bird, Thady Mulrooney, that I set to watch for the ould chap.' (Don't be vexed at *me*, Mr. Esmond, I'm only sayin' what *he* said.) 'But,' says I, ' you misfortunate man, didn't you know the master was at Rose Lodge, an' that it wasn't likely the ould gentleman 'id be goin' to the Hall at that hour o' the night ?' 'Well,' says he, 'I declare to you, Jerry Pierce, I didn't know your master was at the Lodge, however I chanced to miss seein' him, an' the groom at the Lodge tould Thady, an' him ladin' the roan up an' down, that *Mr. Esmond* was goin' to the Hall, an' Thady never thought of askin' which he meant, knowin' well that the roan didn't belong to young Mr. Esmond ; sure, myself never misdoubted but it was the ould lad was goin,' an' I thought I'd do the business at onst an' have it over.'"

Here the widow's emotion became so violent that she was

taken from the room by Mary Hennessy and Aunt Martha, both of whom soon returned, as she begged to be left alone.

"Go on with what you were saying," said Mr. Esmond sharply; "we have no time to wait for your crocodile tears to dry!—go on, I say."

"Ah, you ould rap!" muttered the vanithee between her teeth; "it's a pity it wasn't you was in it, an' not your nevy!"

"Now, I'll tell you what it is, Mr. Esmond," said Pierce, with manly firmness, "if you don't keep your tongue off me, I'll keep my mouth shut, an' you may bring in the peelers as soon as you like."

"Pray go on, Pierce," said Dean M'Dermot, anxious to prevent Mr. Esmond from speaking the still harder words that were on his lips.

"I will, your reverence, when you bid me," said Pierce, "but I wouldn't do it for *him*. Anyhow, there isn't much more to tell. I was tryin' hard to get Tim away before any one 'id come, but someway or another I couldn't get him inseused into the danger of stayin' there; he was so stupefied when he seen what he had done, an' that Mr. Esmond wasn't comin' to, that you might as well talk to a big stone, an' I was 'most out o' my mind wid grief an' trouble, dreadin' every minnit that somebody 'id come an' catch the misfortunate man, an' still watchin' for some one to help to take the poor master home. God only knows what I went through in that little while, till Tom Mulligan an' Barney Breen came up on the look-out for Mr. Esmond. They were passin' us by, as one or two others did before, on account o' the dark shadow of the trees over where we were, when I called out to them, an' they came over, an' och, och! but there's where the cryin' an' clappin' of hands was, when they found the poor master, that we all had our hearts in, lyin' there dead——dead——dead in my arms. An' when they asked who done it, at all, sure myself, thinkin' to screen poor Tim, said I didn't know, that it was somebody from behind the fence, what do you think of Tim but he spoke out an' said, 'Now, don't be tellin' lies, Jerry Pierce!—you know well enough who done it. *It was me*,' says he to Tom; 'I'm the unlucky poor crathur that shot him—thinkin' it was the ould fellow I had, on account o' the horse,—*I* shot him, an' I'm willin' to die for doin' it, for hangin' is too good for me!'

'You'll not die now, then,' says Tom Mulligan back to him; 'I see plain enough that it wasn't him you meant to shoot, an', anyhow, it wouldn't bring him back to life. So go off wid yourself, now, an' quit the country as fast as you can, you poor, unfortunate man!—God forgive you this night, for you've done a bad deed!—but I'm not the man to prove agin you when I and you're troubled enough.' Barney Breen said the same, an' between us we persuaded Tim to go off an' hide somewhere till we'd see how things 'id go. "Och, och!" says he, goin' away, 'if it was only the ould fellow was in it, what 'id I care—what 'id I care?—but *him* of all men—him that was so good an' kind to every one!' Well, sure, Tom Mulligan wanted me to go back home wid them, but I tould him what I had in my mind in regard to doin' for my sister's poor little orphans, an' that now they'd need some one to do for them more than ever they did, on account of their father havin' to go away from them altogether. 'But,' says Tom, 'if you don't come home,' says he, 'an' if you keep out o' sight that-a-way, how do you know but it's yourself they'd be suspectin'?' 'Is it me?' says I; 'is it anybody 'id suspect me of shootin' my own master, an' the best master, too, that ever a poor boy had?—oh, bedad, Tom,' says I, 'there's nobody 'id be fool enough to think o' that.' 'I don't know,' says he, shakin' his head. So then I ups an' I tells him how I wanted to screen poor Tim on account o' the childer, an' made him an' Barney promise that they'd never let on that they knew anything at all about who fired the shot, or how it happened, until I'd give them lave. Tom was mighty loath to promise, but at last he did. And then he says to Barney, 'Barney,' says he, 'run across the fields there to Jack Phelan's an' tell them what has happened, an' let them bring the wheel-car wid some straw an' a quilt or somethin' over it. Och, wirra, wirra!' says he, 'but it's the poor home-comin' for the master——the glory of heaven to his sowl this night!' So with that we heard some of the others that were out on the sarch comin' up the road, an' I got away into the wood afore any more o' them 'id see me. Sure enough, next day the whole countryside had it that it was Jerry Pierce shot Mr. Esmond, an' though it was worse than death for me to lie under sich a black deed, an' to have people cursin' an' hatin' me for a murder I had no more to do with than the priest of

the parish, still I made up my mind——ay, an' I swore it, too——
that I'd never make any one the wiser for what I knew myself,
an' that I'd get away out o' the country as soon as I could, if
Tim 'id only stay wid the childer an' keep his own saycret. It
was hard to get Tim argued into it, but still I did, myself an'
Ned Murtha, my cousin there, an' Tim's cousin too,—an' he
can tell you as well as myself that it's God's truth I'm tellin'
ye all."

"An' sure I can, Jerry," blubbered Ned, his eyes streaming
over ; "an' sure, Mr. Moran——long life to him!——can bear witness
that I gave him a hint of it when he wanted me to make out
the warrant for you, Jerry. But I wouldn't make it out,
Jerry. I couldn't write a line of it, if I was torn in pieces for
it, bekase I knew it 'id be a black sin, an' a burnin' shame."

"I remember your strange conduct very well, Ned," said
Moran kindly, "and even the hint you speak of—a hint that
often puzzled me then and after. So, Jerry, you got Tim persuaded to keep his secret and remain in the country ; but how
did it happen that you remained yourself too, as it appears
you did ?"

"Well, I'll jist tell you that, sir," Pierce promptly replied.
"Somehow or another I always had a sort of a notion that God
would see me rightified in His own good time, an' there was
some I didn't care to lave behind me."   Here he began twirling
the caubeen again.   "An' another thing, Mr. Moran, that made
me stay here wid my neck in the halther was the black thought
that was still in Tim Murtha's mind." He glanced at Mr.
Esmond, and saw that there was a thunder-cloud on his brow
and a livid lightning in his eyes.   But still he went on——

"I have tould ye already how I saved Mr. Esmond's life
twice in one night, but I didn't tell ye that there was another
night, when he knew nothing about it, that he was jist as near
death as he was that night, only for one that dashed the
pistol out of Tim's Murtha's hand, an' knocked himself down
——that was me again, an' it happened the very night, Mr.
Moran, that *you* were part of the way wid his honour there,
comin' from Dr. Hennessy's in Cashel, till you turned off from
him at the cross-roads."

Here looks of surprise and consternation were exchanged
between Esmond and Moran, but neither spoke, and Jerry

went on: "God Himself only knows how grieved I was for the poor master, an' the mistress, an' her little orphans. I was walkin' round an' round the outside o' the house, like a ghost, the first night o' the wake, watchin' my opportunity to slip in an' get a sight of him before he'd be put in the coffin, an' at last I ventured in"—

"Liar!" cried Mr. Esmond furiously; "you impose on our indulgence in listening so long to your lying story."

"I'm no liar," said Jerry proudly; "an' I think there's one in this room that seen me there that night."

Here Bryan Cullenan advanced, and, placing himself between Mr. Esmond and Pierce, raised his hand solemnly and said—

"Before God, Mr. Esmond, I tell you he speaks the truth. I was kneelin' beside the bed that time when the quality all went into the other room abroad, when Jerry Pierce came in, wid the cape of his coat over his head, an' stood a little while lookin' at the corpse, an' heavy grief was on him, I could see that, though the life was 'most scared out o' myself, an' me takin' him for a sperit till I got sight of his face at his off goin'; an' another thing I can tell you, Mr. Esmond, that Jerry Pierce went to the Island an' made his station there for the benefit of his poor master's sowl. Now, what do you think of that?"

"I think you're an old fool to believe it, that's all."

"Mr. Esmond," said Dean M'Dermot, "it is not for me to say whether a man is guilty or innocent, when I only know him in the confessional, but I can certify that Jerry Pierce did go to Loch Derg this summer, and with the very intention Bryan has just stated."

"Wisha, glory be to God!" cried Cauth again from her corner, and she clasped her hands and looked upwards.

"Now," said the vanithee, with an exulting nod and a fierce look at Mr. Esmond, "there's a nut for you to crack. Liar, inagh! it's yourself is the liar to say it to one that never could a lie—never, never!"

With difficulty the excited old woman was silenced by the pitying kindness of the Dean and Mr. Moran; as for Esmond, he looked from one to the other with a glazed and half-conscious stare that was more frightful than his previous burst of passion.

"And do you really mean to say, Pierce," said Moran very earnestly, "that you have borne for so long a time the shame and the obloquy of such a crime, merely to screen the father of your sister's children?"

"That's what I say, Mr. Moran, an' as I have God to face, I say the thruth."

"And were you never tempted to betray him all that time, or rather, to clear yourself?"

"God knows I was, many an' many's the time! He had an ugly way wid him of late, poor Tim had, an' he'd say things to me that 'id cut me to the very heart, but then I forgave him, for I knew it was the trouble that done it all. The night he tore the things off his dead child bekase Mrs. Esmond gave them, I was mad enough to kill him"—

"How—what?" cried Mr. Esmond. "What's that you say?"

Mrs. Esmond by a look and a sign warned Pierce to give no explanation on that point, but Mr. Esmond imperiously repeated his question, and whilst Pierce was hesitating, looking from one to the other, uncertain how to act, the vanithee burst into a wild and rapid description of the awful scene, calling on Ned Murtha to verify her account, which he did. The hearing of this strange tale of deadly passion had a different effect on Mr. Esmond from what his wife, at least, expected. During the recital he stood with his eyes cast down, his chest heaving, and the muscles of his face working after a strange fashion; when the cracked voice of the fairy-woman ceased, and Ned Murtha had confirmed her wondrous tale, the old man sank heavily in his chair, and heaved a long deep sigh then closed his eyes wearily.

Meanwhile Moran hastened to finish the examination, if such it could be called. He suddenly assumed a sternness little usual with him, and said to Pierce—

"And are we to understand that after all this forbearance and patient endurance, you have at length made up your mind to turn King's evidence against Tim Murtha, and give the gallows its due?"

Pierce's face was crimson in a moment. He turned on Moran with the fierceness of a roused lion, while the aged crone at his side laughed loud in scorn.

"Mr. Moran," said Pierce, "you're a gentleman, an' I'm only

a poor man—a very poor man. You can say what you like to me, so, but it's aisy seen you don't know much about me, or you wouldn't say the likes o' that. No, sir, I'm not turnin' King's evidence, for only I know that Tim Murtha is out of the reach of the law, it isn't here I'd be now."

"Why, where is Tim Murtha?"

"Oh, bedad, sir, that's more than I can tell," said Pierce, with a grim smile; "but anyhow, he's where the peelers can't catch him"—

"Why, surely the man is not dead, is he?"

"He is, sir—as dead as ever you or I'll be. He died last night of the faver, an' more by token, he left it on me before he died, that I'd come this very day an' give myself up, an' tell all about the murder. The vanithee here, that says she's my mother, though I never knew I had a mother livin',—which is remarkable, but I suppose she knows best,—anyhow, her an' Ned Murtha was to the fore when—when Tim lied."

"That Tim Murtha is dead," said Mary Hennessy, "I can bear witness, for Miss Markham and myself were conducted yesterday evening by this good woman, whom Pierce calls the vanithee, to her little cottage on Gallows Hill, where the poor fellow had died a little before in the greatest misery and destitution." Here Mr. Esmond groaned audibly and moved uneasily in his chair.

"And do you mean to say, Jerry," said Mr. Moran, "that you would never have given information against Murtha had he still lived?"

"Is it me, Mr. Moran," and Pierce turned on him with a flashing eye and a burning cheek—"is it me 'id give information against my sister's husband, an' the father of her poor little orphans?—No, not if I was to be hung myself for the murder,—an' sure, that same was what I laid out for myself, an' nothing else!"

"And you were content to bear all the shame of so foul a crime rather than betray the real culprit?"

"Well, I'll not say I was *content*, your honour!—oh, bedad, I wasn't content at all, for it went to my very heart to have e'er a one, an' especially the poor dear mistress, thinkin' me guilty of sich a crime—me of all men livin',—but still I'd raythor lie under it than have poor Kate's little ones left without their father. That was the short an' the long of it, an' I'd have died without ever lettin' on who done it."

"Then you would have died with a lie in your mouth?" It was the Dean who spoke this.

"No, your reverence, I wouldn't—but I'd have kept my mouth shut, an' then I'd tell neither lies nor truth. But in regard to Mr. Esmond—that's my master—barrin' Mrs. Esmond herself, I'll take my bouk oath on it there wasn't one livin' that his death was so sore a crush to as it was to me. An' sure, didn't I watch the vault ever since he was put into it, an' keep the grass smooth an' green on the top of it above, an' the place all about it as clane as a new pin? An' didn't I say my prayers there for his poor sowl, many an' many's the night when you were all asleep in your beds?"

"Poor Jerry!" said young Mrs. Esmond, who had entered just in time to hear the last words,—"poor Jerry! how much we wronged you! and how glad I am to find not only that it wasn't you—one of our own household—that—that fired the fatal shot, but that no one ever meant to kill my dear husband. It is true my loss is the same, but it is something—oh, much, much!— to know that he was not killed designedly."

"And pray, madam, where's the difference?" cried Mr. Esmond sharply. "Didn't the villain mean to shoot me, only he happened to shoot Harry instead? Wasn't his crime all the same? Tell me that, now! But I see how it is,—I—see—how it is,"—and his passion began to rise—"my life is of no account amongst you—if I had been shot, as the villain intended I should, I don't believe one of you would have cared a rush! Well, here I am, you see, in spite of the murderous crew, and for all Jerry Pierce's fine story I'll have blood for blood before all's over. Now that his partner in crime is out of the way, he thinks to get out of the scrape by lying, but he'll find that lying won't save his neck."

"But if he has good evidence, Mr. Esmond," suggested Moran.

"He evidence?" repeated the old man scornfully. "He has no evidence that will be worth a button—that I'll answer for!"

"Haven't I Tom Mulligan an' Barney Breen?—you're forgettin' that, Mr. Esmond."

Here the sound of carriage wheels was heard without, and Aunt Winifred, going to the window, said, "'Talk of—some-body, and he'll appear,'—there's Tom Mulligan now, come with the carriage for Henrietta."

"Bring him in, then, at once," said young Mrs. Esmond.

"But do you hear, you, Pierce," said Mr. Esmond, "not a word—not a look at Mulligan—mark me, now!"

Pierce had only time to nod assent when the door opened, and in came Tom Mulligan, looking confused and bewildered. He had heard nothing of what had occurred till he drove up and saw the police at the door, then learned from a groom, in answer to his brief inquiry, that "Jerry Pierce was within." That was the amount of his knowledge when the summons to the parlour came to complete his bewilderment. What he saw there was not calculated to reassure him. His eye fixed first on his former fellow-servant, and he involuntarily exclaimed—

"Ah, then, Jerry, my poor fellow, is this the way wid you at last?—sure, didn't I tell you how it 'id end if you didn't take advice?"

Pierce made no answer, but Mr. Esmond called out in his sternest tones—

"Never mind Pierce, but tell us what you know of the murder of your master."

This put Mulligan all in a tremor.

"Is it me, your honour?—is it me know anything of the murder?—Lord save us an' bless us! what 'id I know of it?"

"Come, come, now, Mulligan, tell the truth," said Mr. Moran gently but firmly. "We *know* that you have some knowledge of how it happened, and we must hear it."

Still Mulligan spoke not—his great round eyes vainly seeking some instruction from those of Jerry Pierce, but Jerry Pierce took care to look every way but at him.

"Dolt!" cried Mr. Esmond, stamping on the ground, "why do you not speak?"

"Why, then, that I mayn't sin, Mr. Esmond!" began poor frightened Mulligan, then, by a sudden impulse, he addressed himself to Jerry—"Wisha, Jerry, man alive! what'll I say at all?"

"Tell the truth, every word of it," said Pierce in his deep, quiet voice, "as if you were goin' before your God! Tim's dead now himself, an' he laid it on me to tell all."

"Tim's dead?" shouted Mulligan, much excited; "an' they can't hang you bekase you're as innocent as the child unborn! Oh, then, it's myself 'ill tell every word of it now—an' no mistake!"

"Compose yourself now," said Dean M'Dermot, "and tell us what you saw and heard the night you went out to look—to look for your master."

"I will, your reverence; I'll tell it word for word as if it was at my confession I was."

He then proceeded to narrate the occurrences of that fatal night as far as they came under his knowledge, and his account was found to tally in every, even the smallest particular, with that of Jerry Pierce. With the single exception of Mr. Esmond, all present testified their satisfaction, and openly expressed their conviction of Pierce's innocence.

True to his own harsh character, Mr. Esmond gruffly commanded Mulligan to leave the room. The poor fellow obeyed, not unwillingly but very timidly. As he closed the door he heard Pierce say, "Mr. Esmond, I hope you're not vexed with Mulligan?"

"That's my business—not yours," was the answer. "Have you any more to say?"

"Not a word, your honour—not a word more."

"In that case, Moran, you may as well tell the sergeant to step in."

Here an angry chorus of remonstrance arose from the ladies.

"My goodness, Harry! you're not going to send him to prison?" said his wife.

"If you do, I'll never forgive you, Harry Esmond, never—never!" cried Miss Esmond.

"Dear me, Mr. Esmond, how could you think of such a thing?" from Mary Hennessy.

Henrietta Esmond arose, though with difficulty, from her seat, her face now pale, now flushed—every eye was fixed upon her as she crossed the room in the now deepening twilight. She stopped in front of Jerry Pierce, and then spoke in a voice broken and tremulous as the ripple of the ocean wave—

"Jerry Pierce," said she, "as the party most concerned in

the sad story you have told—as the widow of Harry Esmond— I think it right to assure you that I believe every word you have spoken; I believe you did what you could to avert the dread catastrophe which your fears foresaw, and for that you will accept my heartfelt thanks. I know, too, that but for you, another Esmond would have gone to his account as suddenly as my poor husband—for that too I thank you."— She paused, and Dean M'Dermot spoke.

"And for the honour done our common nature by your heroic fortitude—your generous devotion to your guilty relative and his family—I thank you, Jerry Pierce;" and taking his hand he shook it warmly, whilst the tear that trembled in his eye told the depth and sincerity of his emotion.

"Well," said Kate Costelloe, coming forward, "if everybody thanks him for something or another, I have to thank him for *not killing the young master*, because there's one black villain less than I thought. And, Jerry Pierce, before all the quality, I humbly ax your pardon for all I said to you, and all the hard names I called you this while back, an' for comin' here a purpose to get you taken."

"An' was that what brought *you* here!" screamed the vanithee. "Oh, the curse o' the crows on you for an ould rap! Wasn't it enough for you to hang"—

"Mother! mother!" said Jerry Pierce, laying his hand on her mouth, "don't talk that way. Let the poor woman alone; sure, she was only doin' what she thought she had a right to do—an' she would, too, if I had been guilty, as *she* thought I was—let her alone now an' for ever!"

"I will, Jerry. I will, aroon, when *you* bid me,"—and the crone wiped her eyes with a dilapidated old apron; "but— but"—she darted a fiery look at Cauth—"but—*I'll not forget it to her!*"

"Couldn't I say a word, Mr. Esmond?" inquired Bryan timidly.

"Yes; what have you got to say? But mind, I've a crow to pluck with *you* for harbouring Jerry Pierce on the Rock when you had every reason to suppose him guilty of horrible murder."

"But sure I didn't suppose him guilty, Mr. Esmond," said Bryan anxiously; "indeed, I didn't, your honour! He knows himself that the first time I got sight of him there I was frightened 'most out o' my wits, just for fear he'd be hidin' himself there. I followed him from place to place among the ruins till I came on him at last, an' then he tould me how it was—only makin' me promise that I'd never give information again' poor Tim. From that out, I own I did give him the run of the Rock, an' I'm not sorry for it now, though I ask your honour's pardon, Mr. Esmond, if you think I done wrong."

"Humph! I see I'm left in a minority of one," said Mr. Esmond, looking round with a scowl of defiance; "still, I'll do my duty. Here, Sergeant Kollett,"—that personage had just appeared at the door,—"here is your prisoner," pointing to Pierce, who made no effort at resistance as the rigid policeman placed his hand on his arm.

"Go home, mother," said he to the old woman, "and don't fear for me—if man is ungrateful, God is not, and He'll protect me! Not a word, now—for my sake, I ask it."

He was led away to prison in virtue of the warrant issued months before for his apprehension. The party left behind were proceeding to comment on the strange scene just witnessed, lamenting in no measured terms that Jerry Pierce should have been sent to prison. They were silenced by a stern "It couldn't be helped," from Mr. Esmond, who soon after left the room, and appeared no more that evening.

CHAPTER XXI.

PHIL MORAN TRIES HIS LUCK.

THAT same night, when the stars were in the sky and the shadows deep and dark on the earth, a gentleman knocked at the low door of the fairy-woman's hut. No answer was returned. The knock was repeated, and, after another brief delay, the door was opened very softly, and the stooping figure of the vanithee was visible by the dim light from the crackling brambles on the hearth.

"So you came?" said she. "Well, stay where you are—there's death and poverty inside, an' maybe the faver too—so don't come in." Stepping out on the road, she closed the door after her, and moved close up to her visitor, who was no other than Phil Moran, as the reader will probably have surmised.

"Well now, vanithee," said the lawyer, dropping his voice to a whisper, "what have you got to say to me?—or was it to me you spoke when you said 'Come to my place this evening'? I had half a mind not to come, but still I thought I would—though it does seem foolish, after all."

"Foolish, inagh!" said the hag sharply; "maybe you'll not think it so when you hear what I have to tell you, an' it's only a word or two."

"In the name of God, what is it, then?"

"Put down your head here, an' I'll whisper it in your ear You don't know who may be listenin'."

Smiling to himself at the absurdity of his position, and rather by way of humouring the old woman than anything else, the young man bent his head to a level with her face, and she whispered something in his ear, then drew back and fixed her keen eyes on his face through the gloom of the summer night, as if to mark the effect of her words.

And the effect was like magic. Moran started, gasped for breath, and caught the hag by the arm with a force that made her reel.

"Say that again!" he exclaimed in a thrilling whisper; "or did I hear you right?"

"You did—an' I'll not say it again—I said it onst, an' that's enough."

"But how—where—when—I mean, how do you know that?"

"No matter to you how I know it. If you don't find it true, never b'lieve me again—that's all. You put in a word for me this evenin' at the Lodge below, an' I thought I'd do you a good turn. Away wid you now from here, an' see if you don't find my words come in true. If they do, I know you'll be thankful to the ould vanithee, an' I hope you'll do what you can for that poor boy of mine."

"In any case, my good woman, I will do that; but have no fears for *him*—with God's help there is no doubt but his innocence will be established."

"God bless you for that word, anyhow!" And, dashing away the tears that were gathering in her eyes, the old woman hobbled back into the hut, leaving Moran to retrace his steps down the hill in a state of mind very different from that in which he ascended it.

Whether it was accident or design that led his steps to the old house in Friar Street it is not for me to say; but it so happened that some twenty minutes after, Attorney Moran plied the heavy, old-fashioned knocker on Dr. Hennessy's door with such good effect that admission was almost instantaneous, and our friend was ushered into the parlour, where, "as luck would have it," he used afterwards to say, Mary Hennessy sat alone, with a volume of Lingard's *England* in her hand, and a cloud of some kind shading the sunny brightness of her features.

Very natural was the inquiry, "Where is Maurice?" and no less natural was the answer, "Gone to Kilbraa, or somewhere there, on professional business." But not so natural was the pause that followed, a pause which seemed rather embarrassing to both, though why it should be so perhaps neither could tell.

At last Moran spoke. "Perhaps I ought to apologise, Mary—Miss Hennessy, I mean—for interrupting your studies. May I ask what you were reading?"

"A very sad story," said Mary, drawing a long breath, as if much relieved, "the story of that unhappy wife and most admirable woman, Catharine of Arragon. What a strange fate it was that gave her to that inhuman monster, Henry the Eighth!"

"Very strange indeed," said Moran, so absently that Mary smiled; but the greater his abstraction the more rapidly she talked on, gliding from one subject to another, in the vain hope of drawing him into conversation on some ordinary topic. The piano stood open, and all at once Moran said—

"It's a long time now since I heard you play, Miss Hennessy,—won't you play something now, pending Maurice's return?"

"Certainly, Mr. Moran," was the cheerful answer, though the round, rich voice trembled a very little. Several pieces were played,—noisy, showy pieces, too,—and then Mary turned with an arch smile on her face and asked, "How do you like that, Mr. Moran?"

"I don't like it at all, Miss Saucebox," said Moran, laughing, "and you know that as well as I do. Why not play some of my old favourites, and keep those show-off affairs for those who like them?"

"True enough, Mr. Moran, if I only could remember your favourites—what were they?—oh, now I have one!" and she started off at the full speed of her nimble fingers with "I'm the boy for bewitching them!" at which Moran laughed heartily, and said, "I wish I *was* the boy for bewitching them—I know one I'd bewitch, anyhow."

"Is it possible?"

"It is possible, Miss Prim; and I have just made up my mind to try my luck this very night, and know for certain what I have to expect."

"As how?"

"As how? Oh, the pretty innocent! Mary Hennessy can't possibly guess who it is that has stolen the heart out of Phil Moran! Now seriously, Mary,"—and he drew his chair nearer to the music-stool on which she sat,—"now seriously, how long is this to go on? You know as well as I do that I love you better than I do myself, and yet you continue to appear as innocent of the fact as—well, no matter what! But human patience—even Phil Moran's patience—can't possibly last for ever, and I'm determined to know the worst, or the best, before I leave this house to-night."

Mary laughed, but she blushed too, and besides, her laugh was not the light, careless, ringing laugh that was wont to come straight from her merry heart.

"By Jove!" said Phil to himself, "the hag may be right after all," and his eye brightened and his fresh cheek grew ruddier still.

"Mary," said he, "I know you'll not deceive me, but give me a straight answer to a straight question."

"I'm entirely obliged to you for your good opinion, Mr. Moran," archly said Mary, and she began twisting the handkerchief in her hand into various comical shapes.

"You are, eh?—well, I hope you'll prove yourself worthy of it. Now, answer me this little question—what do you think of Phil Moran?"

"Why, of course, I think very well of him," laughed Mary. "He's a good fellow enough in his way—for an Irishman—and as a limb of the law"—

"But what would you think of him for a *husband?*" and Phil shut one eye inquisitively, and turned his head to one side.

"Oh, a husband! That is quite a different thing. Having never seen the gentleman in that capacity, I am not prepared to give an opinion."

"Well, but, *badinage* apart, Mary, I wish to know what I am to expect at your hands. It is for you to make me the happiest or the most miserable of men? Will you share my fortunes for good or ill? Can you love me?"

The colour came up brighter than ever in Mary's face, and she cast her eyes down to hide the moisture that began to suffuse them.

"Mr. Moran," she said, "if you come to speak so seriously, I suppose I must answer you as seriously. I do not think I can love you in the sense to which you allude—but be content with *friendship*, and I will love you—yes, as a brother."

"Friendship!" quoth Phil in huge disdain; "who cares for

friendship 'in the sense to which *you* allude'—ahem? But I'll tell you what I'll do—no, confound it! I can't tell it—but I'll make Tom Moore tell it for me;" and forthwith he began singing in a voice that was pleasant to Mary's ear, from the many pleasant associations connected with its rich liquid tones—

"'A Temple to Friendship,' said Laura, enchanted,
'I'll build in this garden, the thought is divine.'
The Temple was built, and she now only wanted
An image of Friendship to place on the shrine.

"Just like you, Mary!

She flew to a sculptor, who set down before her
A Friendship the fairest his art could invent,
But so cold and so dull that the youthful adorer
Saw plainly this was not the god that she meant.

"Just like me, Mary!"

"A novel *refrain* you are adding, surely," said Mary, with a smile bright as a houri's.

"Never mind, it suits my purpose.

'Oh no, then, I never could think of enshrining
An image whose looks are so joyless and dim;
But you little god upon roses reclining,
We'll make, if you please, sir, a Friendship of him!'

"Shall I go on?"

"As you will, Mr. Moran."

"The bargain was struck, with the little god laden
She joyfully flew to her shrine in the grove,—
'Farewell!' said the sculptor; 'you're not the first maiden
Who came but for Friendship and took away Love!'

"Now, what if the image you have enshrined should turn out, after all, to be the sly 'little god upon roses reclining,' instead of the other, 'whose looks are so joyless and dim,'—ah, Mary? Suppose you look into the shrine in the grove, and by the light of my burning heart examine the features of the image aforesaid?"

Mary laughed again at the oddity of the conceit; she paused a moment, looked down on the floor, coloured violently, tapped with her little foot on the carpet, and at last looked up in Moran's face with the brightest smile in the world.

"Well?" said Phil, smiling too, and managing to get possession of her hand.

"Well, I've been to the shrine you speak of"—

"And there you saw"—

"No, I didn't! There's knowledge for you! Be good enough to convey yourself home now, Phil Moran, for another word I shan't speak to you to-night—except two—Good-night! au revoir!"

And before Moran had recovered from the bewildering effect of her words, and still more of her looks and gestures, she had bounded off like an antelope, leaving the delighted lawyer to compose his thoughts at leisure, and bless his stars and the fairy-woman to his heart's content. He was too happy just then for ordinary conversation, so, leaving a message for Maurice that he would see him some time next day, he retired to indulge the thick-coming fancies which the newly-awakened hope of happiness will conjure up at eight-and-twenty! A happy man was Phil Moran that night, and as his eye scanned the uncertain future, not one cloud could he detect on his life's horizon. All was fair and bright and glad as the image that smiled over all.

That same evening, about the same hour, Harriet Markham and Lady Pemberton were walking to and fro in the verandah off Lord Effingham's study, engaged in that desultory sort of conversation common between persons whose minds have but small affinity one to the other. A sort of intimacy had sprung up since the Earl's departure between the two ladies, notwithstanding the ten or twelve years of seniority on the part of the noble widow. Her ladyship seemed to have taken a fancy to her brother's governess, especially since she found that the Markhams were not unknown to heraldry, and had quarterings on their shield from the peerage itself.

Lady Pemberton had been speaking of her brother's late wife, and she said, "View the matter as I may, I cannot see how Fergus ever came to marry her. It is true my father had arranged the affair for him when he was still a minor, and I suppose he had not the courage to resist, for my father was a man who ruled all around him, if not with a rod of iron, at least with a strong hand. Poor Priscilla was a dismal creature, pretty and gentle, but a dreadful bore on account of the confirmed hypochondria that had taken possession of her. To tell you the truth, my dear, we were all glad—that is, myself and the other members of the family—when Priscilla, Countess of Effingham, was consigned to the tomb of the Capulets, piously hoping, of course, that the poor dear soul had found beyond the grave the rest and peace which her own dreary temperament denied her here. As for my brother, no one knew how he felt, for he kept his thoughts and feelings to himself. I hope sincerely that neither of the children will resemble their mother, though I sometimes think that Emma looks like her, and has some of her odd ways, as far as such a mere child can have them."

"Well, of course I cannot say," observed Harriet, as if to fill up the pause, "what resemblance Lady Emma bears to her mother, but I think her, on the whole, an amiable child, though more shy and sensitive than her sister."

"The worst of it is, however," resumed Lady Pemberton, "that there seems to be as little chance for happiness, as far as my brother is concerned, in the alliance he is forming himself as there was in the one over the forming of which he had little or no control."

"Does your ladyship really think so? I sincerely hope you will find yourself mistaken."

"Possibly I may, but I fear—oh, I very much fear. It is true Lady Jane de Montford (they're an old Norman family, that of the Marquis ———) is a beauty, and somewhat of a wit,— no very great recommendation, I think, for a woman,—I believe she loves my brother as much as she can love any one, but— but—I fear she is not the woman to make him happy; in the finer qualities of mind and heart I believe her sadly wanting. However, time will tell—there is no help for it now," she added in a melancholy tone.

There was a long pause; then Harriet said, with some hesitation—

"Did I understand your ladyship to say that Lord Effingham's name is Fergus?"

"Certainly, my dear, that is his name. Why do you ask?"

"Because the name—excuse me, Lady Pemberton—is so very *Irish*, so peculiarly Irish, indeed I might say."

"Oh," said Lady Pemberton, with a careless laugh, "you do

not know, then, that our mother was Irish?—yes, and very Irish, too,—descended, I believe, from some old Milesian family, and very proud, I assure you, of her ancient lineage. Fergus was her father's name, and had been a favourite name in the family since the Deluge for aught I know; and, truth to tell, my very dear and right noble brother has not his name for nothing. With some of the more amiable traits of my father's sternly-commanding nature—the old Danish-Norman-English type—he has in him many of the most prominent characteristics of the Celtic people—so my father used to say, when he meant anything but flattery. For me, I never gave much attention to the distinctive traits of one people or the other, but I know that the very qualities my father complained of in his heir were precisely those that endeared Fergus to all our circle—wider than than it is now."

As if the last words had awoke in her mind a train of saddening thought, Lady Pemberton lapsed into silence, and Harriet, equally thoughtful, made no effort to resume the conversation. The night-breeze began to wax chill, and the stars twinkled brighter through the clear, cool air, so after a few turns up and down the verandah, Lady Pemberton proposed to return to the drawing-room, where they had left Mrs. Pakenham and the chaplain hotly contesting the honours of the chessboard, to the great amusement of a young clergyman whose first sermon, delivered in Cashel Cathedral on the previous Sunday, had quite won Mrs. Pakenham's heart, and the hearts of ever so many other dowagers. A clerical *petit-maître*, he was one of those pulpit orators so happily described by the trenchant satire of Cowper's verse—

> First we stroke
> An eyebrow, next compose a straggling lock;
> Then, with an air most gracefully performed,
> Fall back into our seat, extend an arm,
> And lay it at its ease with gentle care,
> With handkerchief in hand depending low.

Whether this delicate pillar of the Church by law established was or was not aware of Miss Markham's being a Catholic, he seemed well inclined to cultivate her acquaintance; but Harriet, with the perversity natural to her wayward sex, shunned the super-elegant minister in the same proportion that he sought her. It is probable that with Cowper, in the passage before cited, she thought to herself—

> In man or woman, but far most in man,
> And most of all in man that ministers
> And serves the altar, in my soul I loathe
> All affectation. 'Tis my perfect scorn,
> Object of my implacable disgust.

But whatever she thought, she certainly bade Lady Pemberton good-night at the drawing-room door, and sought in the quiet of her chamber the more congenial company of her own thoughts.

Long she sat in pensive musing, her head leaning on her hand, whilst many a troubled thought flitted over the fair surface of her face, like shadows from the summer clouds falling on the hills and valleys of some lovely landscape. Once or twice a pearly tear stole from under her closed eyelids and rolled unheeded down her cheeks, but all at once she raised her head, and, pushing back from her damp brow the rich tresses of her braided hair, she cast her eyes upwards, and remained a moment absorbed in mental prayer, then rose, and, going to the window, gazed out upon the night, where only the stars and the dark canopy they studded were visible. The solemn night was before her, in the majesty of darkness and of silence, and her finely attuned nature quickly rose above the transitory things of earth in the awful presence of the dread unseen. Alone with the mysterious Presence which pervades the universe, self was forgotten, only heaven and its interests remembered, peace like the halcyon descended on her soul, and a strange, undefinable hope diffused a softened light over the deep recesses of her pure and gentle heart.

She was roused from her calm and soothing reverie by a low tap at her chamber door, which hastening to open, she found the nurserymaid, Ellen Mulquin, with another young female wrapped in a light shawl.

"I hope you'll excuse me, Miss Markham," said Ellen, dropping a curtsey, "but this poor sister of mine wouldn't be aisy, at all, till she'd get spakin' to you the night, an' I know you're so good an' so kind that you'll not be angry with us for comin'; for, indeed, miss, it's in the height o' trouble poor Celia is."

"Angry? why, how should I be angry?" said Harriet very gently. "Come in, girls, and let me hear what your trouble is."

"Oh, not me, Miss Markham—I can't stay," said Ellen; "I have got something to do for the young ladies, and I must be off. Celia can tell you herself all about it. Go in, alanna! an' don't be afeard to open your mind to Miss Markham."

The timidity that at another time would have deterred Celia from "opening her mind" to "a rale lady like Miss Markham" now vanished quite in the presence of the sore trouble that was tearing her very heart.

"Oh, Miss Markham dear," said she, before Harriet could speak a word, "can't you do anything, at all, for poor Jerry? Sure, the peelers took him at last, an' he's in gaol, an' I'm sure they'll hang him, for all he's as innocent of what they lay to his charge as the child unborn. Can't you do anything for him? I'm sure you can if you'll only try, an' if you do, you'll have my blessin', an' the blessin' of God, every day you rise."

So eager and so rapid was poor Celia's utterance that Miss Markham could not put in a word till the girl's voice failed her for want of breath.

"Why, my poor girl," she hastened to reply, "this is, indeed, bad news. But tell me, how did it happen? How and where was Jerry arrested? Or are you sure he was arrested?"

"Sure, Miss Markham?—sure! Oyeh! it's me that *is* sure!—doesn't the whole country know it?—an' wasn't I at the gaol myself tryin' to see him, an' the hard-hearted villains wouldn't let me get one sight of him? Oh, wirra, wirra! what'll I do, at all, at all, at all?" And the tears gushed in torrents from her eyes, and she wrung her hands in all the wildness of despair.

"Do try and compose yourself, poor girl!" said Miss Markham, her own eyes full of sympathetic tears. "You have not told me when and where Jerry was arrested?"

"Och, sure, that's the quarest thing of all," said Celia, restraining her emotion with wonderful quickness; "sure, he wasn't arrested at all—he arrested himself!"

"Arrested himself?—what do you mean?"

"Why, miss, he went to Rose Lodge, his own four bones, an' gave himself up, an' tould the ould gentleman an' the rest o' the quality all about how it happened."

"Well, that is very strange," said the young lady thoughtfully; "that would lead one to suppose that he might not be guilty, after all."

"An' sure he isn't guilty, Miss Markham!" cried Celia eagerly; "sure, I knew that long ago!"

"You did?—and pray how did you know it?"

Celia's face was scarlet in a moment, and, casting her eyes bashfully down, she began pulling at the fringe of her shawl with great industry and perseverance. "Well, you see, miss," she stammered out, "he came to see me when he was on his keepin'—a couple o' nights after it happened."

"Oh, he did, eh?" and Harriet smiled pleasantly.

"Well, he did, miss, in regard to a few words that had passed between us—he came to give me back my promise, thinkin' I'd be sorry I ever gave it."

"And did you take it back?"

"Is it me, Miss Markham?—is it me take it back?—oh vo! that 'id be too hard entirely on poor Jerry, an' somethin' tellin' me all the while that maybe he wasn't so bad, after all,—oh no, miss! I tould him that if I wasn't his wife, I'd never be any other one's."

"And you believed him, of course, when he told you he was not guilty?"

"I did, miss," and Celia raised her head and looked the young lady full in the face; "I did believe him, for the raison that I never knew him to tell me a lie—an' the way he said it made me surer again that it was the truth "—— Here she stopped, blushed deeper than ever, and again cast down her eyes.

"Why, how did he say it, Celia?"

"Well, you see, miss,"—the voice fell to a broken murmur,— "it was the first time he ever made so free as to kiss me—an'— an'—he kissed me then for the first an' last time, as he thought, an' says he, 'Celia, that's not the kiss of a murderer!' an' sure, myself knew well he wouldn't say that only it was true; an' ochone! but them words took the heavy load off o' my heart, an' from that forrid I thought I could bear the *worst*; but sure I can't—sure I can't, I see now, for ever sence I heard of him bein' in gaol my poor heart is flutterin' like a bird, an' I've no more strength in me than a little babby. Oh, Miss Markham dear!" she cried, with passionate eagerness, "do you think they'd have the heart to hang him?—do you think they would?"

"My poor girl," said Harriet, with the tenderest compassion, "the law has no heart—knows no pity; if he were found guilty of such a crime, there would be small chance of mercy for him in this world. But do not despair, Celia. I have great hopes, from his giving himself up, that he is, as he says, innocent, though, if so, it is very, very strange that he kept out of the way so long; however, I sincerely hope that all will come right in the end. As for my doing anything for him under present circumstances, it is quite impossible, but I will see Mr. Esmond to-morrow and ascertain how he feels towards Pierce, or whether he still believes him guilty."

"God in heaven bless you, miss! I'm sure your word will go far wid the ould gentleman. I'll go home now wid a lighter heart than I came, an' that you may never know what a sore heart is, an' that happiness may attend you here an' hereafter, is my prayer now and for ever!"

"I thank you kindly for your good wish," said Harriet as the girl left the room. When the door closed after her, she sighed deeply, and murmured softly as she turned away—

"'That I may never know what a sore heart is!'—a kind wish, my poor girl; but it comes all too late—happiness I must try to win for hereafter, by ceasing to look for it here."

CHAPTER XXII

THE COUNTESS OF EFFINGHAM.

ONE of the last days of July was drawing to a close, when Harriet Markham sat with old Bryan on the steep brow of the Rock of Cashel, looking dreamily out on the far-stretching landscape, where the blue mists of evening were coming up from the spacious plain and the rich holmes by the silvery Suir, and the far-off mountain valleys. The old man had been telling her some of the old-time legends she loved so well to hear, and the charm of their wild romance was diffusing itself like the shadowy mist over the fair scene below and the solemn ruins around. It was no uncommon thing for Harriet to find herself alone with old Bryan on the lonely Rock at the solemn hour when night begins to weave her spell of awful silence; at that charmed hour she most loved to hear the Hermit tell of "the sainted men of old," whose memory lingers round the ruined fanes of Cashel, where their mortal bodies returned to dust. The monotonous tone of the old man's feeble voice had such an effect on her sensitive mind as the hum of bees, the falling of water, or the rustling of leaves; there was a ghostly sound, too, in its hollowness that was inexpressibly solemn, reminding the hearer that it, too, would soon be lost in the everlasting silence of that place of death—it, too, would speedily join the voices of the past, to be heard no more of mortal ear. It was a dead voice issuing from living lips, and that fully as much from Bryan's constant habit of self-communion, and his intimate association with the dead, as from the weight of years that was bending him earthward.

That particular evening he had been talking more even than usual, and Harriet, intent on listening, forgot the long walk she had before her, nor heeded the gathering shades. All at once

Bryan started, turned his head in the direction of the gate, and appeared to listen anxiously.

"What's the matter, Bryan?" said the young lady, a little startled by his manner; "did you hear anything?"

"Why, then, I did, Miss Markham—didn't you?"

"I cannot say I did."

"Well, I did—I heard the gate opened and shut—very easy, like. If you wouldn't be afeard, Miss Markham, I'd go an' see if any one came in."

"Well, I don't think I should be afraid to remain here," said Harriet, smiling; "but I have already stayed too long, so I shall accompany you to the gate, and be so far on my way."

"Very good, Miss Harriet; an' after I have taken a look around, I'll go with you down the road."

They had only gone a few yards, and were still in the shadow of the cathedral wall, when Bryan, with a sort of stifled cry, darted off in another direction, and Harriet was left alone. Wondering at Bryan's sudden disappearance, she stood looking after him, when a voice, a familiar voice, spoke near her, and, turning with a start and an exclamation of terror, she saw before her a stately figure with hand outstretched to greet her.

"My lord!—Lord Effingham, you here!—or is it, indeed, you?"

"That is to say," said the musical voice, in which Harriet could not be mistaken,—"that is to say, am I Lord Effingham in the flesh, or only in spirit? Compose yourself, my dear Miss Markham, and, in proof of my corporeal identity, there is my hand."

"But who would have thought of seeing your lordship here? When did you arrive?"

"About half an hour ago."

"And you left—left them all so soon? Why, really, my lord, I am so surprised—so astonished—do pray excuse me!— but you here, of all people—when I thought you in England!"

Here old Bryan approached at full speed, talking audibly to himself about the noise he had heard, and wondering who it was that made it. He was steering right for the spot where he had left Miss Markham, when he came full against Lord Effingham, and started back in amazement, whereat the Earl laughed good-humouredly, and Harriet said—

"Do not fear, Bryan; it is Lord Effingham back from England."

"Lord Effingham?" repeated Bryan, and his bald brow and thin white locks were instantly bared to the first beams of the rising moon,—"Lord Effingham? Mercy on us! was it him opened the gate there now?"

"It was not, my friend; it was the Reverend Mr. Goodchild, who accompanied me. There he is," pointing to the goodly figure of the parson, just becoming visible on the steep ascent. "Would you have the goodness to entertain him a few moments while I speak with your friend, Miss Markham?"

Bryan looked a little surprised, but he said very politely, "With all the pleasure in life, my lord; but he's a mighty quare ould chap that same Mr. Goodchild, or Badchild, or whatsomever he is." And away he posted to meet the chaplain.

"Miss Markham," said the Earl, "I should like to say a few words to you before we return to the Castle. Will you honour me with your attention?"

"Certainly, my lord," Harriet replied as calmly as she could, wondering much the while what Lord Effingham could possibly wish to say to her at such a time and in such a place. She took his offered arm, and they moved on a few paces to an open spot, where the moonlight slept in hallowed sheen on the tombs and headstones and the long dank grass waving so mournfully in the gentle breeze. Bryan and the chaplain were still in sight, but not within hearing. With a beating heart Harriet waited, but as if to break a silence that embarrassed her she said—

"I hope, Lord Effingham, that it was not in search of me you came hither at such a moment? I should feel quite ashamed if I thought so."

"Feel ashamed, then," said the Earl gaily; "for much as I admire these noble ruins, it was certainly not to visit them that I left the Castle almost immediately after reaching it."

"And—the Countess!—what will she think?" said Harriet, more and more puzzled.

Lord Effingham smiled, and answered somewhat evasively, "I did not wait to ask her opinion—at a future time I will. But time presses, my dear Miss Markham, and I must seize the moment so happily afforded me to speak to you on a subject that will perhaps surprise you." He paused a moment, then quickly resumed—"I have a proposal of marriage for you."

"For me, Lord Effingham!—A proposal of marriage for me?"

"Yes, for you. But why tremble so?—you are pale, too,—is it, then, so formidable a thing to be asked in marriage, and for one who will, I am sure, devote his whole life to make you happy? One who knows and loves you as the heart can love but once—as I should have done," he said in a lower tone, "had fate so willed it that I were free."

"Lord Effingham!" said Harriet, withdrawing her arm quickly, while the blush of wounded modesty rose to her cheek, "am I to understand that you came here to insult me?"

"Assuredly not, Miss Markham. Were I capable of insulting any lady, or wounding her delicacy, it would be strange, indeed, if I pitched on you, and that, too, when I come commissioned to offer you the hand and heart, rank and fortune, of my best and dearest friend."

"But who is that friend, my lord?" said Harriet haughtily "I know of no friend of your lordship's who could possibly pretend to my hand and heart—rank and fortune have I none!"

"And yet so it is," said Lord Effingham; "I cannot now tell you who it is: suffice it to say he is neither old nor ugly, stands in good repute amongst his fellows, and, finally, has both rank and fortune to lay at your feet, which he has commissioned me to do"—

"And why you, my lord?—why not himself?"

"That he will explain at the first opportunity, but there are certain reasons which debar him, for the present, from the happiness of addressing you in person"—

"If he loves me, as your lordship says, he may find it no very great happiness to address me in person. I cannot but feel highly honoured by the commission your lordship has deigned to accept in my regard, but"—— There was an acerbity in the young lady's tone that did not escape her noble companion, and he quickly subjoined——

"But you do not feel at all inclined to accept the proposal?"

"Decidedly not, my lord; poor as Harriet Markham is, she knows what is due to a lady, and cannot forget the blood that is in her veins."

"There spoke the sister of Frederick Markham," said the Earl, as if to himself, and he smiled with strange meaning.

Harriet caught his arm suddenly, and, gasping, looked up in his face. "My lord, did I hear aright? Did you speak of Frederick Markham?"

"I did, and much cause I have to remember him. He saved my life once, at the risk of his own, when we met by accident amongst the Bernese Alps, near the foot of the Jungfrau. Did you never hear him speak of Lord Milford?"

"Surely I did, my lord—oh, many, many times. If the Earl of Effingham and the Viscount Milford of poor Fred's acquaintance are one and the same, I believe your lordship and he finished your tour together after the little adventure in Switzerland?"

"We did, and our intimacy ripened into a friendship as lasting as it was sincere. Poor Markham! All the years that have passed since his untimely death have not effaced his memory from my heart; and when I learned accidentally that you were his sister, I regarded you in a different light—as one, in short, who had a right to my friendship and protection."

"I am infinitely obliged to your lordship," said Harriet in a voice quivering with strong emotion. "Oh, Frederick!" she cried, clasping her hands in a sudden burst of passionate sorrow,—"oh, Frederick, my dear, my only brother! what a lonely lot mine has been since strange hands laid you in your far Indian grave! Excuse me, my lord!" and by a violent effort she recovered her composure; "I owe you an apology for this childish outburst of feeling, but the sudden revival of old and very sad memories, long buried in my heart, overcame me quite for the moment. May I beg to know if your lordship has anything more to say, as I am anxious to return to the Castle as speedily as possible?"

"Are you, then, afraid to remain a few moments with me, even though we be not alone?"

"And if we were alone," said Harriet Markham, drawing herself up with the lofty dignity of virtuous womanhood, her eyes flashing with the proud spirit of her race as she fixed them on Lord Effingham,—"and if we were alone, why should I be afraid? The man lives not on earth whose presence Harriet Markham would fear—and you, Lord Effingham, least of all."

"I thank you," said the Earl calmly; "I rejoice to know that I am honoured by your good opinion."

"Nevertheless," said Harriet again, "there is something due

to appearances—no one can afford to despise *them*, a woman least of all. And then," she added in a playful tone, "being a daughter of Eve, I have a natural desire to see the fair brow that is to wear the Effingham coronet through life." She was moving hastily away in pursuit of Bryan and the chaplain, who were only a few yards distant,—disputing, as usual, to judge by the high pitch of their voices,—when Lord Effingham laid his hand gently on her arm, and said in a low, earnest tone—

"You have not told me what I shall say to my friend?"

"Say to him, my lord, that the orphan daughter of Sir Everard Markham is not to be wooed at second-hand."

"But you will see him soon, and hear him plead his own cause."

"Even then he would plead in vain."

"You cannot possibly know that till you have seen and heard him."

"I do know it, my lord; and if you have that friendship for me as Captain Markham's sister which you do me the honour to profess, you will best prove it by telling your friend that I cannot receive his addresses."

"And, as a friend, may I venture to ask why you are so determined? Is your heart, like that of Sarah Curran, buried in the grave of some loved and lost one?"

"I know not, my lord, of any right you have to put such a question," said Harriet, with a quiet assumption of dignity. "I have given such answer as I deemed fitting; your friend must expect no more."

"Miss Markham," said the Earl, after a moment's silence, "I hope you are not displeased with me for having undertaken this embassy? Standing here amongst the graves of the dead, with yon fair moon shining down like the eye of heaven upon us, I solemnly assure you that your peace of mind, your honour, your happiness, are as dear to me as if I were—your brother—more I cannot say."

"I believe you, my lord," said Harriet, with a radiant smile; then, as they hastened to rejoin the chaplain, she added in a lower and more subdued tone, "And now for the Lady Jane that was,—Lady Effingham that is,—I hope she is not over-much fatigued to see me?"

"I hope so," was the reply, and no more passed on the subject. After settling, to Bryan's satisfaction at least, the dispute going on between him and the chaplain,—which proved to be on the alleged banishing of the toads and serpents from the Irish soil by St. Patrick,—the Earl offered his arm to Miss Markham, and the little party left the Rock to Bryan and the dead. As they descended the steep path, the radiant beauty of the moonlit sky attracted their attention, and Lord Effingham said, pointing to the fine aurora borealis that was shooting its splendours athwart the northern sky—

"Does not that remind you, Miss Markham, of Scott's vivid description of just such a scene?—

> The monk gazed long on the lovely scene,
> Then into the night he looked forth,
> And red and bright the streamers light
> Were dancing in the glowing north.
> So had he seen in fair Castile,
> The youth in glittering squadrons start,
> Sudden the flying jennet wheel
> And hurl the unexpected dart.
> He knew by the streamers that shot so bright
> That spirits were riding the northern light.

Apropos to the immortal 'Lay,'" he added, "you, our fair friend, seem to have adopted with regard to Cashel the advice of the Scottish poet as regards Melrose, namely, to 'visit it by the pale moonlight,' and, moreover, to 'go alone the while' to 'view St. Patrick's ruined pile'"—

"And," said Harriet promptly, as she gracefully pointed to the solemn monuments of the long-past ages that rose in lonely beauty on either hand,—"and may not I too, with justifiable pride—

> —— home returning, soothly swear,
> Was never scene so sad and fair?

Ah, would that some Irish poet, great as he, might one day do for St. Patrick's of royal Cashel what Scott did for St. David's of fair Melrose!"

"Pity it was," said Lord Effingham, "that Moore did not attempt some such thing—though, if he had, Cashel might gain little in *prestige*, for Moore was not the antiquarian that Scott is, and to do anything like justice to these magnificent ruins a wealth of antiquarian lore were indispensably necessary. But tell me, Miss Markham, since when have you cultivated these solitary habits?"

"Ever since I have been—in the vicinity of the Rock of Cashel."

A smile shone for a moment on Lord Effingham's face—he had noticed the slight pause in Harriet's answer, and gave it a meaning which might have escaped a less keen observer.

"It is well you did not say, since you came to Effingham Castle."

"And why, my lord?" Harriet asked in some alarm, and, raising her eyes to his for a moment, she found the Earl regarding her with a searching look that brought the blood to her cheek she knew not why.

"You ask me why?" his lordship said, with a pleasant smile. "Because it would speak but ill for the social qualities of the inmates of the Castle were you driven to seek entertainment

> Where the owlet hoots o'er the dead man's grave.

What say you, Mr. Goodchild? This question concerns you amongst others."

"I—I beg your lordship's pardon," began the chaplain, "but really I—I did not catch the purport of your lordship's remark."

The purport being caught, the worthy gentleman began earnestly to protest that he, on his part, had at all times done his utmost to entertain Miss Markham, and if he had not more entertained her the fault was hers, not his. "Nay, more," said he, with a touch of solemn humour little expected from him,—"nay, more, my lord, my reverend brother, lately arrived in the parish, good Mr. Featherstone—a very proper and well-favoured young gentleman, who, moreover, much resembles Absalom of old in the quality and quantity of his hair—would willingly have assisted in making the Castle agreeable to Miss Markham; but truly his efforts, however laudable, seemed as entirely thrown away on the young lady as though he were old Philemon Goodchild instead of Master Chester Featherstone."

A careless inquiry from the Earl as to the qualifications of this new inmate of the rectory, whom he had not yet seen, brought out a playful sketch of his *personals* from Harriet, from the chaplain some critical observations on the manner and matter of his preaching, and by the time the latter were ended, our little party had reached the Castle. As they approached the door, Harriet's heart began to beat fast and faster—a strange tremor was creeping over her; she longed to see the new lady of the mansion, and would have given much to have had an opportunity of questioning Mr. Goodchild as to what manner of person she was, but the presence of the Earl forbade any such attempt, and she was forced to remain on the tenterhooks of curiosity, without even a hint of what was passing in her mind. It might have been that Lord Effingham felt the tremor of the hand that rested so timidly and lightly on his arm, for just as they reached the upper one of the broad white marble steps that led up to the lofty vestibule of the hall, he stopped an instant, looked in Harriet's face and smiled. Oh, how that smile humbled the sensitive girl! yet she could not tell why, even to herself. She would have withdrawn her hand as they entered the hall, but Lord Effingham held it fast, and, with that strange smile on his face, led her on, almost mechanically on her part, across the tesselated floor, and up the grand staircase, to a small apartment opening on the drawing-room. No one was yet visible, and Harriet felt more and more overcome by some undefinable emotion—

Secret in its source as dreams, voiceless as the past.

The colour came and went on her cheek, and tears filled her eyes, though she dared not let one escape from under the burning lids that were studiously cast down to conceal them.

"I think we may find her ladyship here," said the Earl in a careless tone, and he opened the door. No one was there, but voices were heard in the adjacent apartment, and Lord Effingham said, "Have the goodness to remain here, Miss Markham, and I will bring my lady-love"—

"Oh, my lord," said Harriet, without raising her eyes, "that would scarce befit our relative conditions. If you would do me the honour of conducting me to where Lady Effingham is, I shall be too highly favoured."

"I see you are very anxious to make her acquaintance," said Lord Effingham, still smiling; "I must therefore procure you that pleasure at the earliest possible moment."

It appeared very strange to Harriet, and embarrassed her more than a little, that the Earl still lingered, regarding her changing features with the keen scrutiny of one who would read her heart. A burning blush kindled on her cheek, and her eyes involuntarily sought the ground. She felt the piercing glance that was on her, and she was vexed she knew not why, yet neither did she know what she ought to say, and so she remained silent. At last Lord Effingham spoke, and his voice was not so firm as usual.

"Miss Markham, you desire to be presented to Lady Effingham, do you not? Favour me with your hand, and I will lead you to her."

The hand was given, though with a look of wondering surprise, and the Earl, leading her up to one of the large Venetian mirrors that occupied the panels of the wainscoting, bowed with mock ceremony, and said, pointing to her own graceful figure on its brilliant surface, "*There* is the Countess of Effingham that is to be—with Miss Markham's gracious permission. There is, or shall be, no other."

"My lord!" said Harriet, the crimson blush on her cheeks giving place to a ghastly paleness, as she turned with a start and fixed her eyes on the now earnest face that was regarding her with a look of ineffable affection,—"my lord, what am I— to understand—from this?"

"That as I owe my life to Frederick Markham, so shall I owe my happiness to his sister, if she deigns to bless me with her hand."

"Then—you—were not married in England?"

"Certainly not. Lady Jane, taking umbrage at my long delay in going to claim her hand, thought proper to revenge herself by making herself the lawful property of a certain captain of the Guards who had been dancing attendance on her handsome ladyship for full three weeks, and I, finding the family overwhelmed with grief and indignation, retired in apparent discontent, with what *real* satisfaction—with what an exquisite sense of relief—even you cannot understand until you have fathomed the depths of my heart. Say, Harriet, have I rightly interpreted the emotion that you laboured so hard to conceal? Have you guessed the secret that for months has been the charm and the torment of my existence?"

By this time Harriet found herself the occupant of a *fauteuil*, though of how she got there she had no very clear idea; the whole was so like a dream that she could not realise her position. With a sort of half-conscious look she had turned to Lord Effingham and listened in mute wonder; his last question seemed to restore her to full consciousness—the warm blood rushed to her face, crimsoning lip, cheek, and brow, but she did not immediately reply, and Lord Effingham spoke again in a tone half sportive, half serious.

"If I cannot say with Sir Nicholas, the royal standard-bearer, in the ballad, after the woeful day of Marston Moor,

I came to thee a landless man,

I can say what I would give half my lands were it otherwise than it is to say now, 'I come to thee a wifeless man,'—will you wear the rejected coronet?" and he smiled. "Will you accept the heart and hand I am now free to offer?"

"The coronet I value little," said Harriet, covering her eyes with the only hand at her disposal. She paused a moment, then hurriedly added in a lower tone, "The heart and hand I value more than Lady Jane could ever have valued them"—

Ashamed of even this admission, Harriet would have made a hasty retreat, but retreat was just then impossible, and during the next five minutes she heard words, burning words, never to be forgotten—words that were stamped in golden letters on the tablet of her heart, to shine there while life remained. Short as the time was, it sufficed to lay bare to the eager eyes that watched her varying features the innermost depth of Harriet Markham's heart, and to draw from her lips the timid confession that her life would have been a blank, a dreary waste, had Lord Effingham brought back with him his English Countess.

"Then you approve of my taste?" said the Earl, as they rose to rejoin the company in the drawing-room, and he glanced at the brightly-smiling image in the mirror. "I thought you would," he added, with a look that covered Harriet's face with blushes. Then, bending down his stately head, as he drew her arm within his, he whispered—

"Oh, bring to me my Norah Fey—
Hours are days when she's away."

"I see you have not forgotten that simple ballad," said Harriet, with a thrill of joy as she thought of the lone night-watch beneath her window.

"Oh no, nor the pansies,—you remember *them*, do you?"

A look of radiant happiness, of unutterable affection, was Harriet's answer as they entered the drawing-room.

The party there were evidently prepared for what was coming, and when Lord Effingham led Harriet to Lady Pemberton, saying, "Caroline, you have been long years without a sister—there is one whom I commend to your sisterly affection—love her first for my sake, you will soon love her for her own," Lady Pemberton received the blushing girl with a kindness that won her heart for ever, but without any surprise. Mrs. Pakenham was barely civil, freezingly cold, in fact, and supercilious; Mr. Goodchild blander and smoother than ever, and as jubilant, honest man, as though he had himself been the winner of so fair a prize.

It was not till the following morning that the two young daughters of Lord Effingham were made acquainted with the turn affairs had taken; and if aught were wanting to complete Harriet's happiness, it was the delight they manifested on learning that they were to have for their "new mamma," not "that nasty Lady Jane," against whom they seemed to have cherished a most unaccountable prejudice, probably from Mrs. Pakenham's persistent habit of enlarging on that lady's bad qualities, leaving what good there was in her entirely in the shade, but "their own dear, dear Miss Markham." The truth was, as regarded the children, that Harriet had learned to love them for their own sakes, perhaps, too, for their father's, and as a natural consequence they loved her in return. She had devoted much attention to the training of their minds and the cultivation of their naturally good dispositions, and already her assiduous cares began to bear good fruit in the minds and hearts of their little ladyships.

The only clouded brow in Effingham Castle during the happy days succeeding the Earl's return was that of the Hon. Mrs. Pakenham, who lost no opportunity of hinting at *parvenues*, or tendering her unsought opinion on unequal marriages, *mésalliances*, and so forth, to the great amusement of those most concerned. It seemed so difficult to please Mrs. Pakenham in a wife for the Earl of Effingham. If Lady Jane's levity and heartlessness had been her theme before, want of position, etc., was now a more crying sin. Poor Mrs. Pakenham, how are the mighty fallen!

CHAPTER XXIII.

MORE VISITORS TO THE ROCK—THE CONJURER.

The days were gliding on swiftly towards the auspicious one that was to make Harriet Markham Countess of Effingham, when one fervid noon the Earl surprised his lady-love in close colloquy with no less a person than the Old Man of the Rock in a shady part of the avenue not far from the Castle.

"How now, fair lady," he smilingly said; "I did not expect to see you abroad at this sultry noontide hour."

"That is because your lordship is not acquainted with my peculiar habits. I have been walking some time to and fro in this refreshing shade"—

"Musing slow, *à la* 'saint or moralist,' *n'est-ce pas?*"

"I know not that, my lord, but *musing* or not, when our good Hermit here made his appearance, with an invitation to visit the Rock this evening for a very special purpose."

"And what may the purpose be?"

"That he will tell you himself," said Harriet, as she took the Earl's arm and returned his beaming smile.

"I shall be glad to hear it," was the gracious reply. "But first I would have you put on your hat, Bryan; even under this leafy screen the dog-star is not to be trusted."

"Many thanks to your lordship for your mighty great condescension," Bryan returned, with a very low, and indeed a very polite bow, "but I couldn't rest contented wid my hat on an' the best of quality to the fore. Neither sun nor wind ever does ould Bryan Cullenan any harm."

"Well, then, be so good as to let me hear why it is that you wish Miss Markham to visit the Rock this evening."

"Oh, that's aisy done entirely, your lordship,"—another low bow. "Sure, it's in regard of a fine ould gentleman from foreign parts somewhere, that's on the Rock 'most all day. I declare to your lordship he's one of the finest ould gentlemen I ever laid eyes on, an' all the time I'm on the Rock, an' all the ladies and gentlemen I seen there in my time. It does my ould heart good, so it does, to hear him talk about the place, an' I declare he knows more about it himself than I do, an' he tould me things concearnin' it that I never knew myself."

"Is it possible?"

"It's truth I'm tellin' your lordship, an' I tould Miss Markham the same before."

"Yes, Bryan, but you have not told Lord Effingham what your private opinion is in relation to this remarkably 'fine old gentleman.'"

Here Bryan hesitated. "Well, you know, Miss Markham, I'm not sure about that, an' maybe it isn't right for me to say it."

"Let me say it for you, then. You must know, my lord,"— turning to Lord Effingham with that look of arch intelligence that at times lit up her features,—"you must know, my dear lord, that our friend here can in no other way account for this unknown old gentleman's wonderful knowledge of matters appertaining to Cashel save only by the supposition that his knowledge is supernatural. He therefore concludes that he must be some 'great conjurer or another from beyond sea.'"

"And he wishes you to see him?"

"Precisely, my lord."

"And you purpose going?"

"I do—on one condition," the last words in a lower tone; "that is, provided your lordship will summon courage to brave the awful presence of the conjurer."

"Doubt not that, lady mine," the Earl returned in the same tone; "no more solitary rambles now, even on the sacred Rock. Happiness, you know, was born a twin, so I claim my share of your enjoyments."

"At what hour do you think we shall be likely to see your old gentleman, Bryan?" said Harriet, with grave composure.

"Oh, bedad, miss, you can't go wrong for the hour, for I'll go bail you'll find him on the Rock go when you will. Sure, he was there early this mornin' with a company of ladies and gentlemen, an' then he came back again all alone by himself, an' spent as good as three hours with me, lookin' at everything, and huntin' every hole an' corner, sometimes talkin' to himself, sometimes to me, an' more times sayin' nothing at all to any one, but standin' leanin' on a staff he has, or sittin' down on a big stone, lookin' at the arches an' pillars, an' the ould ancient carvin' that's on the stones, till you'd think he'd never take his eyes off o' them. Dear knows, I don't know what to make of him, an' still my heart warms to him if he was fifty conjurers on account o' the great conceit he has in the ould walls and things."

"Very well, Bryan; we shall make it a point to see your conjurer some time this evening. Good morning." And taking Lord Effingham's arm, Harriet said in a low voice, as they turned their faces towards the Castle, "I think I know the precise time when we shall be sure to meet this new acquaintance of Bryan's. If he be, as I suspect, some enthusiastic antiquarian, after spending most of his day on the Rock, when

— the gay beams of lightsome day
Gild but to flout the ruins grey,

he will most probably desire to

— visit it by the pale moonlight.

We shall have no difficulty, I think, in inducing Lady Pemberton to go with us."

"Not the smallest, I will answer for it," said Lord Effingham, with a pleasant smile; "Caroline is a true woman in the quality for which good mother Eve was most remarkable. Say nothing of it, though, to Mrs. Pakenham, who, *entre nous*, is never any very great acquisition—least of all to an exploring party. But lo! here she comes, stateliest of dowagers, and a thunder-cloud on her brow, I protest! Let us turn up this path—I do not think she has seen us."

Harriet was silent, wondering in her own happy heart at the sportive gaiety which now marked Lord Effingham's manner in his intercourse with her, whilst to others he was still the same. Then she thought of his early characteristics, as described by his sister, and her heart swelled and her cheek glowed at the thought that she alone had the key to the inner nature of one so calm and cold and passionless to the outer world.

As Lord Effingham had expected, Lady Pemberton was delighted with the account of Bryan's mysterious visitant, and all anxiety to get a sight of him. In the flush of this new excitement, trifling as it was, her usual listlessness vanished quite, and her brother remarked with a smile, half sad, half tender, "My poor Caroline, I see you are still the same after all that has come and gone."

The sun's last rays had faded from the parched earth that July evening when the Effingham carriage stopped at the gate leading to the ruins, and our party of three, ascending the steep and rugged way to the cathedral door, were guided thence by the sound of voices to Cormac's Chapel, where they found a lady and gentleman busily engaged in examining the quaint, rude sculpture round the arch of the portal, consisting of a double line of bead and zigzag moulding—if that term can be applied to stone. It was easy to see by the wondering look on old Bryan's face, as he stood silent and obsequious a few paces in the rear of his visitors, that the tall old man with his fine massive head, sparsely covered with silver-grey hair, and shaggy brows of the same colour protruding far over eyes that twinkled like stars with the changeful emotions of the mind was no other than "the conjurer." Who the lady might be or whether she had been summoned from the aerial world by his potent art to give record of the men and women of other times, was, of course, beyond the power of speculation. Truth to tell, if she had been brought into existence by the magician's wand, he might have summoned a fairer shape to hold commune with on the solemn Rock, amid the shadows of the past.

The strangers were not long unaware of the new arrivals; for Bryan, feeling a little nervous about his position as the evening shadows thickened, began to look anxiously for the coming of the expected visitors, whose presence might protect him from any malpractices on the part of the conjurer.

"Well, I declare," quoth Bryan, "that's great!"

"What is great, my friend?" said the old gentleman.

"Why, your honour, if here isn't Lord Effingham himself, an' his sister, a grand lady, too, an' Miss Markham. Well, to be sure, isn't it the greatest of luck that brought them now, just in time to have a talk wid yourself, sir, an' this elegant fine lady?"

With the dignified ease and courteous familiarity with which well-bred persons are wont to make acquaintance, the parties exchanged salutations, smiling all round at Bryan's odd introduction. The ice of formality was not there to be broken, for each saw at a glance that the others were of their own order, and probably of their own peculiar tastes in a greater or lesser degree. No introductions took place at first on either side, save the characteristic one of old Bryan, but all were prepared to be pleased with the others, and pleased they were. The conversation, before confined to the strange lady and gentleman, with an occasional word from Bryan, at once became general, and the supposed conjurer resumed the thread of his observations.

"I was just observing, my lord," he said, addressing Lord Effingham, "that this chapel cannot be so old by a century or so, as Irish antiquarians would make it appear. I do not think that the king-bishop, Cormac MacCullenan, could have been its founder."

"Indeed? and what grounds have you for disputing a fact so generally received as I believe that is?"

"That I will soon show you," and, moving round to the lateral door, he pointed to a half-effaced, yet still plainly discernible sculpture on the lintel. It was that of an archer in the act of drawing his bow—the old English crossbow.

"Your lordship sees that rudely-sculptured figure?—know you that such was the cognizance of Stephen of Blois?"

"I have read that such it was, but I should not have remembered it in this connection."

"That is because your lordship has not studied with attention the chronicles which time has traced on mouldering walls. Now we know that Stephen of England ended his mortal career in the year of grace 1101, or thereabouts, whereas Cormac of Cashel departed this life on the bloody battlefield of Moyling in the year 903, nearly two hundred years before."

Here was heard from old Bryan that indescribable sound emitted by Irish mouths amongst the peasantry when anything strange or marvellous falls under their senses. It is enunciated by striking the tongue sharply but slightly against the roof of the mouth.

"Thu! thu! thu!—well, if that doesn't bate all ever I heard!"

"So you infer from this heraldic device," said Lord Effingham, "that the name Cormac's Chapel is a misnomer?"

"Not exactly; it might have been built by another Cormac, though not, I am persuaded, by the great Cormac to whom it is popularly attributed. That it is no older than the days of good King Stephen I am entirely of opinion. Be that as it may, however, it is a rare gem of mediæval art. It is, in all respects, one of the most interesting architectural remains I have anywhere seen, as the entire group exceeds in diversity of interest anything of the kind in these islands."

"I am glad to hear you say so," said Harriet Markham, her face expressing the joy of her heart.

"And why so, my dear young lady?" the old man asked, regarding her with a look of kindly scrutiny from under his half-closed eyelids.

"Why, because, in the first place, I see your tastes are antiquarian, that you speak from knowledge, and—are not an Irishman."

"You are right, young lady, in both surmises. I have devoted some attention to the lore of ancient days, and I have not the honour of being a native of your beautiful island, yet I am fain to declare that I hold it in high esteem, for very many good reasons. Cashel I have long desired to visit, though I honestly confess I had no adequate idea of what it really is."

"I told you so," said his lady-friend, "and I saw you were somewhat sceptical about it. For my part, I have no very great affection for ruins—of any kind."

"Of course not, of course not," said the cheerful old man; "nobody ever accused you of such a weakness. My good friend here, Lord Effingham, and ladies, though a very worthy person in the main, has no respect whatever for other people's hobbies, though, between ourselves, she mounts one herself of an odd time, and ambles off at the quietest pace imaginable. Her hobbies are all agricultural and—shall I say it?—utilitarian. Is it not so, my fair friend?"

"It is; if to live in the present and for the present be utilitarianism, then I am a utilitarian, and I only wish I could get more of my countrymen and countrywomen to live less in the past and in the future, and more in the realities of the present."

"Yes, yes, more of political economy and less of poetry. We know you, chère amie! most amiable of philanthropists that you are!"

"Permit me one remark," said Harriet Markham, "before you dismiss the subject. A thoroughly Catholic people, like the race that inhabits this island, can never be taught political economy in the sense you speak of, because they cannot, if they would, concentrate their thoughts on the present. They *must* live in the past and in the future, for the past is their pride, the future their hope, whilst the present is with them but as the connecting link between them."

"Very true, my dear, very true," said the old gentleman, with an approving nod and smile; "I don't think a Malthus or a Harriet Martineau would ever find favour in this old-world country of yours. Eh, Maria?" and he looked at his friend with a humorous smile.

That bustling little personage, already moving away, made answer, "Possibly not—but perhaps worse doctrines than theirs may prevail in this same *Insula Sanctorum*. Nay, young lady, you needn't look at me so—I do not mean religious, but only social and political doctrines. But come," to her friend, "let us be moving, unless, indeed, you propose remaining all night, meditating, like Hervey, 'amongst the tombs.'"

"And that I would not mind doing," he replied, "would this good Hermit of ours but keep me company."

"The Lord in heaven forbid!" said Bryan, with such simple fervour that every one laughed.

"Why, how is that?" said the old gentleman. "I am told it is nothing new for you to spend the night here as well as the day."

"Do you not know that he takes *you* for a conjurer?" whispered Lord Effingham.

"I should not be surprised if it were so," the other replied in the same tone; "he is a glorious old fellow—quite a study in himself."

"A second Old Mortality?" asked the Earl, with a significant look; whereupon the stranger laughed and said "Almost, but not quite," then nodded and turned again to the examination of the architectural details before and around him.

For some time the party walked on in silence, each one lost, apparently, in their own reflections; at last the supposed conjurer, having stumbled over a fragment of stone, stooped and picked it up, then examining it by the clear light of the full moon, he said to Bryan—

"This is a piece of that tomb in the chancel within—Archbishop M'Grath's."

Bryan eagerly pounced on the precious fragment, expressing his wonder that it came to be outside the walls, and muttering to himself a "Christ save us!" as he glanced furtively at the dreaded stranger whose knowledge of the place so far exceeded his own—at least, so he thought.

Meanwhile, the unconscious object of his terror went on discoursing of all he saw, and of all he thought, admiring, explaining, expatiating, and delighting his wondering auditors.

"Now, my Lord Effingham," said he, stopping in a place which commanded a view of the entire group of buildings, "can anything on earth be grander or more solemn than this? Said I not well that nothing within the British seas can compare to it—Iona of the Hebrides, perhaps, excepted? Look, my lord, at the group, as it stands,—look at the diversity, yet completeness of the whole, the court, the fortress, the abbey precincts, the graveyard, the Bishop's seat, all in one enclosure, perched in isolated grandeur on the summit of this singular Rock. See, there stands the palace where the brave Dalcassian princes of Munster ruled with right royal sway; there minstrels swept the sounding string in praise of beauty and of valour—the Hall of the Minstrels still is there, though its voices are now but the mournful sighing of the wind through the ivy that drapes its walls. Hushed is the harp of the tuneful Gael in the palace of their kings. Yonder is the hall of the vicars-choral, erected by the good Archbishop O'Hedian for the prebends of his cathedral; there is the cathedral itself, majestic even in decay, its altar gone, its glory vanished for ages, only death and ruin within and around it, where stately prelates and stoled priests ministered of old, and men and women wept and prayed and were forgiven. Where the banners of the blessed Saints waved over long processions round the aisles and along these paths, naught now is seen but broken walls and clustering ivy, and the dreariness of desolation—

> Year after year 'tis crumbling,
> And heavily the loose stones fall,
> Long grass and fern hang clustering
> Above the tombs without the wall.

Then yonder is Cormac's peerless chapel, sheltered by the arm of the cathedral transept, and bidding defiance to the stern warfare which time wages ever on the works of man: safe in the solidity of its quaint masonry, it escapes the ruin that is falling deeper year by year on the statelier edifice which has so long sheltered it from wind and weather. Then the little Church of the Apostles, smaller still than Cormac's Chapel, with the twelve venerable figures rudely yet not unskilfully carved on its dilapidated stonework; and as if to crown the interest of the group—to close the solemn record—this mysterious pillar-tower rising over all, pointing back to the very night of time, to a period long anterior to Christianity, and to a race of men whose history has perished from the land, except in so far as the lone cairn on the green hillside or the spectral tower bears record of their passage."

"And the abbey," suggested Harriet, when the old man paused, "you would not willingly omit the cloisters yonder from your enumeration."

"If I did," the stranger replied, with his benignant smile, "it were like leaving the Colosseum out of a description of Rome, or the Temple of the Sun out of Palmyra. That abbey has occupied a good part of the time I have spent on the Rock; for, independent of the interests attached to it as the home of generations of good and holy men, Cistercians and Dominicans (for I find it belonged successively to both), I was endeavouring to find the entrance to the subterraneous passage which is said to have connected it with Hore Abbey, yonder in the vale."

"And did you succeed?" inquired Lord Effingham.

"Alas! no, my lord," and he shook his head; "such good fortune is not for me, and seeing that this worthy man whose days and years are spent amongst the ruins has never been able to discover it, I am bound to believe that such passage never did exist, save in the legends of the country."

"I'll not give in to that, anyhow," said Bryan stoutly, his ire a little roused at this attack on one of the standing traditions of the place; "since the memory of man, or long before it, nobody ever said the likes o' that, for sure every one knows the passage is in it, only we can't happen to light on it; an' sure, maybe there's good raisons for that same," he added significantly.

"And what do you suppose the reasons to be?" inquired the old gentleman.

"Why, then, maybe it's there where the ould monks hid away all their goold and traisures at their off-goin', and then don't you think but they'd build up the openin' to keep people from findin' it out?" Another reason Bryan had, which he chose to keep to himself, deeming it unfit to make the Sassenach quality as wise as himself in the matter, and that was that the passage was closed by powers supernal to reserve it as a hiding-place for the persecuted Catholics of the neighbourhood in some of those desperate emergencies to which the finger of prophecy—local and legendary prophecy—points for aye as awaiting the oft-tried children of the soil.

"What wonder is it," said Lord Effingham, after a short silence, "that the Catholic people of Ireland are so wedded to their own religious belief? With such monuments as these ever before them, how could they forget the faith of their fathers, associated as it is with all the past, and interwoven with the history of their race?"

"And with all their hopes for the future, my lord," added Harriet quickly. "Were it not for this one ray of light, shining ever from the veiled future through the portals of religion, how could they have journeyed so patiently through the darkness of many ages of suffering and desolation? Faith alone it is that has cheered their dreary path of life—given them strength to live, and courage to die when life itself was a lingering death, and death the last act in a lifelong tragedy."

"I believe you are right, young lady," said the old gentleman, and a thoughtful, even a melancholy look settled on his features. "It may be that the possession of this strong, hopeful faith more than counterbalances the many hardships which have fallen to the lot of the Irish people."

"Hardships, inagh?" put in Bryan almost indignantly; "athen, only for them maybe so many wouldn't go to heaven,

an' when they get there isn't it all past?—Much about the
hardships, an' far less!—doesn't every one know that no one can
get to heaven without sufferin', an' sure, the blessed and holy
Scripture itself tells us that? If it wasn't the will of God, do
you think England could ever have kept us down as she has
done, starvin' crathurs off the face of the earth when there's full
an' plenty for them to eat, an' givin' them only the height of
bad usage when a body 'id think that it 'id be for her own good
to have them better all? God knows what's best for us, an' He
can change His hand in His own good time, an' raise up them
that suffered so much for His sake, an' bring England as low,
maybe, as she ever brought poor Ireland. He has great power,
the God we serve—praise and glory to His name for ever!"
And Bryan went on in advance of the others, shaking his head
defiantly and muttering to himself, "Sure, God loves them He
chastises—the whole world knows that."

The old gentleman stood looking after him with a good-
natured smile on his large features. "What a glorious old
fellow that is," said he, turning with a smile to his lady-friend;
then, lowering his voice, he added, "I have had the richest
treat all day in his company. He is an antiquarian by nature,
if you can understand what that is, devoting his life to the care
of these magnificent ruins, yet actuated chiefly by pious venera-
tion for the sacredness of the place. He is to this Catholic
necropolis what Old Mortality was to the graves of the Scottish
Covenanters."

The last remark was overheard by Miss Markham as she and
Lord Ellingham came up close behind. "What a pity it is,"
said she, "that Ireland has no *Scott* to make her natural
beauties or her ancient monuments classic, as that great master
has made those of Scotland. The same elements of romance
are here—the same wealth of legendary lore—the same loveli-
ness of lake and river, wood and mountain—the same diversity
of races in her history—the same intestine wars"—

"And a much more poetic temperament in her people," added
the stranger earnestly. "In all and each particular, Ireland
presents as rich a mine for the novelist as ever did Scotland,
and I marvel much that no great national writer of fiction has
yet risen above your horizon. Why, this Cashel alone would
furnish material for a first-class historical tale. A world of

romance lies sleeping amongst these ruins, were the dry bones but imbued with life by the wand of imagination."

"And who so fit to do it as—*the conjurer*—a cousin-german, I suspect, of the renowned Jonathan Oldbuck of Monkbarns?" archly said Harriet; whereat the strangers both laughed, and the old gentleman, tapping with the glove he held in his hand the fair cheek of the young lady, said, "Were I thirty years younger, I know who might, could, and would be *a conjurer*, and furnish a type for the heroine of a tale of Cashel—one that might have inspired the minstrel's lay, and nerved the warrior's arm, and made pious souls more pious still by word and by example."

Lord Effingham smiled fondly on the blushing girl at his side, and expressed his hope that one day or another might be given to the world a grand historic novel illustrative of the history and antiquities of Cashel.

The two strangers smiled on each other, and the lady said, "What think you, Signor Conjurer?"

"Nay, my friend, I should rather ask you that question," the old man said evasively. "I am almost angry with certain persons of my acquaintance for neglecting Cashel so long."

"Ah, but you know the 'certain persons' are not the persons to treat that subject effectively. Their prosy ethics would make dry work of the shadows you spoke of a while ago."

"I know not that," said the old man, with a thoughtful shake of the head; "yet still, every one has their *forte*, and perhaps yours is *not* the poetry of history. We will see, however, what can be done for Cashel, at least, pending the appearance of the national novelist who is to complete the work of Sydney Morgan and Maria Edgeworth!"

"Thanks," said the lady; "our visit here has not been for nothing."

The evening was now far advanced, and the visitors prepared to leave the Rock, the strangers, especially the old gentleman, with evident reluctance. He requested Bryan to come forward, and, having placed in his hand a silver crown, told him he need not fear to keep it.

"So you're no conjurer, after all?" eagerly asked Bryan.

"I can lay claim to no such honour."

"Who on earth are you, then?—for if you're not a conjurer,

you're something past the common altogether, an' I'd be entirely obleeged to you if you'd tell me your name."

"I know not that the knowledge would benefit you much," said the kindly old gentleman, with his humorous smile; "such as it is, however, you are welcome to it. I am *Sir Walter Scott* —and this lady, my very dear friend, is called *Miss Edgeworth*. Good-bye, Bryan; and I hope you will not forget the conjurer, who, at least, can never forget Cashel and the Hermit of the Rock."[1]

Bryan was not very profuse in his expressions of gratitude, but he raised his hand to wipe the tears from his eyes, and retreated to the rear to hide the emotion for which he could not account. He had never heard of Sir Walter Scott or Maria Edgeworth, but, as he had said before, his heart warmed to the amiable antiquarian.

When the two parties now exchanged their formal yet very cordial greeting, it was found that Lord Effingham and Miss Markham had both guessed the identity of the distinguished strangers.

"I began to think," said the Earl, "that old Bryan was not so far wrong, after all. I suspected that his conjurer might prove to be the Wizard of the North." And he bowed with courtly grace.

"And I," said Harriet, "over and above the testimony of the printed likenesses I had seen of the author of *Waverley*, made up my mind full soon that if the host of Abbotsford were above ground he was on the Rock of Cashel this very night—and Miss Edgeworth too!" and she bowed to the lively little lady, who was talking with quick, animated gestures to Lady Pemberton. The authoress of *Castle Rackrent* nodded her head and smiled, then resumed the animated account she had been giving her silent but admiring listener of some amusing incidents in the tour from Edgeworthstown thither, which she and Sir Walter, with some other friends, had made in company.

---

[1] It is well known that Sir Walter Scott, on the occasion of his visit to Cashel, in the summer of 18—, was so impressed by what he saw there, during a two-days' stay in the vicinity, and after a minute and critical examination of the ruins, that he declared his intention of making it the subject of a novel. Unhappily, the intention was never carried out. Would that it had!

Lord Effingham would fain have persuaded the distinguished strangers to go at once to the Castle, but that they declared impossible for that evening, as the other members of their party having gone to visit other places in the vicinity, would naturally expect to find them at the hotel in Cashel where they left them.

"In that case," said the Earl, "we will hold you excused, on condition that the whole party dine with us to-morrow."

To this a right willing assent was given, and the Effingham carriage rolled away towards the old borough, leaving to the quiet inn two personages whose names will live while Ireland and Scotland have a literature to boast of.

CHAPTER XXIV.

THE CLOSE OF THIS EVENTFUL HISTORY.

COURTEOUS reader, my tale is almost told : we have reached the term of a journey which I meant to make a pleasant one for you. I know not how far I have succeeded, but you will, I hope, give me credit for the intention. Before the curtain falls on the widely-diversified group of characters I have placed before you, many things remain to be told, in brief. The last scene of the drama is closed, but I must crave the reader's kind attention while I tell how Harriet Markham discovered that the "proposal" conveyed through Lord Effingham was but a ruse to sound the depths of her heart ; how Lord Effingham, after two weeks of blissful preparation, placed his coronet on the brow of Harriet Markham, with the express understanding that he was to continue the study of Catholic doctrines, already privately commenced ; how, after a few months, the newspapers chronicled the fact—in terms varying with the party and denominational views of the several writers—some that the Earl of Effingham had "gone over to Rome," others that he had "embraced the holy Catholic faith,"[1] etc. etc. ; how Phil Moran, in due time, led Mary Hennessy to the hymeneal altar, accompanied thereto, on their own account, by Dr. Maurice Hennessy and Bella Le Poer, who had been carrying on a little affair of the heart "on the sly," as Mary said, for some months previous to the happy event, which came off in form of a "double

[1] To those who might be disposed to object to Lord Effingham's conversion, we will "vouchsafe" so far as to remind them that the conversion of an Irish earl is nothing new,—even later than the period of our story, the Earl of Dunraven, whose principal seat is at Adare, County Limerick, became a convert to the Catholic faith. It was but the other day, moreover, that the Marchioness of Downshire, an Irish peeress, was received into the Church.

marriage" in Cashel Church, under the ministry of Dean
M'Dermot. How the trial of Jerry Pierce came off at the
Clonmel Assizes, in presence of a vast multitude, comprising
the highest and the lowest in "sweet Tipperary;" how old
Harry Esmond astonished the whole country, and none more
so than his own kith and kin, by giving his testimony in
favour of Jerry Pierce, and expressing his opinion that he was
really as innocent of the crime as he professed to be ; how the
sturdy old Trojan was thenceforward regarded with little less
enthusiasm than Jerry himself ; how Jerry, being honourably
acquitted, was "chaired"—i.e. borne on men's shoulders—
through the streets of Clonmel, and the hills around re-echoed
with the wildest shouts of joy and exultation ; how Mr. Esmond,
on approaching his own residence, was greeted with a similar
ovation, the horses being taken from his carriage, and he conveyed to Rose Lodge in triumph, amid the vociferous cheers of
the multitude ; how, from the steps of his hall-door he made a
speech as remarkable for its characteristic brevity as Dean
Swift's famous charity sermon. "I see I was mistaken in you,"
said he to the assembled peasantry—"in fact, did you gross
injustice. I promise, therefore, to be from this day to the last
day of my life what I never was before—a good landlord !"
He kept his word, and ever after, people used to say that the
loss of one good Esmond gained them another, just as good a
magistrate and as good a landlord as ever *he* was. To none was
this change more gratifying than to Henrietta Esmond, who
could now look up to her husband's uncle as a friend and a
protector. She had no immediate relatives of her own, and had
from the first attached herself to the Esmonds—at least, the
ladies of the family, who were all, Aunt Winifred by no means
excepted, as kind to the orphan-heiress as heart could wish.
Miss Esmond, with all her peculiarities of character, was in the
main a good soul, sound at heart, and the occasional acerbity of
her temper never led her so far as knowingly to inflict pain on
any one. Indeed, the good old lady was rather a favourite with all
the family,—even her brother, on whose corns she trod the oftenest, had a very sincere affection for "Winny," and on ordinary
occasions seemed rather amused than otherwise by "her little
odd ways," as he was wont to call them. As years rolled on,
the hopes and affections of all the Esmonds were centred in the

little son and daughter of their lost Harry, and the children amply repaid their mother's devotion and the tender care of their uncle and aunts, for they grew up full of promise, bright and beautiful as fair flowers opening to the sunbeams. Surrounded by none but the kindliest and most healthful influences, their good qualities were all largely developed, and their bad ones repressed, if not overcome. But in all the tranquil happiness that marked her life, and made the days like one long summer-noon, Mrs. Esmond never lost sight of her irreparable loss—never forgot him who was her first, last love—him whose bright young life had been so cruelly extinguished—

> Not quietly into the silent grave stealing,
> But torn like the blasted oak, riven away.

The heart-crushing load of grief that had bowed her to the earth during the first months of her widowhood yielded gradually to the soothing influence of time, but the tender melancholy that took its place never passed away, and although it could not be said of the gentle Henrietta, as it was of Henry the First of England, after the loss of his son and daughter at sea, that "she never smiled again," it was nevertheless true that, as the poet sings of the fair Queen of Scots in Holyrood Palace—

> The touch of care had blanched her cheek, her smile was sadder now,

and so it was her life long till she left this weary world to join her loved one beyond the skies.

It remains to tell how Jerry Pierce wed his faithful Celia, and took up his abode with her in her uncle's cottage, as neither could think of leaving the old man lonely in his age, his boys having taken to themselves helpmates some time before, and gone housekeeping on their own account. By the generous kindness of young Mrs. Esmond, the vanithee—now no longer the "fairy-woman"—and the two orphan children of the unhappy Tim Murtha were established in a comfortable little cottage, with a potato garden attached, close to that of Larry Mulquin, and it was Jerry's pride and pleasure to cultivate, before and after working hours, his mother's little spot of ground, from which he managed to raise not only an abundant supply of the favourite esculent, but of other vegetables, which added considerably to the comforts of the little family. A few fruit-bushes were there too, and some flowers annually obtained from the gardeners at the Lodge or the Hall, for Jerry Pierce and his family "had the run of both houses," as the worthy fellow used to boast with innocent and very justifiable pride. Indeed, it was well known to all the countryside that Jerry and all belonging to him were under the special protection of the Esmonds, and "were sure of never knowing a day's want." It was much to Mr. Esmond's praise that he lodged a small sum of money in bank for the Murtha children, to lie with accumulated interest till such time as they were come to an age to be settled in life. In the light of an awakened conscience he saw that the misfortunes of the Murthas were all due to him, in the first place, and that thus by a terrible but just retribution he was indirectly to blame for the untimely death of the nephew whom he had loved as a fond father might love a dear and only son. In this, as in all the important acts of his later years, he was guided by the wise paternal counsels of Dean M'Dermot, then as ever the common father of all his people, their friend, their guide in matters temporal no less than spiritual. Poor Mabel, after wandering around Holy Cross and Cashel for a few more weary years, died at last in the vanithee's cottage, well cared for during the long illness that closed her mortal life by the kind hands of Celia Pierce and her mother-in-law, and provided with comforts and even delicacies from Rose Lodge and Esmond Hall. Many an hour did the ladies from both houses spend by the bedside of the interesting maurne, and their charitable cares were rewarded by a lucid interval of some hours immediately before the poor girl's death, during which she received the last sacred rites, then died in full consciousness, with the Holy Names on her lips, mingled with a prayer "for poor Patrick's soul," and a blessing on the kind friends, high and low, who had made her path to the tomb a pleasant one. She was waked for two nights, and amongst the crowd of friendly neighbours that filled the house "inside and outside," as Jerry Pierce said, was Shaun the piper and his dog Frisk, the former entertaining all that came with the best music in his pipes and the best jokes in his budget of fun. And it was the general opinion that Shaun "kept them all alive, betwixt himself and the pipes, more power to them." At our last hearing of Shaun he was himself alive and merry, minus poor Frisk, however, who went the way of all dogs a year or so after Mabel's wake, and was laid at rest "under the greenwood tree" by the kindly "neighbour boys," friends of Shaun and admirers of his dog's fidelity.

Ned Murtha, sheepish and awkward as ever, was nevertheless making his way in the world better than might be expected when last heard from. He had attained the honourable post of confidential clerk to Attorney Moran, and was said to have "money in the bank—enough to keep him all his days." Kate Costelloe, ever the same wayward, moody creature, remained in dutiful attendance on Bryan Cullenan, the comforts of both duly cared for by the pitying kindness of "the young mistress," as Kate persisted in calling her. The woes of squalid poverty thus happily banished from their little cabin, the two old people jogged quietly on together—contentedly on Bryan's part, for Bryan was always contented—with dogged tranquillity that was not resignation on the part of Kate Costelloe, whom no effort of her kind protectress could draw from her lifelong stupor of dull remembrance. Life was to her but a dreary blank—no hope for the future—no joy in the past—nothing but gloom and drear despondency, save where an occasional glimpse of the bright world beyond the tomb came like a far-off gleam of light making the surrounding and nearer darkness all the more sensible. There came a time, however, when the benign influence of religion reached the stubborn heart of Kate Costelloe, and by slow degrees the crust of dark despair and stolid misery crumbled away, and the far-off light came near and nearer in the wake of true contrition, till at length the unhappy woman raised herself from the earth on which she had so long lain grovelling, and dared to look her transgressions in the face, not as she had been wont to do, as merely bearing on her own fate, but as violations of the Divine law. From that moment her life was one long course of penance,—not of idle, unavailing regret,—and when her day of life was ended, she departed in the hope of a joyful resurrection, purified by years of patient suffering and the fervour of sincere conversion.

Lastly, we are bound to put on record how it fared with old Bryan Cullenan in the closing years of his mortal life. We have failed in portraying his worthy character if the reader requires still to be told that the old man lived in peace with himself and all the world to the last hour of his life. "The peace which surpasseth all understanding" had its throne in his heart of hearts, and even had his life been more chequered than it was, had the trials and vicissitudes of man's fallen state and its many tribulations fallen to his lot, Bryan Cullenan would still have enjoyed that inward peace which is the most priceless of all blessings—yea, more precious than the gold of Ophir, or the gems of Eastern mines. Calm and serene as a summer evening sky, his days glided by on downy pinions, unmarked in their tranquil passage. With but one worldly object in view— the preservation of the ruins on the Rock from the slow but certain ravages of time, and the ruder and swifter destruction dealt by the hand of man—Bryan's devotedness to that self-imposed task increased with every passing year, till at length he remained at his post night and day and in all weathers, coming down only to hear Mass, or comply with his other religious duties. His kind friends—and they were many—often visited him on the Rock, and took care that he wanted for nothing, but he never now went to any of their houses as he sometimes did in former days. Alone with God and the hallowed memories of the place, he spent his last years, wasting his little remaining strength and the last expiring energies of his nature in the service of the Saints of Cashel, keeping watch and ward over their mouldering fanes, their neglected shrines. Stoutly and bravely did the lone old man battle with the all-subduing power of decay, vainly striving to arrest its progress, yet working ever, despairing never—satisfied when he could but replace a fallen stone, clear away the rubbish that will accumulate in places abandoned to the empire of ruin, or pick the moss that ventured to make its appearance amongst the half-effaced letters of the quaint Latin inscription on the tomb of some venerable "man of eld," prelate, priest, or warrior-prince. And ever as he worked he held communion with the spirits of the place, and pondered over the solemn teachings of mouldering bones and grinning skulls. Shunning more and more the company of his fellow-beings, Bryan looked with greater yearning day by day and year by year to the invisible world on whose threshold he stood. Silence and solitude were his sole delight, and the voices of earth grated harshly on his eat. Yet his outward bearing was unchanged, and the few kind friends who would not be kept from visiting him were always sure to find on his face the same calm smile, on his lips the same fervent blessing. The grosser elements of his body evaporated, as it were, by slow degrees, and only the shell remained. The joints were stiff and the limbs feeble—the infirmities of age began to prevail over Bryan's hardy nature. A ghostly sight he was in those latter days, for

> His form was bowed and bending,
> His fleshless hands were thin and spare,

and the light of his eyes was all but quenched. Yet still he worked on at his cherished task amongst the graves and the tombs and the dreary ruins—on, on to the last. But the end came. One grey cold day in autumn, old Cauth ascended to the Rock, hoping to induce Bryan to eat some little delicate morsel which she had prepared with anxious care; she found the old man on his knees in the chancel of the cathedral, dead and cold—his beads in his hand and the large crucifix appended to them clasped close to his breast. He had fallen forward, and so lay before the place where the high altar had been of old. Great was Cauth's sorrow, but still she consoled herself with the thought, "He was at his duty a Sunday last, and sure, anyhow, it's the happy change for *him*—the Lord have mercy on him!" So died THE HERMIT OF THE ROCK, and they made him a grave amongst its honoured dead, and laid him down to rest for ever in the scene of his pious labours. But after him, for years long, the sacred ruins were left to the undisputed power of decay; no man was found to take the place which death had left vacant; storm and tempest aided the gradual process of decay—the stones fell and there was none to replace them; the long grass waved unheeded on the place that had been the Holy of Holies, and the green moss crept slowly over the names of the illustrious dead, and the people of the neighbourhood used to say with sorrowful emphasis, as they pointed to the sad ravages of time and neglect, "Och, it's aisy seen, sure, that poor Bryan isn't on his feet—if he could only see the ould place now, it 'id break his heart, so it would. It's a wonder he can rest in his grave and things goin' to wrack and ruin that-a-way all around him."

For years long it almost seemed to them as though the old man ought to return to save the ruins from the destruction to which they were evidently hastening, but he came no more; the grave had claimed its own, the farther shore was gained, and even the departing glories of the holy place could not waken one throb in the dead, cold heart of THE HERMIT OF THE ROCK. Peace to his soul for ever!

THE END

www.ingramcontent.com/pod-product-compliance
Lightning Source LLC
Chambersburg PA
CBHW030757230426
43667CB00007B/998